ON RELIGION:
A STUDY OF THEOLOGICAL METHOD
IN SCHLEIERMACHER AND NYGREN

ON RELIGION:
A STUDY OF THEOLOGICAL METHOD
IN SCHLEIERMACHER AND NYGREN

BY

WILLIAM ALEXANDER JOHNSON

PhD, Teol. Dr.

ST. JOSEPH'S UNIVERSITY   STX

BTQ 11 .J6
On religion: a study of theological meth

3 9353 00083 8209

113973

LEIDEN
E. J. BRILL
1964

Copyright 1964 by E. J. Brill, Leiden, Netherlands

*All rights reserved. No part of this book may be reproduced
or translated in any form, by print, photoprint, microfilm
or any other means without written permission from the publisher*

PRINTED IN THE NETHERLANDS

TABLE OF CONTENTS

PREFACE

This book has been written within the context of two universities and two faculties, the University of Lund, Sweden (the Faculty of Theology) and Columbia University, New York City (the Graduate Faculties of Philosophy and Religion). I am indebted to many people for this work. First of all to Prof. Carl Michalson of Drew University, Madison, New Jersey, who first introduced me to the study of Theology and suggested that the excitement generated in theological school carry over to a European graduate education. Prof. Gustaf Wingren, Professor of Systematic Theology at the University of Lund, was my instructor during the earliest period of my graduate studies. It was he more than anyone who encouraged me to deal with the problem of theological method in Schleiermacher and Nygren. The work which follows appeared first as a doctoral dissertation at Columbia University entitled "The Religious A Priori: The Philosophy of Religion of Anders Nygren, with particular reference to his dependence upon Schleiermacher" (1959). The dissertation was completely revised and modified in order to analyze the theological methodology of these two thinkers, and this work is therefore a supplement to the work done for the doctorate. Professors Horace L. Friess and Wilhelm Pauck guided my research in Schleiermacher and Nygren, and helped me bring my original work to completion. My sincere appreciation is expressed to them, for they more than any other American scholars were able to relate the unique philosophical and theological problems of the United States to my European research.

My research in Schleiermacher is dependent upon the work of two men: Wilhelm Dilthey (and his studies, *Leben Schleiermachers* I, 1870; *Denkmale der inneren Entwicklung Schleiermachers, erläutert durch kritische Untersuchungen; Schleiermacher, Allgemeine Deutsche Biographie 31. Bd.,* 1890; *Leben Schleiermachers I,* 2. Aufl. hrsg. v. H. Mulert, 1922), and Hjalmar Lindroth, of the Faculty of Theology of Uppsala University, Sweden. The latter scholar has written what I consider to be the finest work of Schleiermacher-analysis yet published, *Schleiermachers Religionsbegrepp: Förutsättningar och Konsekvenser* (I-II, 1926-1930). Lindroth's influence upon my interpretation of Schleiermacher will be apparent and I acknowledge readily my dependence upon him.

Many individuals close to me participated in the completion of this work. Miss Carol Steiman, Secretary of the Department of Religion, Trinity College, Hartford, Connecticut, typed the manuscript for publication. My wife, Carol, labored and suffered with me through all of the stages of the book, and it is proper that this book be dedicated to her – to express the fondness of the author for her contribution and continued presence.

Madison, New Jersey   WILLIAM A. JOHNSON
Christmas, 1963.

INTRODUCTION

The following is an attempt to analyze the theological methods used by Schleiermacher and Nygren. To do so one must take seriously the conception of religion found within both of their systems. Schleiermacher and Nygren began their theological tasks by referring first to the category of religion. When they found a place for religion within the "human consciousness", they then performed their specifically historical-theological tasks. Schleiermacher attempted to answer the question, "What is religion?" by reference to a "description of the religious consciousness, so far as it was concerned with the relation between the world and God", and he executed this task from "within the faith of the religious community." As Rudolf Otto wrote in the preface to his edition of the *Reden*:

> One is time and again enthralled by his (Schleiermacher's) original and daring attempt to lead an age weary with and alien to religion back to its very mainspring; and to reweave religion, threatened with oblivion, into the incomparably rich fabric of the burgeoning intellectual life of modern times.

The category of religion had to be resuscitated before modern man would take seriously the church and the theologians. Once religion was shown to belong to the "essence of life" and that without it mankind could not fully develop, then modern man could find it acceptable. Schleiermacher's challenge to the thinking of his day brought about revolution in theological thought. Religion was unlike the distorted and perverted figure the intellectualism and moralism of the Age of Reason made it out to be. Religion was not metaphysics nor morals neither was it to be confused with the emerging "science of religion" school, nor was it identifiable with "natural" religion, a theology of Rationalism, nor Kant's *Die Religion innerhalb der Grenzen der blossen Vernunft*. Schleiermacher discovered that religion possessed a valid, normal and normative quality, a unique and independent nature, which had to be recognized by the intellectual of his time. Otto summarized Schleiermacher's attempt:

> Religion is a new, unique, and independent area of human experience and the spiritual life, and that it possessess its own special worth with respect to knowledge and action; further, that religion should not be stunted and that it belongs to knowledge and action as a necessary third factor. For it is religion that first completes the circle of the truly human; it is religion that first endows knowledge and morality with true value, significance, depth and content.

Nygren, too, attempted to find a place for religion within human consciousness. Nygren's call to his generation to re-evaluate religion is found in his book, published in Sweden in 1921, *Religiöst Apriori*. In this work, he proposed to "demonstrate religion as a necessary and universal experience, inseparable from the nature of man." Gustaf Wingren, in his book *Theology in Conflict*, describes Nygren's task in the following way:

> The religious question is an independent question, and so is the ethical. Scientific study can never help or destroy a religion or an ethos. These answers to the questions of eternity or fellowship are at hand – we simply meet them as actual convictions. The only task of scientific scholarship is simply to describe them correctly. Philosophy of religion and philosophical ethics have done enough when they have demonstrated that there are questions which are essential without being scientific. They plurality of questions is the only thing which critical philosophy is able to demonstrate. This is sufficient for theology. Now theology knows what its task is: to describe as accurately as possible the answer of Christianity to a couple of eternal, unscientific, but inescapable questions; the question about the eternal, or communion with God; and the question about the good, or human fellowship. The task of systematic theology is to characterize these answers, nothing else. It is necessary to avoid all problems which would lead beyond the purely descriptive and characterizing task.

Nygren's earlier philosophical works indicate that he stands directly within the Schleiermachian tradition, and that he cannot be understood without this assumption. He designates Schleiermacher as "the philosopher of religion par préférence", and by so doing reveals his philosophical bias.

This study attempts, therefore, to deal with the conception of religion in Schleiermacher and Nygren's thought. It is my contention that the theological methodologies of both Schleiermacher and Nygren can be understood only by the recognition that they both attempted to substantiate religion as a positive philosophical category before they attempted to function as theologians.

The conclusion of this work demonstrates that Nygren's philosophy of religion is dependent completely upon Schleiermacher's, and that without Schleiermacher the search for the "religious a priori" itself would not have been undertaken.

SCHLEIERMACHER'S CONCEPTION
OF RELIGION

SCHLEIERMACHER'S CONCEPTION
OF RELIGION

In the history of thought, there are two ways by which the Absolute may be known. First, there is the immanental way, which presupposes that reason is identical with being. Secondly, there is the transcendental way, which presupposes that God makes himself known by revealing himself to the religious subject. Each method has its apparent difficulties; the first can effect a denial of the efficacy of reason; the second threatens to make the concept of God an object of knowledge comparable to other knowledge. Schleiermacher, in his philosophical program, attempted to avoid both of these dangers.

To attempt to describe Schleiermacher's conception of religion by a simple analysis of his *Reden* of 1799 is not sufficient. There are very precise and distinct periods in Schleiermacher's philosophical and religious development, and each of these must be analyzed and described before Schleiermacher's conception of religion can be understood in its entirety. First, there is the *period of his youth*, (to 1796), during which time Schleiermacher was developing the basic philosophical presuppositions for his later thought; second, there is the *intuitive period*, (1796–1802); third, the *critical period* (1802–1806), and finally the *systematic period* (1806–1834), in which period Schleiermacher matured as a scientific theologian and dogmatician.[1] Each period is separate and distinct, nevertheless, there is a general development and continuity between these periods in Schleiermacher's life.[2] Furthermore, it must be recognised that Schleiermacher is a synthetic thinker – he is able to use contrasting philosophical and theological ideas, without, at the same time, losing the unity of his system.[3]

---

[1] W. Dilthey, *Leben Schleiermachers*, Mulert ed. (2 Aufl.; Berlin and Leipzig: De Gruyter, 1922), Vol. I, p. 422ff; cf. Fr. Ueberweg, *Grundriss der Geschichte der Philosophie* IV neu bearb. u. hrsg. v. K. Oesterreich (11 Aufl.; Berlin: Reimer, 1916), p. 107; (12 Aufl.; 1923), p. 119.

[2] Schleiermacher related his philosophical position to his life throughout his works. Upon meeting Fichte in Berlin in July 1799, Schleiermacher reflected, "Philosophie und Leben sind bei ihm – wie er es auch als theorie aufstellt – ganz getrennt"; see *Aus Schleiermachers Leben – In Briefen*, hrsg. v. L. Jonas u. W. Dilthey, (Berlin: Reimer, 1858?1963), Vol. IV, p. 53.

[3] The richness of Schleiermacher's scientific construction is expressed by J. Wendland, "Neuere Literatur über Schleiermacher," *Theologische Rundschau*, (1914), p. 135.

CHAPTER ONE

THE EARLY PERIOD OF SCHLEIMACHER'S THOUGHT

I. THE YOUTHFUL PERIOD

A. *The Positive and Negative Influence of Moravianism upon Schleiermacher's Religious Development*

Long after Schleiermacher left the circles of the Moravians he still called himself a Moravian, although he considered himself "a Moravian of a higher order."[1] Schleiermacher, even to the end of his life, expressed his thankfulness for the influence of the Moravians upon his religious development.[2] It was within Moravianism that he discovered religion, and found religion to be something more than the religion of reason.[3] Religion became, for Schleiermacher, the expression of that which is most authentic about human existence. From the Moravians, Schleiermacher was influenced primarily by: 1) the insistence upon the identity of life with religion;[4] 2) the emphasis upon religion as an expression of a rich and inner experience of the heart.[5] The piety of the Moravians was always characterized by an "experience" of salvation; 3) the orientation of the Christian faith about the "community of the pious," which had as its center the person of Jesus

---

[1] Br. I, p. 309.

[2] "Ja, was hätte aus mir werden, wohin hätte es mit mir kommen können, wenn nicht die Gemeinde gewesen wäre." E. R. Meyer, *Schleiermachers und C. G. von Brinkmanns Gang durch die Brüdergemeine* (Berlin: Reimer, 1905), p. 58.

[3] Religion was for him, "die mütterliche Liebe, in desen heiligem Dunkel mein junges Leben genährt wurde." Fr. Schleiermacher, *Über die Religion – Reden an die Gebildeten unter ihren Verächtern*, hrsg. v. R. Otto, 1920 (1 Aufl.; Berlin: Reimer, 1799), p. 14.

[4] Schleiermacher criticized the philosophical religious position of Fichte in 1800; "Richte – der nun auch nicht mehr hier ist – habe ich freilich kennen gelernt: er hat mich aber nicht sehr afficiert. Philosophie und Leben sind bei ihm – wie er es auch als Theorie aufstellt – ganz getrennt, seine natürliche Denkart hat nichts Ausserordentliches, und so fehlt ihm, so lange er sich auf dem gemeinen Standpunkt befindet Alles was ihn für mich zu einem interressanten Gegenstand machen könnte. Ehe er kam, hatte ich die Idee, Über seine Philosophie mit ihm zu reden, und ihm meine Meinung zu eröffnen, dazu es mir mit seiner Art, den gemeinen Standpunkt vom philosophischen zu sondern, nicht recht zu gehen scheine." Br. IV, p. 53.

[5] Dilthey – Mulert, *Leben Schleiermachers* I, p. 35 ff.

Christ, who was personally and intimately involved in the life of every believer.

However, Schleiermacher also reacted negatively to the Moravians. He rejected the esoteric elements of their conception of the Christian faith. He also rejected the orthodox theological formulation of the content of the Christian faith. Furthermore, Schleiermacher questioned why the Moravians were isolating themselves from the world, fearful of culture, prohibiting a natural and free expression of one's faculties,[1] when at the same time, religion was to be supposed a positive expression of existence. In Moravian circles, Schleiermacher found a piety which laid great stress upon a rich emotional and imaginative life.[2] Schleiermacher's father felt that this kind of religious concern might awaken within his son the desire for the same kind of spiritual life, and which, in addition, might "save" him from the skeptical world in which he lived. For Schleiermacher during this period, feeling and imagination became constitutive for the religious experience, and as a result religion took on the character of "immediate experience."

When Schleiermacher identified himself with the Moravians, he found for the first time that religion was something real in human experience as it was in the life of the religious community, the Church. The expression of a rich and intimate community could be seen within the Schleiermacher family circle, and later in Schleiermacher's relationship to a group of personal friends and comrades.[3] The community life of the Moravians was oriented to the life of Jesus Christ. A community of love was to be sought for among its members at all times. The Savior, Jesus Christ, his love, his suffering, were to be always in the center of the religious life of the individual as well as of the

---

[1] In his discussion of freedom, we have the decisive moment in Schleiermacher's young life, with the result that he decided to leave the Moravians: "Im schönen Genuss der jugendlichen Freiheit hab ich die grosse That vollbracht, hinwegzuwerfen die falsche Maske, das lange mühsame Werk der frevelnden Erziehung." Dilthey – Mulert, *Leben Schleiermachers*, p. 108. For the fullest expression of this period of decision, cf. The following source materials; his own letters from the moravian period, his curriculum written in 1785 as he left the school in Niesky, the description of "die Wasserfahrt" (1786), his autobiography of 1794, his *Diarien der Brüdergemeinen, Nachrichten aus der Brüdergemeine, Protokolle*, etc.; cf. Meyer, *Schleiermachers und C. G. von Brinkmanns Gang...*

[2] He himself could say in his Autobiography, "der Grund zu einer Herrschaft der Phantasie in Sachen der Religion die sich bei etwas weniger Kaltblütigkeiwahrscheinlich zu einem Schwärmer gemacht haben würde." Br. I, p. 7.

[3] Cf. Meyer, *Schleiermachers und C. G. von Brinkmanns Gang...*, p. 3 ff; also Carstenzen, *Individualitetatanken hos Schleiermacher* (Lund: Gleerupska Universitetst Bokhandeln, 1924), p. 169 ff.

community. On the one hand, the Savior was *transcendent* to the believer. The believer was wholly dependent upon Him for his subsistence. On the other hand, the Savior seemed to be identical with the religious experience of the believer, and in this way He became *immanent* to the believer. The believer had an objective assurance that the Savior had once lived as a historical figure and that He now lived transcendently with His heavenly Father. In feeling, as the immediate self-consciousness of the self, and in imagination, as "objective consciousness," Jesus Christ was at one time both immanent and transcendent to the religious subject.[1]

Schleiermacher found, however, that it was psychologically impossible to maintain the religious experience which the Moravians insisted upon. When the religious "feeling" began to wane, the "objective consciousness" had to maintain the whole of the religious life. For the believer, the Savior became the transcendent God. It was He who preserved the objective quality of the religious life. What happened next was inevitable: the religious life had to be dogmatically formulated in order to be promulgated. The Savior became, therefore, "the divine One, who had humbled Himself in the form of a man," who had suspended His relationship with the divine. In order for man to achieve communion with Him, man must transcend himself. That is, man could attain communion with God only through "supernatural feeling" („übernatürliche Gefühle"). Piety is therefore

---

[1] Schleiermacher's reaction to this, in his early period may be seen by: "Ich weiss gewiss, dass Du mit mir ... ihm, dem gnädigen und guten Heiland, danken und ihn mit mir bitten wirst seine Gnade besonders in den 14 Tagen bis zum grünen Donnerstag, da ich sein Fleisch und sein Blut im heiligen Abendmahle geniessen werde, von Tag zu Tag grösser und herrlicher werden zu lassen. 'Ich will sie alle zu mir ziehen' hiess es in der gestrigen Losung; das wird er in Gnaden auch an mir erfüllen; er ist auferstanden, zu helfen allen Elenden auf Erden, das giebt mir auch ein Recht an ihn; er ist meine Zuversicht allein, der Gott, für mich am Kreuz erblasst." He says in another letter; "Wir wollen uns immer fester an ihn (der Heiland) halten, je weniger Kraft wir haben, deste mehr will Er uns schenken, so wir darum bitten; je mehr schlechtes wir bei uns fühlen, deste mehr Gnade dürfen wir holen aus seiner Fülle Gnade um Gnade. Wenn man sich nur immer an Ihn halten kann, wenn man in so einem Umgange mit Ihm steht dass man auf jede Warnung, jeden Wink acht giebt und gleich weiss was Er uns sagen will, wenn uns nichts aus der Gemeinschaft rücken kann, so dass man zum Leichtsinn, zum Stoltz, zum Zorn sagen kann, da für hing mein Herr am Kreuz, da wird einem alles leicht. Das muss man sich alle Tage schenken lassen, das ist mein tägliches Gebet, besonders seit dem letzten Abendmahl." Br. I, p. 30; Br. I, p. 34; *Neue Briefe Schleiermachers aus der Jugendzeit*, hrsg. v. J. Bauer, Zeitschrift 31, Vol. 4, 1910, p. 591.

the only adequate attitude in response to the transcendent God.[1]

Schleiermacher's subsequent transfer to the seminary in Barby in 1785 added to his doubt as to the sufficiency of "supernatural feeling." The result of the doubt was an increasing dissatisfaction with the Moravians. During his first term at Barby, Schleiermacher expressed openly his distrust of the quietistic, monastic-type life of the Moravian community.[2] He looked forward to the possibility of becoming a "Lehrer der Wissenschaften," but realized that this was not possible within a Moravian framework.[3] He felt that he could not even become a "Lehrer und Vorsteher der Gemeinde." At the end of the first term at Barby, Schleiermacher could acknowledge "Jesu Frieden und Liebe,"[4] but he did not possess the full confidence necessary, as determined by the Moravians, to allow the Jesus Christ to direct his future life.[5]

---

[1] Schleiermacher had come upon this divergence in Moravian thinking before, cf. Br. I, p. 30; N. Br. p. 590 ff. During his time in Niesky he had seen this tendency toward an orthodox formulation of the content of faith. As well, Spangenberg's *Idea fidei fratrum* was used in the worship services; cf. Meyer, *Schleiermachers und C. G. von Brinkmanns...* p. 23.

[2] Schleiermacher saw how passive the community really was. This was indicated by his conversation with a member of the Moravians: "Es thut Dir leid, aus Deiner Seligen Ruhe herauszukommen, und ich kann Dir nicht ganz Unrecht geben; aber liebe Schwester, Pflicht ist Pflicht und man muss sich immer freuen sie zu thun. Ich denke, wenn Du Dich auch von Morgens um 5 bis Abends um 10 im Hause und Garten herumtummelst, so kannst Du eben so selig sein, eben so sehr des Heilands Nähe fühlen, als in Deiner ruhigen Unthätigkeit (wenn Du mir das Wort erlaubst), die Du in Gnadenfrei genossest." Br. I, p. 30 ff.

[3] He saw them as "ein unerträglicher Cirkel, etwas zu lernen um es Anderen zu lehren, die es wieder nur um des Lehrens willen lernten." He found "in der Brüdergemeinde keine recht sich auf das Leben verbreitende, der Mühe lohnende Anwendung der Wissenschaften." Br. I, p. 10.

[4] Br. I, p. 31.

[5] Schleiermacher expressed his feeling in his autobiography: "Wir jagten immer noch vergeblich nach den übernatürlichen Gefühlen und dem, was in der Sprache jener Gesellschaft der umgang mit Jesu hiess; die gewaltsamen Anstrengungen unserer Phantasie waren unfruchtbar und die freiwilligen Hülfsleitungen derselben zeigten sich immer als Betrug." Br. I, p. 10. The old battle continued: "durch die Art, wie die Lehre von dem natürlichen Verderben und den übernatürlichen Gnadenwirkungen in der Brüdergemeinde behandelt und fast in jeden Vortrag verwebt wird." Br. I, p. 7. cf. also: "Der Glaube ist ein Regale der Gottheit, schrieben Sie mir, Ach, bester Vater, wenn Sie glauben, dass ohne diesen Glauben keine, wenigstens nicht die Seligkeit in jenem, nicht die Ruhe in diesem Leben ist, als bei demselben, und das glauben Sie ja, o, so bitten Sie Gott, dass er mir ihn schenke, denn für mich ist er jetzt verloren. Ich kann nicht glauben, dass der ewiger, wahrer Gott war, der sich selbst nur den Menschensohn nannte, ich kann nicht glauben, dass sein Tod eine stellvertretende

The second term in Barby brought about Schleiermacher's second spiritual "crisis." Okley, an Englishman, who was a member of "der philosophische Klub," to which Schleiermacher also belonged, had become very impressed with the rationalistic philosophy of the Enlightenment.[1] "Selbstdenker" now became an honorific title in "The Philosophical Club." Okley very blatantly expressed his hatred for the theological orthodoxy of the Moravians. What was more, the freedom of rational inquiry was declared to be essential to the life of the members of the group. Letters began to be exchanged with the secular universities of Germany. Volumes which were representative of rationalistic thinkers, although frowned upon by the Moravian authorities, were read with great interest.[2] At this time, too, Schleiermacher came under the influence of his uncle, Stubenrauch,[3] who was professor of theology in Halle. He also became interested in the writings of Moses Mendelssohn and Jacobi. As a result, he began to read Spinoza.[4] Of all the philosophers he studied, Kant became more and more significant to him.[5] The break with Barby and the Moravians had been made![6] It was impossible for Schleiermacher any longer to believe in the divinity and substitutionary atonement of Jesus Christ as dogma. As well, it became increasingly impossible for him to identify "supernatural feeling" with the activity of God's grace. In his correspondence with his father, he assured his distressed parent that the lack of faith he had for the Moravian interpretation of the Christian faith did not mean the rejection of the Christian religion completely.[7] Rather than seek for supernatural perfection, which

Versöhnung war, weil er es selbst nie ausdrücklich gesagt hat, und weil ich nicht glauben kann, dass sie nöthig gewesen; denn Gott kann die Menschen, die er offenbar nicht zur Vollkommenheit, sondern nur zum Streben nach derselben geschaffen hat, unmöglich darum ewig strafen wollen, weil sie nicht vollkommen geworden sind." Br. I, p. 45.

[1] Cf. Br. III, p. 12, Okley wrote: "Noch erfreulicher war mir Dein Versprechen gegen die stockdumme Orthodoxie anzugehen."

[2] Br. I, p. 11. *Jenaer Literaturzeitung* and *Berliner Monatsschrift* gave the young students an opportunity for intellectual rapport with the thought-world of the time.

[3] Cf. Br. I, p. 37.

[4] Cf. Br. I, p. 70.

[5] Cf. Br. I, p. 70. After Okley left the Moravians, he thanked Schleiermacher "für ... Nachrichten von der Kantischen Recension", Br. III, p. 10, also p. 12.

[6] Br. I, p. 10; also "Vergeblich versuchte man nun meine Bekehrung durch alle Mittel; ich konnte den Pfad nicht mehr verlassen, den ich einmal betreten hatte." Br. I, p. 11. Also the significant letters written to his father first in January 1787. Br. I, p. 45.

[7] Schleiermacher himself maintained this to his father: "Warum, bester Vater,

Schleiermacher felt was impossible for him or any man to attain, his objective in life became to attain to "die Menschheit."[1] It was now valid for Schleiermacher to begin with the concepts of the world and reality as such, and to seek to discover the Absolute within them. As the Absolute had been given in that which is most characteristic of natural life, no supernatural relationship was necessary.[2] Schleiermacher had seen, however, during this period, that religion was wholly dependent upon supernatural feeling. His reaction against this approach to the religious life included a conception of religion which recognized that in the many and varied experiences of human life, a religious experience may be born. The divine could be found, he believed, within the internal structure of man's being. Religion was intimately related to the aesthetic, moral and intellectual experiences of man. Furthermore, he felt that the capacity for these experiences was a gift of divine providence. Religion became an aspect of "a higher consciousness," the consciousness of the relation of man to a higher world. Schleiermacher could consider himself still a Moravian, but now, "of a higher order."

B. *Schleiermacher's Criticism of the Faith of Rationalism*

Dogmatic Rationalism, which asserted that reason was adequate to determine at all times the nature of truth and falsity, conceived of the Absolute from an immanental point of view. Reason was considered to be perfectly independent and complete within itself and needed nothing to fulfill itself.

Schleiermacher, after leaving Barby, went to the University of Halle, where the metaphysical system of the Leibnitzian-Wolffian school were still in prominence. With Kant, they represented the most influential intellectual system of the period. Religion had to be dealt with in terms of categories which were intelligible to these "authorative" philosophers.[3]

---

sagen Sie ich bete nicht Ihren Gott an, ich wolle fremden Göttern dienen? ist es nicht Ein Gott, der Sie und mich erschaffen hat und den wir beide verehren? warum können wir nicht mehr vor einem Altar niederknien und zu unserem gemeinschaftlichen Vater beten? Br. I, p. 56.

[1] Cf. Br. I, p. 45.

[2] Cf. Schleiermacher's brilliant piece "Wasserfahrt", in which he described his relationship to life and nature.

[3] Schleiermacher's relationship with his uncle is important to note at this point. Stubenrauch, professor in Halle, was a moderate representative of he Enlightten-

The most important representative of the Enlightenment and the Wolffian School of the period was J. A. Eberhard, who was professor of philosophy in Halle. He became Schleiermacher's teacher in philosophy. He had been influenced both by Mendelssohn and by British empiricism.[1] Eberhard was a strong critic of Kantian philosophy, and particularly of Kant's proofs for the existence of God.[2] Eberhard, unlike Kant, did not make any distinction between the ideal and the real, but instead identified them. From such a standpoint, the "old metaphysics" with its rational psychology, cosmology and theology, was preserved.[3] It is certain that Schleiermacher, even before he left Halle, read with great interest the debate between Eberhard and Reinhold, who was a leading Kantian disciple of the time. During a later period of seclusion in Drosson it is also certain that he read the *Allgemeine Literatur Zeitung*, and kept in close contact with the scientific and literary world by means of it.[4] This debate between Eberhard and Reinhold prompted Schleiermacher to continue his studies of Kant, which had begun earlier during his Moravian period.[5] It was

---

ment position, who combined a warm understanding of religion with a wide tolerance of different opinions. cf. H. Hering, "Samuel Ernst Timotheus Stubenrauch und sein Neffe Friedrich Schleiermacher," *Beiträge zur Forderung Christlicher Theologie*, 34 Bd., (1919), p. 16 ff., cf. also Dilthey, *Leben Schleiermachers* I, p. 37 ff.

[1] Eberhard prepared an introduction to Ontology, Cosmology, Psychology and Natural Theology in his textbooks, *Vorbereitung zur natürlichen Theologie* (Halle 1781) and *Kurzer Abriss der Metaphysik, mit Rücksicht auf den gegenwärtigen Zustand der Philosophie* (Halle 1794). These works indicate clearly that he was a disciple of Wolff and Baumgarten.

[2] Cf. Eberhard's criticism in *Philosophisches Magazin* (Halle, 1788–92) and *Philosophisches Archiv* (Halle, 1792–95).

[3] Cf. Kant's answer to Eberhard in *Philosophisches Magazin*, 1790, "Über eine neue Entdeckung, nach der alle neue Kritik der reinen Vernunft durch eine ältere entbehrlich gemacht werden soll." PM III: 2, 1790, p. 148 ff., p. 205 ff., cf. also ALZ II, 1789, p. 596.

[4] Cf. Br. IV, p. 8.

[5] It is interesting that Schleiermacher's father, during his son's study in Halle, recommended the study of Kant: "Da Du nun bei Eberhard die Metaphysik hörst, so empfehle ich Dir, dabei des Professor Kant Kritik der Vernunft und seine Prolegomena zur Metaphysik für Dich zu studieren und gründlich durchzudenken, damit Du in die unabsehliche Wüste transcendentaler Begriffe nicht ohne einen sicheren Führer Dich wagen mögest." Br. IV, p. 8 ff. Schleiermacher's answer in August, 1787, "Was die Kantische Philosophie betrifft, die Sie mir zu studieren empfehlen, so haben ich von je her sehr günstige Meinungen von ihr gehabt, eben weil sie die Vernunft von den metaphysischen Wüsten zurück in die Felder, die ihr eigenthümlich gehören, zurückweist. Ich habe deswegen schon in Barby mit ein paar guten Freunden die Prolegomena gelesen, aber freilich nur soviel davon verstanden als man verstehen kann, ohne die Kritik der reinen Vernunft gelesen zu haben. Ob ich nun gleich, weil ich die Kritik nicht kriegen könnte, nicht im

Kant who more and more attracted his interest and his study.[1] Schleiermacher's first philosophical works *(Über das höchste Gut,* and *Über die Freiheit des Menschen)* dealt primarily with Kant.[2] By 1789, Schleiermacher was able to write his father and say that he had read and studied all of Kant's works.

In Eberhard, Schleiermacher met a proponent of the old "dogmatic rationalism." The ultimate principle of philosophy was reason in and for itself. Upon this principle, Eberhard constructed an elaborate metaphysical system, and defended the ontological and the cosmological proofs for the existence of God. This he did basically because he asserted that reason was *norma veri et falsi.* Eberhard did not distinguish, therefore, between the ideal and the real, but included the real within the ideal and made it immanent to reason. In the light of the critical Kantian epistemology which demanded a transcendent object for real knowledge, Schleiermacher began to realize the incongruity of the dogmatic rationalistic standpoint. He realized that if one could construct a metaphysics from the starting point of reason, the resultant construction would necessarily rest upon reason alone without any object. The Kantian critical method had maintained that reason had the ability to form a content of knowledge. On the basis of this, Schleiermacher could reject the Wolffian metaphysic. As well, Schleiermacher realized that any attempt to discover the Absolute by an immanental method alone would result in failure.

We must realize, however, that whatever influence the critical philosophy of Kant had upon Schleiermacher, the Kantian system, in fact, rests upon a rational principle. Every activity of reason presupposed the intuitive faculty. Intuition presupposes the subjective intuitive forms, space and time. The objectivity of knowledge presupposes ultimately the unity of apperception. The rational aspect of Kantian philosophy reveals itself primarily in the area of moral philosophy. Kant, who rejected the presuppostions of the older dogmatic metaphysics, permitted reason to be used in his practical philosophy in the form of the practical postulates.

Stande gewesen bin während des Eberhard'schen Collegii die Wolf'sche Philosophie mit der Kantischen zu vergleichen, so soll doch solches in diesen Michaelis-Ferien geschehen." cf. Br, IV. p. 5.

[1] To his father in December 1789 he wrote : "Ich habe in Drossen einen grossen theil der Kantischen Schriften wieder durchstudirt", Br. I, p. 84.

[2] Cf. ALZ II, 1789, p. 577 ff., re: "Die Reinholdsche Recension"; also Br. IV, p. 40 ff., also Br. I, p. 83, 84, for a discussion of the locus of Schleiermacher's affection during the Eberhard-Reinhold discussion.

Eberhard, as a typical representative of the Enlightenment, permitted religion to be subsumed under morality.[1] Furthermore, he had defined human perfection in a way which was identical to the divine perfection.[2] The ideal of the human is not a transcendent goal nor is it, for that reason, unattainable. Morality is a striving toward perfection.[3] Under the influence of Shaftesbury, Eberhard accepted the concept of "the moral sense," which he identified with moral feeling.[4] Schleiermacher was influenced a great deal by the Eberhardian ethical position, and, in particular, by Eberhard's criticism of Kant. This fact may be seen most clearly in reference to the Kantian practical postulates of the immortality of the soul and the existence of God. We find this criticism in *Über das höchste Gut* (which Dilthey dates as belonging to the last period in the university, that is, 1789).

In *Über das höchste Gut*, Schleiermacher developed the idea of the highest good in an historical way, and gave particular attention to Kant's definition of the *summum bonum* and the relation of this concept to religion. Kant had defined duty in the *Kritik der praktischen Vernunft* as "the highest good," but included the concept of happiness within his definition.[5] Kant sought to validate the practical postulates of the immortality of the soul and the existence of God by reference to this concept of happiness.

Schleiermacher criticized Kant for his assertion that duty and happiness could be unified by reason. He discovered, too, that there was a dualism within Kant's moral system. The moral law was held to be absolutely binding, although one was never able to realize i fully. Schleiermacher rejected this dualism.[6] The moral goal could

---

[1] Cf. his *Neue Apologie des Sokrates oder Untersuchung der Lehre von der Seligkeit der Heiden* I–II, (Halle, 1772, 1778). Schleiermacher during this period was strongly influenced by the subordination of religion to morality.

[2] *Sittenlehre der Vernunft*, (Halle, 1786), p. 17; cf. *Neue vermischte Schriften*, (Halle, 1788), p. 208.

[3] Cf. *Neue Apologie des Sokrates* I, p. 341.

[4] Cf. *Neue vermischte Schriften*, p. 196; *Sittenlehre der Vernunft*, p. 50 ff.

[5] Duty is "das oberste Gut", but not "das ganze und vollendete Gut", "denn, um das zu sein, wird auch Glückseligkeit dazu erfordert, und zwar nicht bloss in den parteiischen Augen der Person, die sich selbst zum Zwecke macht, sondern selbst im Urtheile einer unparteiischen Vernunft, die jene überhaupt in der Welt als Zweck an sich betrachtet." Immanuel Kant, *Kritik der praktischen Vernunft* (Leipzig: Reclam, 1788), p. 133.

[6] Schleiermacher, writing to his father, who represented a Christian moralistic and absolutistic position, said: "Sie schreiben mir, wenn ich auf mich selbst Acht gäbe, würde ich wohl gewahr werden, dass ich mich selbst von meinen Fehlern nicht los machen kann. Ich sehe das tagtäglich, liebster Vater; aber ich glaube auch

not be other than that which can be realized, he maintained. Furthermore, Schleiermacher asked, how could duty and happiness, as aspects
of the highest good, be unified by reason?[1] A moral system, he asserted, could not have happiness as its highest good and at the same
time remain rational. The highest good in Schleiermacher's ethical
system could never be the moral law in relationship to its goal.[2] But
rather the highest good, for Schleiermacher, was the removal of the
dualism between the ideal and the real in the ethical life.[3] Unlike Kant,
who maintained that happiness must be included within the practical
reason, Schleiermacher insisted that happiness is of an experiential
character and for that reason could not be a part of the practical
reason. Happiness could never be the highest good.[4] In this way
Schleiermacher was able to demonstrate that the Kantian postulates

---

[1] Plato had taught Schleiermacher that the idea of happiness was to be eliminated from the idea of the highest good: "Der ganze Zweck seiner so oft miss-
nicht, dass das Gott verlangt. Er kann nicht wollen, dass wir hier schon ganz
fehlerfrei werden sollen, denn das ist nicht möglich." Br. I, p. 69.
verstandenen Republik, unstreitig einer der herrlichsten Compositionen des Alter-
thums, ist zu zeigen, dass es schlechterdings nothwendig sei uns selbst zu regieren
und dass dies auf keine andere Weise geschehen könne, als wenn wir unbedingt
alle übrigen Theile unsrer Seele dem regierenden Vermögen der Vernunft unter-
werfen. Diese höchste Vernunftmässigkeit unter dem Titel der göttlichen Wahr-
heit, war der einzige Bestandtheil seines eigentlichen höchsten Guts." Br. III,
p. 20 ff. "Es ist der Vernunft wesentlich, dass sie überall, wo sie allein handelt, mit
Verachtung eines (Partikularen und) Subjektiven in der grössten Allgemeinheit
schliesst und beschliesst." Br. III, p. 20 ff.
  "Dies ist der Charakter des reinen Sittengesetzes, so wie ihn uns Herr Kant
aufstellt und wie er hinreichend ist um dem Begriff des höchsten Gutes zum Grunde zu liegen." *Denkmale der inneren Entwicklung Schleiermachers, erläutert durch kritische Untersuchungen.* (Appendix to Dilthey, *Leben Schleiermachers*), p. 10.
  [2] "das heisst ein Gegenstand des Begehrungsvermögens, um dessentwillen wir
auch etwas anderes wollen was eigentlich nicht in demselben enthalten ist."
Dilthey, *Denkmale* ... p. 9.
  [3] Schleiermacher's answer to the question, "What is the highest good?":
"Nichts Anderes als der vollkommene Inbegriff alles dessen, was nach gewissen
Regeln in einer gewissen Verfahrungsart nämlich der ungemischten, rein ratio-
nalen, zu erlangen möglich ist. Wir wollen uns vorstellen, dass uns das Sittengesetz als eine algebraische Funktion gegeben sei, so werden wir unter dem
höchsten Gut nichts Anderes zu denken haben als diejenige krumme Linie, welche
Alles ist und Alles in sich enthält, was durch jene Funktion möglich ist." Dilthey,
Denkmale ..., p. 9.
  [4] Schleiermacher's remark: "Allein sollte sie in jener Welt sich eher als möglich
denken lassen? Ich denke nicht. Nimmt man an, dass uns in jeden andern mög-
lichen Zustand die Sinnlichkeit auch ankleben wird so werden auch die Natur-
gesetze unsres Begehrungevermögens immerfort von den Geboten der praktischen
Vernunft unterschieden bleiben. Nimmt man das Gegentheil an, so ist nicht er-
weislich dass es uns alsdann noch um so etwas als Glückseligkeit ist zu thun sein
werde." Dilthey, *Denkmale* ..., p. 13.

could not be maintained.[1] The practical postulate of immortality was related to the concept of duty as the highest good. The concept of happiness required the practical postulate of the existence of a God. However, immortality was tied up with "the eternal progress of morality," and, therefore, the perfect identify of the will to the law of the practical reason was never possible for man without the postulate of immortality.

Schleiermacher directed his criticism to the Kantian postulates even in their purest form. The demand to realize the highest good was absurd from a human standpoint, he maintained. The highest good as the inclusion of all that is in the moral law did not consider man as a sensuous being, but considers man only as a participant in the practical and rational life.[2] The highest good can therefore only be "a regulative principle" and not "a constitutive principle" as Kant wanted it to be.

Schleiermacher has attempted to show in his criticism of Kant that man is not pure practical reason but is determined by a purpose and is bound up with the sensuous conditions of life. Schleiermacher rejects, therefore, what he considers is the "new" metaphysical system built upon the practical postulates. The practical postulates of God and immortality do not have more necessary value for us than the principles of the theoretical reason. Religion, for Schleiermacher, during this period, became a kind of projection of the ethical into the infinite. As long as ethics stood in the center of his thought, religion could only be a kind of complement to it.[3]

---

[1] Cf. Dilthey, *Denkmale*, p. 13.

[2] Schleiermacher's criticism is expressed so: The highest good as that which is included in the moral law, "ware nothwendig in einem Willen, der schlechterdings allein durch das Sittengesetz bestimmt werden müsste, möglich in einem solchem, der ohne Widerspruch auch bloss von der praktischen Vernunft bestimmt werden könnte, aber nicht möglich in einem Willen wie der unsrige, der nicht unmittelbar, sondern nur vermittelst subjektiver von dem Sittengesetz abgeleiteter Bewegungsgründe durch dasselbe bestimmt werden kann. Herr Kant scheint hier im praktischen seinen Fehler selbst nicht vermieden zu haben, den er uns im speculativen aufgedeckt hat." Dilthey, *Denkmale* ..., p. 12 ff.

[3] He wrote to Brinkmann in 1789: "Ich glaube, dass was mir nach diesem Tode bevorsteht, die zweckmässigste Vervollkomnung meines Zustandes sein wird, welche dermalen möglich ist, und wenn ich vermuthe, dass hierzu die Verbindung mit denjenigen Seelen nothwendig ist, in denen ich dadurch eine gewisse innere Aehnlichkeit meiner eignen Existenz gleichsam verdoppelt sehe, und an denen ich mich wie eine schwächere Rebe an einer stärkeren auf die beste und innigste Weise immer höher hinaufranken kann, so glaube ich wenigstens nicht zu träumen." Br. IV, p. 11. Yet this type of thinking was not constitutive for him at this time.

C. *Schleiermacher's Attempt to Solve the Dualism in Kant between:*

1) *Phenomenal Necessity and Transcendental Freedom*
2) *The Thing in Phenomenon ("Erscheinung") and the Thing in Itself ("Ding an sich"):*

Schleiermacher worked on *Über die Freiheit des Menschen* from 1791 to the fall of 1792. The book discussed the problem of freedom, particularly in terms of the way Kant had defined the term. Schleiermacher attempted to remove the dualism in Kant of the element of necessity which belonged to the phenomenal world, and the element of freedom which belonged to the intelligible world. In his attempt to deal with this dualism, Schleiermacher took a step in the direction of solving a deeper and more basic dualism in Kant, that is, the dualism which existed between the phenomenal and the intelligible worlds. Kant had maintained that the element of necessity belonged to the phenomenal world. He presupposed, however, that there was moral freedom in the practical life. Schleiermacher asked the following questions about the relationship between necessity and moral freedom:

1. Is the concept of necessity compatible with the practical (moral) life?
2. Is transcendental (intelligible) freedom compatible with a real event?

Schleiermacher answered the first question in the affirmative and asserted, furthermore, that moral obligation could only be maintained on this basis. The element of necessity belonged to the practical life as well as it did to the theoretical life. Nonetheless, Schleiermacher could introduce the idea of moral responsibility. He formulated it by asking the question, "How must the desire be constituted so that it can be compatible with moral responsibility?" His answer was threefold:

1. There must be a moral "impulse" of some sort;

2. This moral impulse must have an equal opportunity with every other impulse to become the determining factor in human activity; and,

3. The cause which made this impulse determinative in a particular action must lie within the self, not outside it.

That is, in all cases of moral responsibility, the cause must lie "within the totality of present impressions."[1] Schleiermacher was not satisfied

---

[1] Dilthey, *Denkmale ...*, p. 25.

with Kant's rationalistic ethic and demanded that there be an emotional element within ethical decision. The purely rational ethic could not be effective, nor could it be realized, Schleiermacher believed.

The second question was also answered in the affirmative. Transcendental freedom for Kant was not something negative, such as "the absence of compulsion," but was rather something positive, such as "the ability to transcend oneself." Schleiermacher rejected Kant's conception of transcendental freedom, but at the same time answered in the affirmative the question: Is transcendental freedom compatible with a real event? He denied practical freedom but maintained rather a practical *determinism*. He referred the transcendental freedom to the theoretical area of man's experience, and presupposed an absolute starting point for a real event.[1] At the same time he maintained that the question of freedom and necessity were answered both from the theoretical as well as the practical areas of experience. Schleiermacher's rejection of the Kantian dualism between necessity and freedom may be seen most clearly in his synthesis of these two opposing elements. This synthesis is of fundamental importance to his ethical system, as well as to his ideas of "spontaneity" and "growth." An event for Schleiermacher was not made up of an infinite number of causal relationships, but it had rather an absolute origin, that is, an Absolute, a thing in itself.

The removal of the dualism in Kant's conception of necessity and transcendental freedom meant that Schleiermacher had begun to overcome the deeper dualism in Kant, that is, the dualism between the thing-in-phenomenon ("Erscheinung") and the thing-in-itself ("Ding an sich"). Already by 1796[2], Schleiermacher had been working with the Kantian conception of the "Ding an sich." For Kant, the "Ding an sich" is the objective correlative of sensuous experience. Without the "Ding an sich," the content of perception would be only subjective. The world would become an illusion and sensuous experience would be impossible[3] Kant separated the thing-in-itself (the "Ding an

---

[1] Dilthey, *Denkmale* ..., p. 45. cf. p. 40: "die ganze Frage ist eine Frage darüber wie etwas geschicht, und diese kann niemals aus Veranlassung der praktischen Ideen allein aufgeworfen werden, denn diese besagen nur, dasu etwas geschehen soll."

[2] Dilthey, *Denkmale* ..., p. 45 ff.

[3] Kant maintains, "dass es ausser uns Körper gebe, d.i. Dinge, die obzwar nach dem, was sie an sich selbst sein mögen, uns gänzlich unbekannt, wir durch die Verstellungen kennen, welche ihr Einfluss auf unsre Sinnlichkeit uns verschafft." Immanuel Kant, *Prolegomena zu einer jeden künftigen Metaphysik, die als Wissenschaft wird auftreten können*, hrsg. v. K. Schulz, (Leipzig: Reclam, 1783), p. 67.

sich") and the thing-in-phenomenon ("die Erscheinung"). The thing-in-itself, he said, is the necessary presupposition for the thing-in-phenomenon. The thing-in-phenomenon, however, can never become the object of our knowledge. Because the senses are bound to the a priori subjective forms of time and place, the object given to us in perception is not the "Ding an sich" but "die Erscheinungen," i.e., the "Ding an sich" in its relation to the subject's manner of intuition.[1] The thing-in-itself has reality in intuition only as phenomenon. In itself it must be thought of as non-sensuous. This is the negative sense of "das Noumenon." However, if something is to be described as phenomenon, there must be the possibility to think of a thing-in-itself. This is the object of non-sensuous intuition, "das Noumenon" in its positive sense, which is, however, never an object of our experience, and remains therefore problematic. On the positive side, it is a necessary idea which limits the intuition to phenomenon.

Kant's sharp dualism between "das Ding an sich" and "die Erscheinung" was structured in such as way that the former gave an objective quality to the latter.[2] The question then arose for Kant, if the thing-in-itself is never an object of our knowledge but only a thing-in-intuition (the thing-in-itself in relationship to the subject's mode of intuition, "die Erscheinung"), how can the thing-in-intuition represent a real object? Does it become merely an illusion? For Kant, the thing-in-itself in relation to the subject's mode of intuition only corresponded to a real object when it was determined by the a priori categories of time and space, and ultimately by the "unity of consciousness." We have already seen that "das Ding an sich" is defined as the objective correlative of sensuous perception. Intuition is, therefore, determined by "das Ding an sich," as well as by the pure synthetic "unity of apperception." However, these a priori presuppositions were never brought together into any kind of a unity by Kant. It is this deeper dualism, between the pure synthetic unity of apperception and "das Ding an sich," (which is the background for the dualism between "die Erscheinung" and "das Ding an sich") with which Schleiermacher had to concern himself during this period of his development.[3]

---

[1] Immanuel Kant, *Kritik der reinen Vernunft*, hrsg. v. K. Kehrbach, (2. Aufl., Leipzig: Reclam, 1787), p. 235.

[2] Cf. Kant, Kr. d. r. V. p. 676; cf. Immanuel Kant, *Grundlegung zur Metaphysik der Sitten*, hrsg. v. Th. Fritzsch, (Leipzig: Reclam, 1785), p. 91.

[3] Dilthey, *Denkmale* ..., p. 65; cf. Br. IV, p. 49.

Schleiermacher turned next to Spinoza for a solution to the problem of the dualism in Kant.[1] The year 1793 marked the point of the shift from his dependence upon Kant to that of Spinoza.[2] It is quite clear, however, that Schleiermacher had come into contact with Spinoza's thought earlier in his philosophical career. In *Kurze Darstellung des Spinozistischen Systems*, Schleiermacher acknowledged his agreement with the principle features of Spinoza's system.[3] For Spinoza, the infinite is similar to the unlimited and the finite to the limited. Such a conception had some correspondence to Kant's idea of "die Noumena" and "die Phänomene."[4] The noumenon ("die Verstandeswelt") is the cause of phenomenon ("die Sinneswelt") for Kant, in the same way as the infinite is the cause of the finite for Spinoza.[5] But, in Spinoza, there is no possibility of a causal relationship between noumenon and phenomenon, because the category of causality is only valid for the phenomenal world, whereas the concept of identity is determinative for the relationship between the noumenal and phenomenal worlds. As well, the concept of identity is determinative for the relationship of the "Ding an sich" and "die Erscheinung," the thing-in-itself and the thing-in-phenomenon.[6]

Schleiermacher had now discovered the principle of identity. The Absolute was no longer considered to be the thing-in-itself, because now the object was included within the subject. The Absolute was defined in terms of the identity of subject and object. The Kantian "Ding an sich" was thereby excluded from the Absolute. In this way, Spinoza had enabled Schleiermacher to overcome the Kantian dualism. Nonetheless, Kant remained important for Schleiermacher because the concept of the "Ding an sich" was used to interpret Spinoza's *substance* as an irrational and transcendent category.

---

[1] Dilthey, *Denkmale* ..., p. 65; cf. also Br. I, p. 70, 137.

[2] Dilthey, *Denkmale* ..., p. 65.

[3] "Es muss ein unendliches geben, innerhalb dessen alles endliche ist," which negatively expressed is: "Es ist unmöglich dass die endlichen Dinge für sich bestehen können." Fr. Schleiermacher, *Sämmtliche Werke* (Berlin: G. Reimer, 1835–1884), III:4,1, p. 287. Schleiermacher is also impressed with Spinoza's formula: "Es sei kein anderes unbedingtes möglich, als der ganze Inbegriff des bedingten." S.W. III:4,1, p. 294.

[4] S.W. III:4,1, p. 292.

[5] "Spinoza meint, es sei kein anderes unbedingtes möglich als der ganze Inbegriff des bedingten" ... "die Welt der noumena ist gerade auf eben die Art die Ursach der Sinnewelt, wie Spinoza unendliches Ding die Ursach der endlichen Dinge ist." S.W. III:4,1, p. 294.

[6] S.W. III:4,1, p. 294.

D. *Schleiermacher's Attempt to Investigate Critically Kant's "Ding an Sich" and Relate it to Spinoza's Substance*

Jacobi, who with Hamann and Herder were called "the faith and feeling philosophers," criticized the rationalistic philosophy of the Enlightenment. Rationalism was similar to the older "Dogmatic" Rationalism because of the assertion that reason was an independent and autonomous faculty inherent within man. The Absolute was identified with reason itself. Jacobi proposed that Spinoza's *substance* could only be properly understood in the light of Rationalistic philosophy.

Schleiermacher agreed with Jacobi that Spinoza's conception of *substance* had a rationalistic basis, but it was not entirely a rational category.[1] He maintained, overagainst Jacobi, that Spinoza's *substance*, (defined as "the infinite comprehending the finite") was not entirely rational.[2] Schleiermacher asserted that Spinoza did not consider God to be "a universal Being," but insisted rather that, "de ejus essentia universalem non possumus formare ideam."[3] Spinoza's *substance*, Schleiermacher asserted, was not defined primarily in a rational and immanental way, but rather it was an indefinite and inaccessible category, similar to the concept of the transcendent, or Kant's "Ding an sich."

Schleiermacher went on to correct Jacobi's interpretation of Spi-

---

[1] F. H. Jacobi, *Ueber die Lehre des Spinoza in Briefen an den Herrn Moses Mendelssohn* (2 Aufl., München: 1785), p. 121 ff. Schleiermacher recognizes Spinoza's polemical point of departure as "subjectiv"; "subjectiv ist der polemische (Theil) zuerst da gewesen, denn das ist der Gang eines jeden Systems". S.W. III:4,1, p. 285 also S.W. III:4,1, p. 286 ff.

[2] Schleiermacher asserted that Spinoza's rationalism did not rest upon "der Satz vom Grunde" as Jacobi believed. There is therefore no reason to believe that he is wholly a representative of rationalism, who confused logical being with real being. He expressed it so: "Das unendliche Wesen kann seinem Wesen nach nicht durch diejenigen Prädicate bestimmt werden, welche das Wesen der einzelnen Dinge ausmachen, sonst käme ihm auch seinem Wesen nach kein eigentliches Sein zu, sondern eine beständige Succession des Werdens." S.W. III:4,1, p. 290. One can therefore not say anything more than that the infinite is that which "eigentlich existere." cf. S.W. III:4,1, p. 291 ff.

[3] S.W. III:4,1, p. 292. "Das unendliche Ding" can therefore be understood from a double viewpoint: "bald abgesondert von den endlichen Dingen per se," "bald wieder in der untrennbaren Verbindung mit ihnen." It is therefore so, "dass man von ihm sagen kann sowol Es hat keine Vorstellung, als auch Es sind alle Vorstellungen in ihm; sowol Es hat keine Bewegung, als Es ist alle Bewegung in ihm." *Substance* became for Schleiermacher something similar to Kant's *Ding an sich.*

noza's *attributes*.[1] The attributes were not so much "attributes of the Godhead" as they were "characteristics of the perceived."[2] On the basis of this distinction, Schleiermacher was able to find a close relationship between Spinoza and Kant.[3]

Schleiermacher's definition of the Absolute as the *identity of subject and object* had been attained by his attempt to overcome the Kantian dualism of the "Erscheinung" and the "Ding an sich." He could, however, also identify the Absolute with the "Ding an sich," (but when he did so he defined the "Ding an sich" as "the Absolute as one and unchanging").[4] This dual definition of the Absolute will become constitutive for his later philosophical position.[5] The oscillation between these two definitions did not mean, however, that Schleiermacher held a double Absolute, one which was immanent, and the other which was transcendent. Schleiermacher's entire argument in *Kurze Darstellung des Spinozistischen Systems* revealed that he conceived of the Absolute as both immanent and transcendent. He continued to do so until the more mature expression of his conception of Religion in the *Reden* of 1799. It is quite clear that before 1799, Schleiermacher's conception of Religion was identified with a rationally constructed ethical system.[6] Reason for Schleiermacher at this time was conceived to be an independent and active principle, but it could not grasp the

---

[1] Cf. Jacobi, *Ueber die Lehre des Spinoza*, p. 132; cf. Schleiermacher, S.W. III: 4,1, p. 292.

[2] Dilthey, *Denkmale ...*, p. 66 ff. S.W. III:4,1, p. 300.

[3] Ibid., "Hätte er nun hiervon den leichten Uebergang genommen zu der Einsicht, dass Raum und Zeit das eigenthümliche unserer Vorstellungsart ausmache: so würde er nicht gesagt haben, Ausdehnung und Denken wären die Attribute, vielweniger die einzigen Attribute des unendlichen. Hierauf beruht die einzige Differenz zwischen ihm und Kant."

[4] The Absolute is "das unbedingte, welches nicht ausserhalb der Reihe, sondern nur in dem ganzen Inbegriff derselben zu finden ist," and "ein unendliches, innerhalb dessen alles endliche ist." S.W. III:4,1, p. 290 ff.

[5] Schleiermacher wrote, in reference to Leibnitz: "Hier scheint mir Spinoza in jeder Rücksicht siegreich. Man modificire die Monadologie wie man will, am Ende muss doch immer die unendliche Monade die endlichen geschaffen haben, also der ärgste Verstoss gegen das Ex nihilo nihil fit ... Aber noch mehr. Mit welchem Recht gehört denn die unendliche Monade nicht zur Welt?" S.W. III: 4,1, p. 293. Also, "Leibnitz war weder gemüssigt noch veranlasst, eine Mehrheit des existirenden anzunehmen, ja er ist nicht einmal im Stande, jene Mehrheit auf eine haltbare Weise zu constituiren, und Spinoza würde ihm leicht den Uebergang zu seiner Meinung von der Einheit des unendlichen abtrozen." S.W. III:4,1, p. 296; Schleiermacher in relation to Kant: S.W. III:4,1, p. 295, 299 ff.

[6] Cf. Dilthey, *Denkmale ...*, p. 34 ff. Religion, for Schleiermacher during this period, is the projection of the ethical into the eternal. However, this is *not* constitutive for his later moral theory.

Absolute as both immanent and transcendent. The Absolute, as a thing in itself, had to be separate from the human subject. However, on the other hand, the Absolute impressed itself upon the human subject, and functioned as the subjective imagination of the mind. The Absolute, therefore, for Schleiermacher, was 1) the thing-in-itself, and as such it was *transcendent*; 2) the identity of subject and object, and was therefore *immanent*.[1]

E. *The Development of Schleiermacher's Ethical Theory Before* 1796

Schleiermacher's ethical theory, influenced as it had been by Kantian philosophy was up to this point primarily rational. A theory of religion had to fit into his ethical system, which was nothing more than "the practical consequences of the maximus."[2] His definition of Christianity included, of necessity, categories which were ethical in character.

However, an emotional element was soon to introduce itself into the development of Schleiermacher's thought. This emotional element can already be seen in *Über die Freiheit des Menschen*. In *Über das höchste Gut*, where Schleiermacher discarded happiness as the highest good, he could nonetheless recognize that the concept of happiness did not necessarily damage morality.[3] The introduction of an emotional element in his ethical theory was occasioned by the happy experiences he encountered when he stayed with the Dohna family in Schlobitten.[4] In Schlobitten, Schleiermacher did not have too much time for his scholarly pursuits.[5] Instead, he spoke of the "sociable life" which he enjoyed there.[6]

---

[1] S.W. III:4,1, p. 300 ff.

[2] Br. IV, p. 9.

[3] Dilthey, *Denkmale* ..., p. 11. cf. also his letter to Brinkmann, Br. IV, p. 36.

[4] Schleiermacher spoke of this to his father: "Sie können sich leicht denken, wie sehr schwer es mir in vieler Rücksicht wird, Schlobitten zu verlassen. Sie wissen, wie viel Glückliche Stunden ich hier gelebt habe, und wie ich die meisten Menschen hier in einem hohen Grade liebe und ehre." Br. I, p. 123. His enthusiasm runs to this, "Es sind alles so gute Menschen, und es ist eine so lehrreiche und zugleich so liebe Schule. Mein Herz wird hier ordentlich gepflegt und braucht nicht unter dem Unkraut kalter Gelehrsamkeit zu welken, und meine religiösen Empfindungen sterben nicht unter theologischen Grübeleien." Br. I, p. 100.

[5] Cf. Br. III, p. 42, he says *"Ich lerne mich und andre kennen,* ich habe Muster der Nachahmung und fühle, dass ich sein besserer Mensch werde." Br. I, p. 100 ff., also Br. I, p. 92.

[6] "Ich bin fähig selbst innerlich glücklich zu sein, indem mir mein Herz sagt, dass ich das Gute und Edle aufrichtig liebe." *Ibid.*

Schleiermacher subsequently described moral freedom as a spontaneous outpouring or effulgence from the being of man. The concept of freedom was related directly to his conception of "Menschheit." "To be inwardly happy," he said, involved not only man's consciousness of himself as well as his emotions, but could be seen also in man's free and spontaneous expression of the moral life. It could also be expressed in the general sense that life could be called good and valuable.[1]

Schleiermacher asserted that the experience of "composure" ("Gemüthsruhe") must be one's own, and must be an immediate and natural experience.[2]

It is important to note that during the period Schleiermacher was in Schlobitten, he considered the emotional experiences which entered his life to be corollaries to the rational life of man. He began, however, to relate the emotional and the rational aspects of experience together, and by so doing, has taken another decisive step away from the Kantian ethical system.[3]

In his New Year's sermon, *Die wahre Schäzung des Lebens*, Schleiermacher identified the objective of man with that which is most human, which he said could be found within man's own nature.[4]

---

[1] Ich habe immer viel von einer wahren und einer falschen Glückseligkeit gehört, aber es ist keine Saite in meiner Seele, die diesen Ton entspricht ... Lust ist nichts als Eindruck und Empfindung, aber eben weil sie eine Empfindung ist, ist sie immer wahr, nie etwas andres, als sie scheint ... Sieh! das Vergnügen ist überall sich selbst gleich; es giebt kein wahres und falsches; es ist immer nur der einfache leichte Eindruck des Augenblicks." Dilthey, *Denkmale* ..., p. 55 ff.

[2] "Das ist aber," he wrote to his father, "nach meinen Vorstellungen bei unsrer lieben Charlotte nicht der Fall; sie muss sich mit Gewalt in diese Empfindungen hineinversetzen und eine solche Spannung hält die Seele nicht lange aus. Die Täuschung – denn eine solche erzwungene Ruhe ist doch gewiss für nichts anderes zu rechnen – zerfliesst und so fürchte ich, dass sie bald wieder mit mancherlei Missmuth zu kämpfen haben wird." Br. I, p. 105.

[3] Cf. Schleiermacher's two works, *Die wahre Schäzung des Lebens* and *Ueber den Werth des Lebens*; cf. also, S.W. II, 7, p. 138 ff., 141, 144. The same optimistic outlook toward life prevails; cf. "Da es ist denn gewiss eben so falsch, wenn viele Menschen glauben, dieses Leben sei für den menschlichen Geist ein Zustand der Verbannung, nach dessen Ende er immer schmachte, wo es ihm nicht möglich sei einen Grad der Vollkommenheit zu erlangen. Nein, die Einrichtung dieses Lebens ist voll von Gelegenheiten unsere Kräfte zu äussern und zu üben, zu erhöhen und zu veredeln!".

[4] "Die Vermögen meiner Seele enthalten meine Bestimmung. Was ist nun in mir? In zwei grosse Zweige theilt sich alles Wirken der Seele; Erkennen, Begehren. Diese beiden also muss das Leben in Thätigkeit erhalten." The objective for life must be found: "Erkennen und Begehren soll nicht zwei in mir sein, sondern eins. Vollkommene Uebereinstimmung beider, in dem vollsten Mass, worin beide

"Die Menschheit" became the locus for all of life. We see that Schleiermacher had now overcome the dualism which existed between the rational and the emotional aspects of man's experience. The life of man was most real when he experienced his oneness with the world. The concept of "Die Menschheit" revealed the perfect synthesis of the rational and the emotional. Schleiermacher had discovered, thereby, the unity of man's active and passive natures.

Schleiermacher's religio-philosophical development to this point demonstrated a further divergence from Kantian Rationalism. He had come to the same conclusion as had Hamann, Herder, and Jacobi: that one could not separate reason from sensuous experience, nor could freedom be separated from necessity. Schleiermacher found a new point of departure for his philosophical program. It was not Kant's "pure reason" but reason combined with sensuous experience which he believed was closely related to perception. Schleiermacher called this new conception "die Humanität" or "die Menschheit."[1]

II. The Intuitive Period, (1796–1802)

A. *The Principal Presuppositions for Schleiermacher's Conception of Religion at the Beginning of the* 19*th Century*

During this period, in the development of Schleiermacher's thought, a period in which both the *Monologen* and the *Reden* were published, Schleiermacher continued to define the Absolute in terms of the identify of subject and object and, as well, as the Thing-in-Itself.

When Schleiermacher defined the Absolute as the identity of subject and object, he was, in reality, embracing Transcendental Philosophy, which, of course, preserved much of pre-Kantian Dogmatic Rationalism. The strong rationalistic elements in Kant were propagated most faithfully by Fichte. It is of interest to note the relationship of Schleiermacher to Fichte at this time, at about the year 1800.

Through his association with the Schlegel brothers, Schleiermacher took a lively interest in the literary journal *Athenaeum*.[2] Fichte's

---

in mir möglich sind, Einheit beider in Zweck und Gegenstand, das ist Humanität, das ist das schöne Ziel, welches dem menschlichen Wesen gesteckt ist." Dilthey, *Denkmale* ..., p. 52 ff.

[1] Individuality is for Schleiermacher, "nichts anders, als die Cohäsion, die identische Vereinigung der Kräfte einer gewissen Masse an einem Punkte." S. W III: 4,1, p. 299.

[2] Called by A.W. Schlegel "Kritische Jahrbücher der deutschen Literatur," Br. III, p. 183.

contributions were sought for the journal. Schelling was extremely helpful in bringing this about.[1] Schleiermacher, however, only reluctantly identified himself with "the department of Transcendental Philosophy" which was associated in a conscious way with the *Athenaeum*. Independently, Schleiermacher had come to the position where he identified subject and object in the Absolute. This same identification was, of course, a basic premise of Transcendental Philosophy. At the beginning of the 19th century Schleiermacher could be associated with Fichte primarily at the point of the immanental understanding of the Absolute. In no way was he dependent upon Fichte's philosophical position, and he never agreed with the problems Fichte formulated for philosophy. Although Schleiermacher maintained that the Absolute was to be conceived as the identity of subject and object, he did not, as Fichte, begin with pure reason. Rather, he included the "Thing-in-Itself" as a part of his definition of the Absolute. Furthermore, Schleiermacher could not accept Fichte's starting point for philosophical speculation, that is, pure self-consciousness. This reduction of phenomena was wholly unacceptable to Schleiermacher.[2] He considered this a denial of the reality of the universe.[3] He was conscious of the fact that a rationalistic philosophical system which treated the Absolute as pure selfconsciousness must result ultimately in a nihilism. Schleiermacher demanded "a higher realism," and by so doing, went beyond the Transcendental Philosophy of Fichte.

Schleiermacher believed that pure reason or pure self-consciousness could never grasp the Absolute as both immanent and transcendent. For that reason, Schleiermacher had to find a new point of departure in order to overcome the Rationalism of his time. He was successful in finding another philosophical starting point sometime after 1796, when he conceived of the synthesis of man's active and passive natures. He indicated this radical change in his philosophical position in *Vertraute Briefe über Friedrich Schlegels Lucinda* (1800). It was obvious that Schleiermacher appreciated Schlegel's novel. The most striking

---

[1] Cf. H. Süskind: *Der Einfluss Schellings auf die Entwicklung von Schleiermachers System* (Berlin: Reimer, 1909), p. 93. cf. also the following reference from Br. III, p. 183, p. 224, p. 232 ff., etc., which also indicate Schleiermacher's association with Transcendental Philosophy.

[2] Br. IV, p. 53.

[3] "Er wird das Universum vernichten, indem er es zu bilden scheint, er wird es herabwürdigen zu einer blossen Allegorie, zu einem nichtigen Schattenbilde unserer eignen Beschränktheit." Br. IV, p. 55.

part of the novel was the bold assertion of the role the senses played in love.[1] The sensual, said Schlegel, had a legitimate function within the life of man, and could be considered to be equal to the rational aspects of man's nature. Furthermore, Schlegel had asserted, there could be a harmonious relationship between life and reason. The novel, which described in a very lucid way the sensual aspects of love, did not define love solely in terms of sensuality.[2] To the sensual the spiritual had to be joined. By means of this union the sensual part of love (and life) took on new meaning.[3] Reason and the sensual were united in love, yet they were both intrinsic to love.[4]

Schleiermacher's conception of reason had begun to change too at this time. The youthful period in Schleiermacher's philosophical development saw reason dominated by Kant's conception of the practical reason. However, he began to realize that reason played only a small role in ethical decision. Reason was not itself the creative factor. During this time, too, Schleiermacher could speak of "ratio ignava Kantii."[5] He demanded a concept of reason which would permit

---

[1] In Eduard, there is a representative of this position: "Sie sagen, die Liebe als Fülle der Lebenskraft, als Blüthe der Sinnlichkeit, sei bei den alten etwas göttliches gewesen, bei uns sei sie ein Skandal; ist sie es aber wol aus einem andern Grunde, als weil wir sie immer dem intellektuellen mystischen Bestandtheil der Liebe, der das höchste Product der modernen Kultur ist, entgegensezen?" S.W. III, 1, p. 481. cf. Wehrung's and Dilthey's discussion of Schleiermacher's review of Fichte's *Die Bestimmung des Menschen*, 1800; *Athenaeum* III:2, (1800), p. 281 ff; G. Wehrung, *Der geschichtsphilosophische Standpunkt Schleiermachers zur Zeit seiner Freundschaft mit den Romantikern* (Strassburg: 1907), p. 130; and Dilthey, *Denkmale ...*, p. 93.

[2] "Dagegen habe ich nichts, dass man von der Beschaffenheit eines Kunstwerks einen Schluss auf die moralischen Ansichten und Ideen des Künstlers mache, und eben deshalb habe ich immer den Wieland für eine unedle Natur gehalten, weit mehr als etwa den Crebillon, oder wen Sie sonst von dieser Art nennen wollen. Diese Leute ignoriren den geistigen Bestandtheil der Liebe gänzlich, sie geht bei ihnen immer nur von der Schönheit oder vielmehr von dem Reiz der Gestalt aus, die mahlen immer nur die Sinnlichkeit und sind dabei ganz unbefangen." S.W. III:1, p. 479.

[3] S.W. III:1, p. 446.

[4] "Hier hast Du Liebe ganz und aus einem Stück, das geistigste und das sinnlichste nicht nur in demselben Werk und denselben Personen neben einander, sondern in jeder Aeusserung und in jenem Zuge aufs innigste verbunden." S.W. III:1, p. 431.

[5] S.W. I:5, p. 9. Also "Nach Kant besteht die ganze Tugendprocedur darin, dass man sich in eine permanente Jury constituirt, und immerfort über die Maximen, die sich präsentiren, Gericht hält, oder noch besser wie im Turniergericht, wo die Ritter ihre Wappenprobe ablegen müssen. Kommt ein Turnierfähiger, so wird er in die Schranken gelassen und in die Trompete gestossen gar weidlich, Kommt aber keiner – ja die Turnierrichter können keinen machen." Dilthey. *Denkmale ...*, p. 93.

reason to be creative. This was the presupposition for his proposed "Kritik aller Moral" (1797), and the *Monologen* (1800), and which he also expressed in his mature ethical treatise, *Grundlinien einer Kritik der bisherigen Sittenlehre* (1803).[1]

Schleiermacher asserted that reason did not only have a formal structure, as Kant would have it, but as well it had a positive and creative function. The freedom of reason was therefore not a negative freedom (that is, dominion over the sensuous), but rather a positive freedom, that is, reason as a creative and organizing function.[2]

Schleiermacher was more and more conscious of the great opposition between his own position and that of Kant.[3] The practical reason, which for Kant had become a passive force which always was uniform and abstract, had become for Schleiermacher a vital and positive force for action within the life of man.

Man was defined by Schleiermacher in terms of the opposition between his senses and his reason. Nonetheless, man's essential nature, for Schleiermacher, even during this period, was *reason*. But, with his criticism of Kant's conception of the self he introduced the notion that the self was to be defined both in terms of reason and nature, and, in fact, in terms of their unity.[4]

Schleiermacher's conception of man during this period presupposed the unity of man's spirit and nature, his reason and sensuous experience, his active and passive natures. He had broken with the Kantian conception of pure reason. "Die Menschheit" became the basis for his newly found "anthropological" principle.[5]

B. *The Monologen as an Expression of Schleiermacher's New "Anthropological" Principle*

"Die Menschheit" and "die Freiheit" were interchangeable categories in the *Monologen*.[6] The goal and meaning of man's life was not transcendent and exterior to him, but was found within his own

---

[1] Cf. W. Dilthey, "Schleiermacher", *Allgemeine Deutsche Biographie*, 31 Bd., (Berlin: Reimer, 1890), p. 426.

[2] Schleiermacher, at this time, is working with a general theory of culture; cf. Dilthey, *Denkmale ...*, p. 131, and Br. III, p. 79.

[3] Cf. *Athenaeum*, 1799, and Schleiermacher's criticism of Kant's *Anthropologie* (1798).

[4] *Athenaeum*, II:2, p. 302, 303.

[5] S.W. III, p. 431, also S.W. III,1, p. 447.

[6] Cf. 1 Aufl.

nature.[1] This was so because already in Schleiermacher there was the ultimate unity of sensuous experience with reason. The concept of "Individuality" is the basis for this unity. To realize this unity in one's life became the objective for all of life. However, Schleiermacher realized that he was still dependent in his thinking upon the Kantian categorical imperative. He still recognized no other ethic than the imperative.[2] The categorical imperative had as its only function, "the universality and consequence of the maxim."[3] But in the *Monologen* reason was given a positive and a creative freedom, which corresponded to "die Menschheit," or the whole man. Schleiermacher's discovery of this concept of reason was occasioned, as he said, by an experience of "freedom through the act."[4] He could not be satisfied with anything less than a positive freedom which related itself to both nature and reason.[5] Morality therefore had to have an element of organic growth related to it. The moral law was not analogous to a legal system any longer, but was related instead to the laws of nature. Nature and morality were associated as correlatives.[6] However, freedom did not mean licentiousness or freedom from obligation. Freedom was defined in such a way that it was restricted by "Individuality," as well as by "the foreign freedom," and by "the mystery of nature."[7] "The consciousness of the whole man" is Schleiermacher's conception of man as he is involved in the totality of nature.

The *Monologen* defined reason as "Spirit," that is, reason which is free and creative. With his concept of "die Menschheit," Schleier-

---

[1] Cf. Schleiermacher's position in *Die Wahre Schäzung des Lebens* (1792) and *Ueber den Werth des Lebens* (1792–3), which correspond to the main thesis of *Monologen* (1800). Fr. Schleiermacher, *Monologen – Eine Neujahrsgabe* (1800), krit. Ausgabe v. F. M. Schiele, (2 Aufl., Leipzig: Meiner, 1914).

[2] Cf. *Monologen* 1, p. 33, p. 38 ff.

[3] *Ibid.*, p. 38.

[4] *Monologen* 1, p. 38 also "Von innen kam die hohe Offenbarung durch keine Tugendlehre und kein System der Weisen hervorgebracht." M.1, p. 35; cf. also his reflection on the time in the home of Dohna, "Im fremden Hause ging der Sinn mir auf für schönes gemeinschaftliches Dasein, ich sah wie Freiheit erst veredelt und recht gestaltet die zarten Geheimnisse der Menschheit, die dem Ungeweihten immer dunkel bleiben, der sie nur als Bande der Natur verehrt." M.1, p. 108.

[5] M.1, p. 54, p. 36.

[6] "Ein einziger freier Entschluss gehört dazu ein Mensch zu sein: wer den einmal gefasst, wirds immer bleiben; wer aufhört es zu sein, ists nie gewesen." M.1, p. 35.

[7] Schleiermacher restricts this freedom further by speaking of "Würdigkeit der Glückseligkeit."

macher had defined the nature of the ethical task.[1] The moral life was equated with human life and freedom. Reason was considered to be superior to the senses, but cooperated with them to make the human being a creative organism. Man could never be an abstract or general ethical being, but could only be an "individual." This was his "higher morality."[2]

"Die Menschheit" was defined in the *Monologen* as "the eternal community of Spirits" ("Gemeinschaft der Geister"). "Die Menschheit" always included the unity of reason and sense. This unity was located in *humanitas*, which was for Schleiermacher a collective term. The concept of "die Menschheit" was referred always to the world. Because of the corporate sense of "die Menschheit" (in the ethical sphere), there was an inner necessity to relate one's life to another.[3] "The world" is "die Menschheit" as "the eternal community of Spirits" ("die ewige Gemeinschaft der Geister"). Ethical activity, for Schleiermacher, was always "related to the self" ("Selbstbilden"), but it also shared in the construction of "the world."[4] The formulation of one's "Individuality" was always the highest ethical goal. However, it was primarily an expression of reason. The formation of the self always presupposed the community,[5] that is, the expression of the freedom which belonged to man to relate himself to another. Mans'

---

[1] M.1, p. 19.

[2] M.1, p. 39. cf. Eck's discussion of individuality in Schleiermacher, *Ueber die Herkunft des Individualitätsgedankens bei Schleiermacher*, 1908, p. 26 ff. Schleiermacher's conception of individuality is developed from his study of Spinoza and Plato, cf. *Kr. d. bish. S.* (1803), cf. also M. 1, p. 40, 103, "Es genügte mir nicht, die Menschheit in ungebildeten rohen Massen anzuschaun, welche innerlich sich völlig gleich, nur ausserlich durch Reibung und Berührung vorübergehende flüchtige Phänomene bilden"; "Jeder Mensch soll auf eigne Art die Menschheit darstellen, in einer eignen Mischung ihrer Elemente, damit auf jede Weise sie sich offenbare, und wirklich werde in der Fülle der Unendlichkeit Alles was aus ihrem Schoosse hervorgehen kann." Identity is "die Cohäzion, die identische Vereinigung der Kräfte einer gewissen Masse an einem Punkte."

[3] "Es stösst die Freiheit an der Freiheit sich, und was geschieht, trägt der Beschränkung und Gemeinschaft Zeichen." M.1, p. 17.

[4] Cf. what Schleiermacher wrote to Madame Herz: "Eigentlich giebt es doch keinen grösseren Gegenstand des Wirkens, als das Gemüth, ja überhaupt keinen andern, wirken Sie etwa da nicht? O Sie fruchtbare, Sie vielwirkende, eine wahre Ceres sind Sie für die innere Natur und legen einen so grossen Accent in die Thätigkeit der Aussenwelt ... Sehen Sie nur, was Sie gethan haben und noch thun und thun werden, und gestehen Sie, dass dieses Thun und Bilden unendlich mehr ist, als Alles, was der Mensch über das grosse Chaos, welches er sich zurecht machen soll, gewinnen kann." Br. I, p. 195 ff.

[5] "Ich muss hinaus in mancherlei Gemeinschaft mit den andern Geistern zu

self-activity presupposed the receptive and passive aspect of the community.[1] Self-activity was a presupposition for the activity of the human organism; it was conceived to be the unity of man's active and receptive natures, his spiritual expression, and his participation in nature.

Man's ethical activity, the formation of the self, presupposed at the same time man's consciousness of himself. The act of self-consciousness had been designated by Schleiermacher's man's symbolizing ability (vorstellend). The formation of the self is his organizing ability (darstellend). These two acts presupposed one another and were interrelated to one another.[2]

C. *The Conception of the Absolute*

Schleiermacher had defined the Absolute in both a transcendental and immanental way. There was a further conception of the Absolute which belonged to this period, that is, the Absolute as the "harmony of the immanental and the transcendental." Schleiermacher had arrived at his conception of "die Menschheit" as the unity of man's active and passive natures by an *ethical* analysis. The ethical life expressed the interior life of man. However, the way into the interior life was also the way to the Absolute. During this period, the world of the inner life was conceived to be a part of religion for Schleiermacher.[3] However, Schleiermacher shared the Romantic view of his time and defined Religion not only in terms of the Self ("Selbstanschauung"), but also as in terms of Another ("Anschauung anderer").[4]

The relationship of human self-consciousness and the Absolute may be summarized as follows:

1. In human self-consciousness, considered as active, the Absolute

---

schauen, was es für Menschheit giebt, und was davon mir fremde bleibt, was mein eigen werden kann." M.1, p. 47.

[1] Cf. M.1, p. 44, 45, 47 ff.; 51, 52, also R.1, p. 167.

[2] M.1, p. 24, 34, 50.

[3] "Es ist die Beschränktheit der Philosophie beides (Selbstanschauung-Anschauung des Universums) zu trennen. Ihr Leben ist todt ohne Reflexion, und ihre Philosophie ist ein lebloses Gemälde," Dilthey, *Denkmale* ..., p. 118, also "Meine Religion ist so durch und durch Herzreligion, dass ich für keine andere Raum habe." Br.1, p. 208, cf. also: S.W. II:7, p. 135, M.1, p. 21–24.

[4] Cf. Schleiermacher's thoughts regarding the writing of a romantic novel: Br. IV, p. 537, 540, 538; I, p. 241.

was given in the experience of *freedom*, and was therefore to be understood in an immanental way.[1]

2. In human self-consciousness, considered as *receptive*, the Absolute was given in the feeling of *dependence*, and was therefore to be understood in a transcendental way.[2]

3. In human self-consciousness, considered as the harmonious unity of man's activity and receptivity, the Absolute was understood as the "harmony of the *immanental* and the *transcendental*." The *Reden* of Schleiermacher was an example of this third conception of the Absolute. Religion was located within human nature and added to the harmonious totality of relationships. Religion comprised the unity of the active and passive elements of man's existence.[3]

D. *The Absolute as the "Harmony of the Immanental and the Transcendental" in the Reden* (1799)

The essence of Religion was defined by Schleiermacher to be different from metaphysical and moral structures.[4]

Schleiermacher noted that Religion was often united with a metaphysical system. He warned his listeners not to seek the Eternal Being "beyond the world."[5] Religion should not either be combined with ethics or law.[6] The laws of the state, which were founded upon contract, were not to be identified with morality. However, no ethical or legal system could be identified with Religion.[7] Schleiermacher insisted that even if Religion had the same object as metaphysics and morals, i.e., "the relationship of the universe to man,"[8] Religion could not be identified with them. Metaphysics attempted to discover the Nature of the universe and from it deduce the necessary components

---

[1] "Selbstanschauung und Anschauung des Universums sind Wechselbegriffe; darum ist jede Reflexion unendlich." Dilthey, *Denkmale* ..., p. 118.

[2] cf. also M.1, p. 23 ff., M.1, p. 6. Life is "nur eine flüchtige Harmonie, aus der Berührung des Vergänglichen und des Ewigen entsprungen"; also M.1, p. 12 ff; "Der Geist ist das erste und das einzige," M.1, p. 15 ff.

[3] "Ich bin von einer innern und unwiderstehlichen Notwendigkeit, die mich göttlich beherrscht, gedrungen zu reden." R.1, p. 3; cf. also R.1, p. 5, 69, 105, 118, 120, 133, 234.

[4] R.1, p. 14 ff., p. 123, p. 126, p. 130 ff.

[5] R.1, p. 2; "Die Furcht vor einem ewigen Wesen und das Rechnen auf ein andere Welt, das, meint Ihr, seien die Angle, aller Religion.", R.1, p. 22; R.1, pe 145 ff., also p. 31. 34, 58.

[6] R.1, p. 31.

[7] R.1, p. 33 ff. cf. also, p. 34, 63, 68 ff., 107 ff., 219, 222.

R.1, p. 41.

of reality.[1] Morality developed a system of moral rules from man's relationship to the universe. Neither of these were to be identified with Religion.

Religion never attempted to know the Absolute in an objective way. Religion, for Schleiermacher in the *Reden*, was defined as revelation and "immediate experience." He had never forgotten the lessons he had learned during his Moravian period.[2] The "immediate experience", however, was never a supernatural experience, a fact which Schleiermacher realized after his rejection of Moravians, but Religion was "seeing the infinite in the finite."[3]

Furthermore, Schleiermacher rejected the identification of Religion with ethics as Kant and Fichte had done. Religion had nothing in common with a rational ethic, he wrote. Religion was to be associated with a new kind of morality, in which moral freedom was based upon the unity of reason and sense experience. This new morality was to be characterized by spontaneity and organic growth. Nature was the locus for the moral activity of a spiritual being.[4] Man was considered to be a unity of activity and passivity, reason, and sense experience.

Religion therefore became the expression of that which belonged to the highest expression of the nature of man.[5] The religious consciousness was "the primary consciousness within man."[6] Within the inner life of man, the universe expressed itself.

Schleiermacher continued to define the Absolute in two ways. The Absolute was "the infinite Menschheit"[7] and "the higher World-Spirit."[8] The individual therefore was an "element of the Whole."[9] The Infinite became finite and individual, and appeared in "multi-

---

[1] *Ibid.*

[2] "Anschauen will sie (die Religion) das Universum, in seinen eigenen Darstellungen und Handlungen will sie es andächtig belauschen, von seinen unmittelbaren Einflüssen will sie sich in kindlicher Passivität ergreifen und erfüllen lassen." R.1, p. 50.

[3] "Alle Begebenheiten in der Welt als Handlungen eines Gottes vorstellen, das ist Religion." R.1, p. 57.

[4] R.1, p. 50, 57, 92, 113, 115.

[5] Schleiermacher expressed this throughout R.1, cf. p. 122, 20, 12, 144, 14 ff., 5, 10, 11, 12, 234, etc. Religion "will im Menschen ... das Unendliche sehen, dessen Abdruck, dessen Darstellung." R.1, p. 51.

[6] "Auch die äussere Welt, mit ihren ewigsten Gesezen. Wie mit ihren flüchtigsten Erscheinungen, strahlt in tausend zarten und erhabenen Allegorien, wie ein magischer Spiegel, das Höchste und Innerste unseres Wesens auf uns zurük."

[7] R.1, p. 10.

[8] R.1, p. 103, 108.

[9] R.1, p. 153.

plicity" and "Individuality."[1] On the other hand, the Absolute was
an abstract unity, a quantum, from which "Menschheit" and "Individualität" were obliterated. On the one hand, the Absolute was the
highest consciousness of man, the spiritual Nature of man. On the
other hand, the Absolute was the real object, that which was located
outside of the subject and separate from it. In both cases the Absolute was considered to be an absolute unity. However, in the first
instance this unity was derived from a subjective consciousness, a
Spirit;[2] in the other, the unity was found in the object, in the thing.
Religion, on the one hand, must "be inwardly expressed;"[3] imagination became the form of this expression. On the other hand, the
unity, "das Universum," "das Unendliche," was conceived as something separated from the religious subject.[4]

Schleiermacher had modified the Kantian categories by his con
ception of the Absolute. "Das Ding an sich" and the unity of consciousness were Kant's transcendental presuppositions for the objectivity of
knowledge. Schleiermacher equated these. By doing so, he avoided
the Kantian dualism. His conception of Religion as "Anschauen des
Universums" was for Schleiermacher the "most universal and highest
form of Religion."[5] Religion as "Anschauen des Universums" was to
express the absolute unity as *subjective* (immanent in consciousness),
and *objective* (transcendent to the object). Religion was the synthetic
and harmonious relationship of this dual aspect of consciousness [6]
"Die Anschauung" defined the identity of the active and passive
aspects of man. "Gefühl" was introduced at this point and was also
considered to be constitutive for Religion.[7] "Gefühl" was defined in
two ways: first, as "Ursache der Anschauung," secondly, as "eine

---

[1] R.1, p. 53.

[2] R.1, p. 67.

[3] *Ibid.*, p. 77.

[4] *Ibid.*, p. 56; "Das Universum bildet sich selbst seine Betrachter und Bewun-
derer," R.1, p. 143. *Die Menschheit* is "das grösste Kunstwerk ... welches das
Universum unmittelbar bildet," R.1, p. 173.

[5] R.1, p. 55.

[6] Religion is *Gefühl* "Bei denen das Universum der eine, und auf irgend eine
Art Euer eignes Ich der andre von den Punkten ist, zwischen denen das Gemüt
schwebt." R.1, p. 111.

[7] "Anschauen des Universums, ich bitte, befreundet Euch mit diesem Begriff,
er ist der Angel meiner ganzen Rede, er ist die allgemeinste und höchste Formel
der Religion." R.1, p. 55; also "Endlich, um das allgemeine Bild der Religion zu
vollenden, erinnert Euch, dass jede Anschauung ihrer Natur nach mit einem
Gefühl verbunden ist." R.1, p. 66.

Veränderung in Eurem innern Bewusstsein." "Gefühl" therefore included "Anschauung."[1] "Anschauung" was, furthermore, a presupposition for "Gefühl" and "Gefühl" was a presupposition for "Anschauung."[2]

The religious "Anschauung" had to "generate itself from the fullness of the inner life,"[3] if Religion was to be real, said Schleiermacher.[4] This is "das Gemüth" of man, which appeared in the activity of the religious "Anschauung."[5] This subjective power was also called imagination.[6] The religious "Anschauung" was first, the activity of the object, that is, the universe standing overagainst the subject; but secondly, it was the product of the religious subject, "die Phantasie," "das Gemüt," and in this instance was not separated from the subject.

The religious "Anschauung" was considered to be similar to other forms of "Anschauung" in its association with feeling. Feeling was bound up with every "Anschauung."[7] Feeling was described, first, as a "symptom" of "die Anschauungen," and secondly, as the presupposition for "die Anschauungen." The presupposition for the religious "Anschauung" was the "primal feeling of that which is eternal and living in Nature."[8] Religion was defined therefore by Schleiermacher, sometimes as "Gefühl," and sometimes as "Anschauung," because Religion was a conscious unity of "Gefühl" and "Anschauung." The character of "Gefühl" was more than a subjective experience, however, but was positively related to the universe. The character of "Anschauung" included the relationship it had to the individual. Religion therefore was not only "Anschauen des Universums," but

---

[1] "Anschauung ohne Gefühl ist nichts ... Gefühl ohne Anschauung ist auch nichts: beide sind nur dann und deswegen etwas, wenn und weil sie ursprünglich eins und ungetrennt sind." R.1, p. 73; cf. also, R.1, p. 58.

[2] "Alles Anschauen gehet aus von einem Einfluss des Angeschaueten auf den Anschauenden ... So die Religion; das Universum ist in einer ununterbrochenen Tätigkeit und offenbart sich uns jeden Augenblick. Jede Form, die es hervorbringt, jedes Wesen, dem es nach der Fülle des Lebens ein abgesondertes Dasein gibt, jede Begebenheit, die es aus seinem reichen, immer fruchtbaren Schosse herausschüttet, ist ein Handeln desselben auf uns." R.1, p. 55 ff.

[3] R.1, p. 76

[4] R. 1, p. 80 ff.

[5] R.1, p. 87 ff.

[6] R.1, p. 129.

[7] Ibid., p. 66.

[8] Ibid., p. 53, cf. also R.1, p. 108, p. 299.

also "Gefuhl des Unendlichen,"[1] that is, "Anschauung und Gefühl."[2] The religious experience, Schleiermacher asserted, was found in that conscious moment when "Gefühl" and "Anschauung" were united.[3] Schleiermacher had come, in this way, to an entirely new definition of Religion. Religion was properly neither "Anschauung" nor "Gefühl," but the conscious unity of both.[4]

Furthermore, Schleiermacher rejected every attempt to reduce Religion to a psychological experience. Religion was "something specific."[5] Religion was, therefore, "a highest philosophy" in which both metaphysics and morals were united.[6] Schleiermacher spoke further of Religion as the "Ground" or the presupposition for the different experiences of human life.[7] However, just as Schleiermacher defined Religion as "a highest philosophy," the presupposition for the theoretical and practical areas of experience, he also defined Religion from a standpoint which was independent of science, morals, art, love, and Spirit.[8] Religion became, however, the necessary presupposition for metaphysics and morals. In this positive relationship to these other areas of experience, the transcendental character of Religion was

---

[1] R.1, p. 54, 65; cf. also R.1, p. 111, 68, 108 ff., for the relation of *Anschauung* and *Gefühl*.

[2] R.1, p. 50; also "Vergönnt mir, einen Augenblick darüber zu trauern, dass ich von beiden nicht anders als getrennt reden kann; de feinste Geist der Religion geht dadurch verloren für meine Rede." R.1, p. 71 ff.

[3] "Jener erste geheimnisvolle Augenblick, der bei jeder sinnlichen Wahrnehmung verkommt, ehe noch Anschauung und Gefühl sich trennen, so der Sinn und sein Gegenstand gleichsam ineinander geflossen und eine gewarden sind." R.1, p. 73. "Ich liege am Busen der unendlichen Welt: ich bin in diesem Augenblick ihre Seele ... Sie ist in diesem Augenblicke mein Leib ... Die geringste Erschütterung, und es verweht die heilige Umarmung, und nun erst steht die Anschauung vor mir als eine abgesonderte Gestalt ... und nun erst arbeitet sich das Gefühl aus dem Innern empor ... Dieser Moment ist die höchste Blüte der Religion ... Es ist die Geburtsstunde alles Lebendigen in der Religion." R.1, p. 74 ff.

[4] Cf. R.1, p. 75. In reality, Schleiermacher's conception of religion at this time is a "sliding between" religion defined as *Anschauung* and *Gefühl*, and the conscious unity of *Anschauung* and *Gefühl*. Schleiermacher had attempted to harmonize the double aspect of the absolute unity of *Anschauung* and *Gefühl*.

[5] R.1, p. 47; cf. R.1, p. 50 ff.

[6] *Ibid.*, p. 46.

[7] R.1, p. 20; religion meant, that "der Begriff und das Gefühl, das Gesetz und die Tat bis zu ihrer gemeinschaftlichen Quelle sollen verfolgt, und das wirkliche als ewig und im Wesen der Menschheit notwendig gegründet soll dargestellt werden." R.1, p. 19.

[8] R.1, p. 152; cf. R.1, p. 52, 53; "Spekulation und Praxis haben zu wollen ohne Religion, ist verwegener Übermut, Praxis ist Kunst, Spekulation ist Wissenschaft, Religion is Sinn und Geschmack für das Unendliche."

found.[1] Religion is "the higher realism."[2] Without Religion, man could never discover the basic conditions for morality and individuality.[3] Morality therefore had to be based upon Religion.[4] Religion, as "a highest philosophy," was the transcendental presupposition for metaphysics and morals, knowledge and activity, and interpenetrated them all.

E. *Religion and the Religions in the Reden* (1799)

The essence of Religion which Schleiermacher presented in the *Reden* (the first edition, 1799) was not identified with any particular concrete historical Religion. It was neither identified with a generic concept of Religion, that is, a universal Religion. Schleiermacher had, instead, attempted to present the religious a priori, which was to be the presupposition for all of the particular historical Religions. The religious a priori was that which was specifically religious in every historical Religion. Schleiermacher called the presupposition for every historical Religion "die Religion"[5] and "die wahre Religion,"[6] and "die unendliche Religion,"[7] and "die ewige und unendliche Religion."[8]

The various historical Religions of the world share in that which is the "essence of Religion," said Schleiermacher.[9] This assertion can be validated from Schleiermacher's definition of Religion as "Anschauung und Gefühl."[10] "Anschauung" and "Gefühl" are qualitative terms, singular and individual. Religion as "Anschauung und Gefühl" permitted an infinite variety of religious expressions, but within

---

[1] Cf. R.1, p. 27, 46, 53 ff.

[2] R.1, p. 54. Cf. "das Gegengewicht."

[3] "Das principium individui ist das Mystischste im Gebiet der Philosophie," Br. IV, p. 59.

[4] R. 1, p. 204 f.

[5] R.1, p. 238.

[6] R.1, p. 245.

[7] R.1, p. 238.

[8] R.1, p. 247.

[9] R.1, p. 240, 241.

[10] "Anschauung ist und bleibt immer etwas Einzelnes, Abgesondertes, die unmittelbare Wahrnehmung, weiter nichts; sie zu verbinden und in ein Ganzes zusammenzustellen, ist schon wieder nicht das Geschäft des Sinnes, sondern des abstrakten Denkens. So die bei den unmittelbaren Erfahrungen vom Dasein und Handeln des Universums, bei den einzelnen Anschauungen und Gefühlen bleibt sie stehen; jede derselben ist ein für sich bestehendes Werk ohne Zusammenhang mit andern oder Abhängigkeit von ihnen; von Ableitung und Anknüpfung weiss sie nichts ... alles ist in ihr unmittelbar und für sich wahr. Ein System von Anschauungen, könnt Ihr Euch selbst etwas Wunderlicheres denken?" R.1, p. 58 ff.

each Religion there was "a principle which could individualize itself." Religion was, therefore, based upon the religious a priori. The relationship between the concrete historical Religions and the religious apriori may be summarized in the following way:

1. The particular concrete Religions are the realization of the Religion of the infinite, that is, the "realization of the religious a priori."[1]

2. The particular concrete Religions, are the result of the activity of the World-Spirit ("Weltgeist").[2] Every particular Religion became therefore an individual living organism because of the activity of the World-Spirit upon it.

Religion could never be realized except in a concrete historical form. Historical Religions always possessed, therefore, the quality of imperfection. The religious a priori possessed a positive and necessary characteristic which realized itself in history. In this way, Schleiermacher had asserted that all Religions were both *historical* and *necessary*.

On the basis of this, Schleiermacher could reject all natural Religions, that is, those Religions which were oriented to the faith of the Enlightenment in the adequacy of Reason.[3] Natural Religion could not be real Religion, said Schleiermacher. It did not possess the quality of religious individuality which belonged to real Religions, nor could it ever be historical.[4] Schleiermacher strongly emphasized the principle of individuality,[5] which permitted a positive Religion to be realized in history. The "Grundanschauung" was the eternal character of any particular positive Religion. The "Anschauung" expressed the nature of the relationship of the infinite to the finite.[6]

---

[1] "Wollt Ihr von der Religion nicht nur im allgemeinen einen Begriff haben ... Wollt Ihr sie auch in ihrer *Wirklichkeit* und in ihren Erscheinungen verstehen ... so müsst ihr den eitlen und vergeblichen Wunsch, dass es nur eine geben möchte, aufgeben." R.1, p. 242; also, p. 246, p. 248, p. 237 ff.

[2] "als ein ins Unendliche fortgehendes Werk des Weltgeistes," "Das göttliche Leben ist wie ein zartes Gewächs, dessen Blüten sich noch in der umschlossenen Knospe befruchten, und die heiligen Anschauungen und Gefühl, die Ihr trocknen und aufbewahren könnt, sind die schönen Kelche und Kronen, die sich bald nach jener verborgenen Handlung öffnen aber auch bald wieder abfallen. Es treiben aber immer wieder neue aus der Fülle des innern Lebens." R.1, p. 77.

[3] R.1, p. 243 ff., cf. also R.1, p. 272 ff., 275 ff., 278.

[4] The religious individuality in reference to a positive religion "kann den Geburtstag seines geistigen Lebens angeben und eine Wundergeschichte ersählen vom Ursprung seiner Religion, die als eine unmittelbare Einwirkung der Gottheit und als eine Regung ihres Geistes erscheint." R.1, p. 268.

[5] Cf. R.1, p. 252, 259 ff., 260.

[6] R.1, p. 284.

Every "Grundanschauung" was, therefore, identical with the "essence of Religion," that is, with the Religion of the infinite (which is the religious a priori). Every particular, positive Religion was ultimately founded upon the Religion of the infinite, and from it it received its necessary character. Christianity possessed the quality of being historical[1] because its "Grundanschauung" was identical with Christ's historical appearance.[2] Its "Grundanschauung" was formed from the historical relationship which existed between the infinite and the finite. That is, in the Christian faith the claim was made that the fact of salvation is related to the attempt by the Infinite to unite Himself with the Finite.[3] Christianity, for Schleiermacher, was the highest form of the positive, historical Religions. It was for him "the Religion of Religions."[4]

F. *Religion and Dogmatics as an Example of A Historical Science*

Schleiermacher's concern for Religion during this period was magnified by a concern for the doctrines of the Christian church. Theology became, for Schleiermacher, an example of a historical science.

Positive Religion was "an individual Religion." The positive, historical Religions of the world were organic wholes. The "Anschauung", by which the individual became conscious of Religion was related to the "Grundanschauung" or "Zentralanschauung" of the Religion as a whole. The beliefs of a particular historical Religion were systematized about this "Grundanschauung." Schleiermacher asserted that the religious a priori was realized, or that it "individualized itself," in the multiplicity of what were the positive historical Religions of the World. Both the subject matter and the form of the Religion were derived from Schleiermacher's conception of Religion as an organic whole. The religious a priori, therefore, defined the "essence" of Religion, that is, that which was specifically religious in a given historical Religion.

---

[1] R.1, p. 301.

[2] R.1, p. 293.

[3] This *Grundanschauung* defined "die Gestalt alles religiösen Stoffs in Christentums und seine ganze Form," R.1, p. 291.

[4] For a very cogent presentation of Schleiermacher's conception of religion developed from his preaching (1796–1802) cf. Hj. Lindroth, *Schleiermachers Religionsbegrepp* 2 Vol.; (Uppsala: A. B. Lundequistska Bokhandeln, 1926), I, pp. 241–258.

CHAPTER TWO

THE LATER PERIOD OF SCHLEIERMACHER'S THOUGHT

I. The Critical Period (1802–1806)

A. *Religion and Ethics in Grundlinien einer Kritik der bisherigen Sittenlehre* (1803)[1]

Schleiermacher's use of the Kantian critical method involved "a transcendental deduction of the ethical experience."[2] Schleiermacher had employed a transcendental deduction previously, in the first edition of the *Reden* (1799), in which he insisted upon the transcendental character of Religion in relationship to metaphysics and morals. Without Religion, he asserted, morality could not "raise itself over... strange and traditional forms." Without Religion, speculation could be nothing more than "a rigid and meagre skeleton." Only from the starting point of Religion could metaphysics receive a subject matter.

In *Kritik der bisherigen Sittenlehre*, Schleiermacher's concern was limited to morality, and he did not deal with metaphysics. He began, however, to speak in terms of a "Elementarsphilosophie," in which the ethical experience was but one experience among many. He did *not* say in 1802 that "Physik" and "Ethik" were derived from Religion, but he did write that "Physik" and "Ethik" were both to be considered as sciences, and furthermore that they proceeded from "der Elementarsphilosophie."[3] Schleiermacher had progressed from a definition of Religion as the primary experience of man, that experience from which all of the other experiences were derived, to a position in which he defined Religion as "Elementarsphilosophie" or "Wissen-

---

[1] Fr. Schleiermacher, *Grundlinien einer Kritik der bisherigen Sittenlehre*, krit. Ausgabe N. H. Mulert (Leipzig: Meiner, 1908). Schleiermacher had begun to think about such a work long before this period. Fr. Schlegel in 1797 wrote to his brother Wilhelm that Schleiermacher had surprised him with "Eine wirklich grosse Skizze über die Immoralität aller Moral," *Fr. Schlegels Briefe an seinen Bruder August Wilhelm*, ed. O. Walsel, (Berlin; Reimer, 1830), p. 301; cf. also Hr. 1, p. 356; Br. 1. p. 397 ff.

[2] The critical method, employed by Schleiermacher in the sense of a transcendental deduction, is found first in *Reden* 1, 1799, where Schleiermacher insisted upon the transcendental character of religion in relation to metaphysics and morals. Cf. R.1, p. 53.

[3] Kr. d. bish. S.; S.W. III:, 1. p. 287ff

schaftslehre."[1] Schleiermacher could no longer separate the theoretical from the practical life, or science from life in general.[2] Religion became "a highest philosophy" ("eine hochste Philosophie"),[3] which meant the same as "die Elementarsphlosophie."

Schleiermacher, in *Kritik der bisherigen Sittenlehre*, placed a three-fold task before himself: first, to examine ethical principles with reference to their ability to form a moral system; second, to examine individual moral concepts with reference to their relationship to the highest principle of morality; and third, to examine the moral system with reference to the characteristics of perfection and completeness.[4] Schleiermacher then attempted to find "eine Wissenschaft von den Gründen und dem Zusammenhang aller Wissenschaft."[5] Schleiermacher criticized Kant's critical method in the following way:[6]

1. Kant did not follow the critical method to its obvious conclusion and attempt to find the presupposition for the "Wissenschaftslehre." Instead of questioning, "nach dem Fundament des Gebändes," he attempted rather to articulate the diversity which characterized man's experiences.[7] He separated sharply between "the pure ethic" which is "the legislator of Reason for freedom" and "the pure laws of Nature" which legislated Reason "for Nature's sake." Because Kant had not found a common basis for theoretical and practical philosophy, he had not escaped a dualism. Schleiermacher criticized

---

[1] Cf. Wehrung's comments in *Die Dialektik Schleiermachers* (Strassburg: 1920), p. 12 ff., in which he thinks there is a certain confusion of terms in Schleiermacher.

[2] Schleiermacher, already in his youthful period, in *Ueber den Werth den Lebens*, says "Erkennen und Begehren soll nicht zwei in mir sein, sondern eins," Dilthey, *Denkmale ...*, p. 53; cf. Dr. d. bish. S., S.W.III:1, p. 287 ff.; cf. also M.1, p. 50, "Auch hier im Gebiet der höchsten Sittlichkeit regiert dieselbe genaue Verbindung zwischen Thun und Schauen."

[3] R.1, p. 46; cf. p. 170 ff.

[4] "Es kann nämlich die höchste Idee erst nach den einzelnen Säzen un vermittelst ihrer gefunden worden sein." S.W. III:1, p. 17; also "Es kann auch die höchste Idee dieser Wissenschaft noch einen höheren wissenschaftlichen Grund über sich haben, und entweder als aus ihm durch die reine herabwärts gehende Forschung ohne irgend ein anderes Interesse entstanden, oder doch als an ihn angeknüpft und auf ihn zurükkgeführt vorgestellt werden." *Ibid.*

[5] S.W. III:1, p. 16

[6] Schleiermacher found indications that Kant also attempted to demonstrate the Wissenschaftslehre. He spoke of "mit nicht geringem Nachdruck von einer Architektonik der Vernunft," S.W. III:1, p. 21. He attempted to maintain the primacy of the practical reason and to make, "die Ethik selbst als die ganze Bestimmung des Menschen darlegend zur höchsten Wissenschaft." *Ibid.*

[7] S.W. III:1, p. 20 ff.

Kant for assigning to ethics the characteristics which belonged to "die Wissenschaftslehre."[1]

2. Kant's conception of ethics as the highest "Wissenschaft" and the foundation for all knowledge, would not permit any real knowledge at all.[2]

3. The postulates, freedom, immortality, and God did not belong, said Schleiermacher, to the theoretical or the practical Reason.[3] In order for "the idea of the highest Being" to be identified with ethics, morality ("Sittlichkeit") had to be combined with happiness ("Glückseligkeit"). Schleiermacher, however, had already refused to identify the two in his work *Über das höchste Gut*.

4. Kant presupposed that the ethical experience was "given" with human Nature, and was not derivative from it. Schleiermacher maintained that because of this assertion an arbitrariness had been introduced into the ethical experience itself.[4]

Schleiermacher next concerned himself with Fichte.[5] He found that Fichte went beyond Kant's attempt to construct "an archetectonic of Reason," and presented instead "a derivative ethic."[6] Schleiermacher doubted the adequacy and sufficiency of Fichte's system.[7] What Fichte's deduction meant was that he had found only "an empirical basis" for "Wissenschaftslehre," and not, "a transcendental basis."

Schleiermacher criticized Fichte in the following way:

1. If ethics were "die Wissenschaftslehre" there conld be no identity of the universal and the "purely ethical."

2. If the ethical experience were the particular experience related to the "Wissenschaftslehre" as the universal, an analysis had to be made

---

[1] Cf. Schleiermacher's review in *Athenaeum* 1799 of Kant's *Anthropologie in pragmatischer Hinsicht* (1798).

[2] S.W. III:1, p. 21; Schleiermacher thought, "dass der Ethiker die übrigen Vernunftkünstler anstelle: aber aus seiner Wissenschaft kann, dass jene und warum gerade so gefunden worden sind, niemals begründet werden." *Ibid.*

[3] *Ibid.*

[4] "dass auch Kant die Ethik nur vorgefunden, dass er sonst auch nicht den Gedanken gehabt haben würde sie hervorzubringen und von einem Mittelpunkte des menschlichen Wissens aus zu Beschreiben." S.W. III:1, p. 23.

[5] S.W. III:1, p. 24, also p. 18.

[6] S.W. III:1, p. 24.

[7] If *die Wissenschaftslehre* is to be "die höchste Erkenntniss wie die Wurzel aller übrigen," so there must be a place within *die Wissenschaftslehre* "wo jeder besonderen philosophischen Wissenschaft Keim ihr eingewachsen ist, und von wo aus er, sobald ihm Freiheit vergönnt wird, als ein eigner Stamm in die höhe steigen muss." *Ibid.*

of the manner in which the particular was derived from the universal.[1]

Schleiermacher's basic criticism of Fichte was that he equated the particular formal moral law, with the universal in the "Wissenschaftslehre." To identify the universal character of "Wissenschaftslehre" with the ethical act was an extremely serious error, Schleiermacher insisted.[2] Consequently, ethics did not receive any transcendental character.[3]

Schleiermacher's ethical position in this period may be summarized in the following way:

1. He affirmed a monistic ethic, constructed upon "die Menschheit;"

2. He maintained a concept of freedom, which he defined in terms of spontaneity and creativity, and which was objectified in "die Menschheit;"

3. He held that the moral life must include both action and perception, "darstellendes und verstellendes Handeln," the organizing and symbolizing activity;

4. He asserted that both "the community" and "the individual" were to be unified in the ethical act.

Schleiermacher maintained that feeling and imagination were important constitutives of the ethical life. He returned also to the concept of "Individuality," which, for him, was an expression of "the Infinite in the Finite."[4] It became apparent that he was more and more conscious of the fact that ethical activity was to be related to the religious life. Religion was the necessary presupposition for ethical activity. It became clear, on this basis, that the definition of the transcendental as

---

[1] S.W. III:1, p. 26.

[2] "denn das desezlich nothwendige Denken der Selbstthätigkeit, welches der gefundene Inhalt des Gedenken eigentlich ist, kann doch nicht gleich gelten dem Denken oder sich selbst Geben eines Gesezes der Selbstthätigkeit." S.W. III:1, p. 29 ff.

[3] Further criticism of Fichte may be found in S.W. III:1, p. 26 ff., 32.

[4] "dass alle fast das geistige Vermögen des Menschen nur ansehen als Vernunft, die andere Ansicht dieser Grundkraft aber als freies Verknüpfungs – und Hervorbringungsvermögen, oder als Fantasie, ganz vernachlässigen, welches doch die eigentlich ethische Ansicht sein müsste, und sich eben deshalb auch in der Aus führung nicht ganz übersehen lässt. Denn die Vernunft freilich ist in allen diesel be und das durchaus gemeinschaftliche und gleichförmige, so dass es eigentlich sinnlos ist, von einer individuellen Vernunft zu reden, wenn nämlich dieses mehr bedeuten soll, als die blosse numerische Verschiedenheit der Organisation und der äusseren Bedingungen von Raum und Zeit. Die Fantasie aber ist das eigentlich individuelle und besondere eines jeden." S.W. III:1. p. 269.

"die Wissenschaftslehre" was identical with Religion as the transcendental presupposition for ethics.[1]

B. *Schleiermacher's Conception of Religion in His Lectures on Ethics 1804–05 (Ethics A) and 1805–06 (Ethics B)*

Schleiermacher had developed already by 1802 what might be considered a mature ethical position. The basic principles of his system were virtue, obligation, and the "realized" good. He maintained that the ethical life in its entirety must include all of these concepts. Furthermore, he held that the ethical life appeared both as an organizing and symbolizing activity, which was determined by the universal or the individual.[2]

Schleiermacher's lectures on ethics in 1804–05 *(Ethics A)*, dealt a great deal with an analysis of "the laws of virtue."[3] In *Kritik der bisherigen Sittenlehre*, Schleiermacher has insisted that it was difficult to construct an ethical system upon the concept of virtue. However, he considered it as a necessary starting point for ethics, because virtue was the most universal moral concept which could be found.[4] He attempted to find the relationship of virtue to the concept of the highest good. There appeared immediately, he found, an insolvable antimony between virtue and the highest good. The realization of the highest good presupposed perfect virtue. Perfect virtue, however, was a part of the highest good. This antinomy was solved by reference to the two sides of virtue: an inner side, "sentiment," and an outer, "appearance;" that is, virtue as sentiment ("die Tugend als Gesinnung") and virtue as appearance ("die Tugend als Fertigkeit").[5]

By relating the idea of virtue to the highest good, Schleiermacher arrived at a new definition of virtue. To the highest good belonged, "the true and highest idea of happiness," which was conditioned by

---

[1] We can readily see from Schleiermacher's treatment of Spinoza and Plato that "die Wissenschaftslehre," which was also called "eine höchste Philosophie" (R.1), "die höchste Philosophie" (1802), "die Elementarphilosophie" (1802), "die oberste Wissenschaft" (1803), is identical with religion in the transcendental meaning of R.1; cf. Br.1, p. 328, 343, 353; Br.IV, p. 72; *Platons Werke* von F. Schleiermacher, I:1, 1804, p. 3 ff; S.W. III:1, p. 33 ff.; p. 230–285.

[2] Schleiermacher was working hard on his ethical system in 1804; cf. Br.I, p. 404, Br.II, p. 6, also *Fr. Schleiermachers Briefwechsel mit J. Chr. Gass*, hrsg. v. W. Gass (Berlin: Reimer, 1852), p. 3 ff., p. 26, p. 33 ff.

[3] S.W. III:5, p. XII.

[4] S.W. III:1, p. 149.

[5] S.W. III:5, p. 398.

"the unity of Nature and Intelligence." By "Intelligence," Schleiermacher meant the same as "Reason," the principle of universality and community, which stood in opposition to the particular and individual.[1] Virtue was equated with morality "as the Soul of the particular."[2] Therefore, virtue, by means of its relationship to the highest good, expressed the principle of community, the universal, as well as the principle of identity. Virtue formed the inner side of the moral life, it was its internal (moral) power, which expressed itself as "a condition of the Soul." Religion, from this standpoint, was one side of the power which constituted the moral life. Religion, furthermore, was of such basic significance, that it was presupposed in every ethical act.[3] Schleiermacher's definition of Religion corresponded to his definition of "die Elementarphilosophie" in 1802.[4] Religion corresponded to "die Philosophie" or "die Speculation" as "the symbolic perception of individuality."[5] Because Religion was related to "die Philosophie" as "an individual and universal element," it became the transcendental presupposition for Physics and Ethics. By means of their relationship to Religion, Physics and Ethics possessed the characteristic of *necessity*. Man's speculative ability corresponded to the deepest side of his being, that is, to "the religious intuition."[6] It related itself to "scientific knowledge" as "the universal imagination." The most inclusive, however, of all of the intuitions was the religious intuition.

Schleiermacher's lectures on ethics 1805–06 presupposed his earlier lectures in which he dealt with "the transcendental Postulates."[7] In these lectures, he maintained that "die Physik" and "die Ethik" were derived from "die speculative Philosophie,"[8] and were in close as-

---

[1] "Diese Glückseligkeit nun kann, so lange die Tugend nur in einzelnen wohnt, auch in diesen einzelnen nicht sein. Und so ist demnach der tugendhafte ausser dem höchsten Gute." S.W. III:5, p. 333, cf. also p. 349, 388.

[2] S.W. III:5, p. 341 ff.

[3] "Nicht nur auf das scientifische Wissen geht dies Princip, sondern aller Anschauung liegt es zum Grunde, und ist insofern eigentlich Princip der Religiosität, alles Wissen als Anschauen Gottes oder in Gott gesezt." S.W. III:5, p. 361.

[4] Dilthey, *Denkmale*, p. 134.

[5] S.W. III:5, p. 360.

[6] "nicht nur auf das scientifische Wissen geht dies Princip, sondern aller Anschauung liegt es zum Grunde, und ist insofern eigentlich Princip der Religiosität, alles Wissen als Anschauen Gottes oder in Gott gesezt." S.W. III:5, p. 361.

[7] Br. G, p. 25 ff.

[8] S.W. III:5, p. 41 ff., cf. his letter to J. Chr. Gass: "In meiner Ansicht von dem Ganzen der Wissenschaft und dessen, was sie ausdrükken soll, glaube ich nicht, dass ich je etwas ändern werde," Br. G, p. 32; In reference to Schelling he says, "So gewiss die Ethik wissenschaftliche Darstellung des menschlichen Handelns

sociation with one another and influenced each other.[1] Ethics, therefore, became a historical and descriptive science,[2] and had as its task
(beginning with man as a "natural being") "to realize what belonged
to man as a higher being."[3] Every ethical principle was only "one side
of this intuition."

Schleiermacher used "Idee" and "Vernunft" as synonymous terms
to express what was constitutive to the nature of the good.[4] Reason
was the universal principle, Nature, the principle of individuation. The
good ("die sittliche Dignität"), was found in the identity of the ideal
and the real.[5] The natural aspect of man was the passive principle; the
rational, the active. This dichotomy corresponded to the dichotomy
of "self-contained Being – Community" ("Abgeschlossene Dasein-
Gemeinschaft").[6]

Constitutive for the moral life was a gradual development from
the passive principle of Nature to the active principle of Reason, said
Schleiermacher. "Das Insichaufnehmen" and "das Aussichhervor-
bringen" were recognized in "perception" ("Erkennen"), and "representation" ("Darstellen") as Reason. It was at this point that the
moral life appeared.[7]

---

ist: so gewiss ist sie die ganze Eine Seite der Philosophie, die praktische im Gegensaz zur Physik als der theoretischen Seite der speculativen Philosophie.", S.W.
III:5, p. 41 ff.

[1] Schleiermacher always had a vital interest in nature, even during his Halle
period. cf. Br. I, p. 294 ff., Br. G, p. 8; Br.IV, p. 106, p. 108. "Ist die Ethik abhängig von der theoretischen Philosophie, weil diese ihr den Menschen geben muss,
dessen klare Anschauung das lezte Resultat der theoretischen Philosophie ist.
Diese hängt aber selbst wieder von der Gesinnung ab; also stehen beide in Wechselwirkung." S.W. III:5, p. 57.

[2] "Der Styl der Ethik ist der historische; denn nur wo Erscheinung und Gesez
als dasselbe gegeben ist, ist eine wissenschaftliche Anschauung. Der Styl kann
darum weder imperativisch sein noch consultativisch. Daher ist auch die Form
der Ethik die Entwikkelung einer Anschauung. Die Formel des Sollens ist ganz
unzulässig, da sie auf einem Zwiespalt gegen das Gesez ruht, die Wissenschaft
aber diesen eben als Schein darzustellen hat. S.W. III:5, p. 56, p. 58.

[3] S.W. III:5, p. 216.

[4] S.W. III:5, p. 72.

[5] "Lassen wir einen Augenblikk den Gegensaz von gut und böse hier gelten
zur Erläuterung: so ist böse das Heraustreten aus der Identität der Vernunft und
der Organisation, wenn die Gemeinschaft subjectiv nur auf die Organisation bezogen wird." S.W. III:5, p. 317.

[6] "Das gute ist nun die subjective Seite der Gemeinschaft auf die Identität der
Vernunft und der Organisation beziehen d.h. sie als Beziehung des abgeschlosse-
nen Daseins auf das übrige als ganzes, als Welt sezen; denn nur so hat das Afficirtsein der Organisation eine Beziehung auf die Vernunft." S.W. III:5, p. 318. Also,
cf. S.W. III:5, p. 87; cf. R.1, p. 6 ff.

[7] "Die Wechselwirkung von Erkennen und Darstellen ist die Oscillation des

Schleiermacher, in his lectures in the years 1805 and 1806 *(Ethics B)*, attempted again to describe the nature of the highest good. Both the concept of community and individuality claimed to be the highest good.[1] In this series of lectures, Schleiermacher defined the "Kingdom of God" as the highest good for the first time.[2] God was thought of as "Ruler" of "a Kingdom." God's kingdom as the highest good was made up of activity ("Thun") and observation ("Schauen"), the organizing and the symbolizing activities. The Kingdom of God corresponded to "die Idee einer vollkommenen Kultur,"[3] to which belonged science and thought,[4] language,[5] free society,[6] "Haus und Hof,"[7] art,[8] reproduction,[9] family,[10] state,[11] "der Stand,"[12] "die Freundschaft,"[13] as well as the church and the religious life.[14] The differences in Schleiermacher's ethical system from the first to the second lecture series may be structured in the following way:

Ethics A

	Das Organische:	Das Symbolische:
Das Individuelle:	Selbsterkenntniss Contemplation	Philosophie Speculation
Das Ganze (Allgemeine):	Wissen Weltanschauung Intuition	Kunst Imagination

Ethics B

	Receptivität:	Spontaneität:
Gefühl:	Empfindung Contemplation	Fantasie Speculation
Anschauung:	Erfahrung Intuition	Inneres Bilden Imagination[15]

---

sittlichen Lebens, keines von beiden kann ohne das anders gedacht werden." S.W. III:5, p. 87.

[1] "ohne Gemeinschaft kann die Vernunft im einzelnen nicht zur Identität hinaufsteigen; aber sie muss die Individualität mitbringen." S.W. III:5, p. 102.

[2] "So ist das Reich Gottes die höchste Idee, in der auch totales Erkennen und Organisiren liegt." *Ibid.*

[3] S.W. III:5, p. 101 ff.   [4] S.W. III:5, p. 133.   [5] *Ibid.*, p. 135.
[6] *Ibid.*, p. 151.   [7] *Ibid.*, p. 207.   [8] *Ibid.*, p. 253.   [9] *Ibid.*, p. 260.
[10] *Ibid.*, p. 269.   [11] *Ibid.*, p. 276.   [12] *Ibid.*, p. 309.   [13] *Ibid.*, p. 312.
[14] *Ibid.*, p. 317.   [15] Cf. S.W. III:5, p. 336–360.

In *Ethics* A, Religion was described as Intuition and Speculation, in reference to both its universal and individual character. In *Ethics* B, Religion was dealt with not only in terms of the doctrine of the highest good, but also in relation to the conception of virtue.[1] In *Ethics* B, Religion was defined primarily as "Gefühl," while in *Ethics* A, it was related more to "Anschauung." This was necessary because *Ethics* A related Religion to "das Wissen," "die Weltanschauung," and "die Intuition," and located Religion as part of the objective aspect of life, *Ethics* B related Religion more to the subjective area. However, there are elements in *Ethics* A and B which point both to the objective and subjective sides of man.[2]

The relationship of Religion to feeling in *Ethics* B did not mean that Religion and feeling were to be equated. In order that "the unity of consciousness" take place, feeling must become ethical.[3] Only then can feeling be related to Religion! Feeling must have the characteristic of that which is communal ("gemeinschaftlich").[4] Only on this basis can there be a unity of life and consciousness. Feeling represented, for Schleiermacher, the subjective and personal side of "Gemeinschaft." In feeling, the individual experienced, subjectively and personally, his unity with the World.[5] Feeling became ethical, as it was related to the World in its totality.[6] Religion, therefore, corresponded to the individual's experience of his relationship with the World. Feeling received the same characteristics as did "Anschauung" in the *Reden* (1799). Religion, however, was never defined as subjectivity, because feeling was closely related to the ethical act as well as one's consciousness of the objective World.[7]

---

[1] Cf. C. J. H. Engstrand *Expose och kritik af pligtbegrespet enligt Schleiermacher*, (Uppsala: Uppsala Universitets Årsskrift, 1862), and C. Y. Sahlin, *Kants, Schleiermachers och Boströms etiska Grundtankar*, (Uppsala: Uppsala Universitets Årsskrift, 1877).

[2] Cf. Ethics II, Erkenntniss is understood as "sowol Wissen als Gefühl, wie beides unzertrennlich mit einander verknüpft ist." S.W. III:5, p. 334.

[3] "Die durchgängige Sittlichkeit des Gefühls ist nun eigentlich nichts anderes, als dass jene Einheit auch ... für das Product das höhern Vermögens (die Vernunft, die Idee) erkannt werde." S.W. III:5, p. 244.

[4] S.W. III:5, p. 141.

[5] S.W. III:5, p. 244.

[6] "Das gute ist nun die subjective Seite der Gemeinschaft auf die Identität der Vernunft und der Organisation beziehen d.h. sie als Beziehung des abgeschlossen Daseins auf das übrige als ganzes, als Welt sezen... Hierdurch wird das Gefühl auf die Potenz der Sittlichkeit erhoben, und *dieses Verfahren ist nichts anderes als das was wir Religion nennen*."

[7] S.W. III:5, p. 318.

C. *The Definition of Religion in the Second Edition of the Reden* (1806)

In the first edition of the *Reden* (R 1), Schleiermacher concerned himself with the following problems:

1. The conception of Religion as a separate and distinct human experience, different from metaphysics and morality;[1]
2. The definition of Religion as "Anschauung" and "Gefühl;"[2]
3. The definition of Religion as the unity of "Anschauung" with "Gefühl;"[3]
4. The description of the religious "Anschauung" and "Gefühl" expressed in a concrete historical form;[4]
5. The dogmatic beliefs which belong to a concrete historical Religion.[5]

In the second edition of the *Reden* (R 2), Schleiermacher concerned himself with three things:

1. The conception of Religion as a separate and distinct human experience, different from "Leben," "Kunst," and "Physik," "Metaphysik," "Ethik" and "Pflichtlehre;"[6]
2. The definition of Religion and the religious experience, in relationship to knowledge and morality;[7]
3. The nature of the religious experience and individual religious feelings.[8] Included in the *Reden* (1806), was an appendix which dealt with the nature of dogma and doctrine.[9]

The *Reden* (1806) also distinguished between Religion and the other experiences of life. But Religion was not isolated from these other experiences of life, but instead it was related to action ("Handeln"), life ("Leben"), and art ("Kunst"), and also to science ("Wissenschaft"), thinking ("Denkart"), physics ("Physik"), metaphysics ("Metaphysik"), and ethics ("Ethik"). Schleiermacher defined the "essence of Religion" in terms of its relationship to these other areas of experience.

The *Reden* (1806) attempted to discover what was the "essence" of the religious experience. In order to do this, Schleiermacher had to separate Religion from theoretical knowledge and moral activity.[10] Religion, said Schleiermacher, found the eternal and infinite in all that lived, in becoming and change.[11] Religion lived in the infinite nature of the Whole, in the One and the All, in God.[12] However,

---

[1] R.1, p. 38–50.   [2] *Ibid.*, p. 50–71.   [3] *Ibid.*, p, 71–78.
[4] *Ibid.*, p. 78–115.   [5] *Ibid.*, p. 115–153.   [6] R.2, p. 44–58.
[7] *Ibid.*, p. 58–109.   [8] *Ibid.*, p. 109–153.   [9] *Ibid.*, p. 153–177.
[10] *Ibid.*, p. 58.   [11] *Ibid.*, p. 60.   [12] *Ibid.*

Religion was not only "Betrachtung" but was "Observation" ("Wahrnehmung"). Religion was not identical with "the knowledge of perception of the World or God" ("das Wissen und Erkennen weder der Welt noch Gottes"). Religion was identified with "immediate feeling" ("unmittelbares Gefühl"). The religious individual must be a moral individual, but the manner in which he acted was not to be considered as an ethical act because he was motivated by the recognition that God acted upon man in every historical event.[1] "Kunst" or "Leben" were terms used to express the active and productive character of man's Nature.[2] Religion was an independent experience of man and could not be identified with knowledge or morality.[3] Religion was not simply a third human experience which complemented the others, but was the *necessary presupposition* for them. When Religion was absent, said Schleiermacher, there could be no sense of "die lebendige Natur."[4]

A comparison of the definition of Religion given in the *Reden* (1799) as "Anschauung und Gefühl des Universums," and that given in the *Reden* (1806) as "die Betrachtung" (that is, "die unmittelbare Wahrnehmung von dem allgemeinen Sein alles Endlichen in Unendlichen und durch das Unendlich") and as "das unmittelbare Gefühl," revealed that this latter definition was more adequate to Schleiermacher's overall philosophical position at this period. This definition appeared again in the Third Edition of 1822.

The *Reden* (1799) defined Religion as the action of the Infinite making itself known in the Finite. The *Reden* (1800) treated Religion in terms of the Finite being present in the Infinite. The "Universum" of the *Reden* (1799), that which was the object of Religion, became God and "die Welt" in the *Reden* (1806).

The major interest of the *Reden* (1806) was a description of the

---

[1] *Ibid.*

[2] *Ibid.*, p. 62.

[3] "die Religion sich *neben* beide hinstellt, wird das gemeinschaftliche Feld vollkommen ausgefüllt, und die menschliche Natur von dieser Seite vollendet." R.2, p. 64; also, religion is "das nothwendige und unentbehrliche Dritte *zu* jenen beiden, nicht geringer an Würde und Herrlichkeit." *Ibid.* "wahre Wissenschaft" is defined as "vollendete Anschauung," "wahre Praxis" as "selbsterzengte Bildung und Kunst," "wahre Religion" as "Empfindung und Geschmakk für das Unendliche," R.2, p. 65. "Was ist alle Wissenschaft als das Sein der Dinge in Euch, in Eurer Vernunft? was ist alle Kunst und Bildung, als Euer Sein in den Dingen, in ihrem Masse und ihrer Gestalt? und wie kann beides in Euch zum Leben gedeihen als nur sofern die ewige Einheit der Vernunft und Natur, sofern das allgemeine Sein alles Endlichen im Unendlichen unmittelbar in Euch lebt?" R.2, p. 65.

[4] Cf. R.2, p. 66 ff.

relationship of Religion to "Wissenschaft" and "Handeln."[1] Schleiermacher's analysis of this relationship lead to a discussion of the genesis of consciousness. However, Religion and its relationship to "Wissenschaft" and "Handeln" was never given in consciousness itself. Consciousness was built upon the unity of the active and passive, the spontaneous and receptive elements of man's nature.[2] This unity related itself to the unity of "Anschauung" and "Gefühl" in the *Reden* (1799).[3]

The relationship between "Wissen" to "Handeln" concerned Schleiermacher next.[4] He found that they were related in a direct and positive way to one another.[5] He analyzed next the relationship between "Gefühl", "Erkennen," and "Handeln."[6] Life was not possible with only "Erkennen" and "Handeln." "Das religiöse Leben" was a necessary presupposition for both "Wissen" and "Handeln."[7]

"Wissenschaft" was defined as "Anschauung" and "Erkennen," Religion as "Gefühl." "Wissen" was always primary in relationship to "Handeln." But "Wissen" comprehended "Anschauung" and "Erkennen," as well as "Gefühl." They were united in "the immediate

---

[1] R.2 attempts to show how it relates "mit dieser Einheit der Wissenschaft, der Religion und der Kunst und mit ihrer Verschiedenheit zugleich," R.2, p. 69; "Dort allein findet Ihr das ursprüngliche Verhältniss des Gefühls und der Anschauung." *Ibid.*

[2] Cf. also, "Ihr findet Euch versunken in Euch selbst, Alles was Ihr sonst als ein Mannigfaltiges getrennt in Euch betrachtet in dieser Gegenwart unzertrennlich zu einem eigenthümlichen Gehalt Eures Seins verknüpft. Aber sehet Ihr nicht beim Aufmerken noch im Enfliehen das Bild eines Gegenstandes von dessen Einwirkung auf Euch, von dessen zauberischer Berührung dieses Bewusstsein ausgegangen ist? ... Allein eben weil sie verbleicht und entflicht war sie vorher näher und heller, sie war ursprünglich Eins und dasselbe mit Eurem Gefühl." R.2, p. 70 ff.

[3] Cf. R.2, p. 70, "Erregt- und Bestimmtsein Eurer Selbst durch den Gegenstand" cannot have any other meaning than *Anschauung.*

[4] "Nur als ein Erregtes und als ein Bestimmtes könnt Ihr Euer Dasein ihnen (den Gegenständen) mittheilen; also gebt Ihr nur zurük und befestiget, und legt nieder in die Welt, was in Euch ist gebildet und gewirkt worden durch jene Art des gemeinschaftlichen Seins, und eben so kann auch was sie Euch einbilden nur ein solches sein." R.2, p. 75.

[5] Cf. R.2, p. 76.

[6] "Wie es nun mit diesen beiden sich verhält unter sich, so muss es sich doch auch verhalten mit der dritten in Beziehung auf jene beiden. Und wie wollt Ihr diese dritte wol nennen, die Reihe des Gefühls? was für ein Leben soll sie bilden zu den beiden andern? Das religiöse denke ich." R.2, p. 76 ff.

[7] "Euer Gefühl *insofern es Euer und des Universum gemeinschaftliches Sein und Leben* auf die beschriebene Weise *ausdrükt*, insofern Ihr die einzelnen Momente desselben habt als ein Wirken Gottes in Euch durch das Universum, dies ist Eure Frömmigkeit." R.2, p. 77.

Unity of the Universe with Reason" ("die unmittelbare Vermählung des Universum mit der Vernunft"). This moment was for Schleiermacher the genuine religious experience. It was the basis for "Erkennen" and "Anschauen" (which was "Wissenschaft") and "Gefühl" (which was "Religion") as well as for "Handeln." The religious experience was thereby demonstrated to be necessary for "Wissenschaft" and "Handeln," but also for "Religion." It was clear that Schleiermacher was dealing here with two different conceptions of Religion, one which defined the relationship of the Self to the Universe, the second which was "Gefühl." These two conceptions of Religion corresponded to the conception of Religion found in the *Reden* (1799), where Religion was defined as "Anschauung und Gefühl" as well as the conscious unity which existed between them. Schleiermacher, in the *Reden* (1806), gave priority to the definition of Religion which included this original and immediate moment which recognized the unity of the self and the universe. The religious experience became therefore the transcendental presupposition for the theoretical, the practical, and the religious dimensions of life.

Schleiermacher also defined the a priori and a posteriori elements of Religion. Feeling, he said, was the a posteriori expression of the Self, that is, the Self and the consciousness it had of its unity with the universe. Religion, as feeling, had nothing to do with the knowledge of the nature and being of the universe.[1] Feeling itself was not the object of investigation.[2] Everything which was included in Religion had to be an immediate experience. But feeling was not related to objective knowledge.[3] Feeling was related instead to the unity of the Self with the Universe.[4] This was the relationship of the a posteriori expression of Religion to the transcendental religious a priori, upon which all conscious life, the theoretical, the practical, and the religious areas of experience rested.[5] This a priori character of Religion was much clearer in the *Reden* (1806) than it was in the *Reden* (1799). This was so because Schleiermacher's basic interest in the *Reden* (1806) was

---

[1] Cf. R.1, p. 56.

[2] R.2, p. 79.

[3] "die Gottheit ... als eine Erkenntniss zu behandeln ... gewiss in der Religion nur leere Mythologie." R.2, p. 84 ff., cf. R.1, p. 57 ff.

[4] i.e., which is an expression for "Euer und des Universum gemeinschaftliches Sein," R.2, p. 77.

[5] Summarizing this: "Alle diese Gefühle (Ehrfurcht, Demut, Liebe etc.) sind Religion, und ebenso alle anderen, bei denen das Universum der eine, und auf irgend eine Art Euer eignes Ich der andre von den Punkten ist, zwischen denen das Gemüt schwebt." R.1, p. 110 ff., Cf., R.2, p. 150.

to relate Religion to the areas of "Wissenschaft" and "Handeln," and to present in this way the necessary character of the religious a priori.

There appeared to be a close resemblance between the definition of Religion in *Ethics* B and the *Reden* (1806). Religion in *Ethics* B had been identified with "the life of feeling" ("das Gefühlsleben"). In the *Reden* (1806), "das religiöse Leben" corresponded to "the range of feeling" ("die Reihe des Gefühls").[1] Feeling, in *Ethics* B, was not a subjective experience, for the subjective quality of feeling always had an objective counterpart. "Wissen," as well as "Gefühl," was included under "Erkenntnis." But "Gefühl" was never equated with "Erkenntnis." Feeling had to be raised to "Erkennen." Although feeling represented the subjective and the individual, it also possessed the characteristics of community, rationality, and objectivity. When feeling was placed in relationship to "Vernunft," "Idee," and to "die Welt," an objective element was introduced.[2]

In *Ethics* C, Schleiermacher began with "Gefühl" and demonstrated its objective character by relating it to Reason. As we have seen, Schleiermacher's main concern in the *Reden* (1806) was to relate Religion to the other areas of experience. He therefore defined "Gefühl" in reference to that moment in experience which formed the unity of consciousness. In this moment "Gefühl" was related to "Anschauung."[3] Therefore, when Schleiermacher defined Religion in the *Reden* (1806) as "Gefühl," "Gefühl" referred back to this elemental moment of consciousness. This was "a Being for itself" ("ein Sein für sich") and "a Being in the whole" ("ein Sein im Ganzen"). By relating it in this fashion, Schleiermacher had introduced into "Gefühl" the concepts of community, rationality, and objectivity.[4]

In *Ethics* A, Schleiermacher defined "Wissenschaft" as "Anschauung" and defined Religion as a form of "die Anschauung" which related to "Wissen," "Intuition," and "Weltanschauung." The most characteristic feature of *Ethics* B was that "Anschauung" was wholly omitted in the definition of Religion. "Gefühl" became the most significant category. "Anschauung" replaced the objective knowledge of *Ethics* A. In the *Reden* (1799), "Anschauen des Universums" was

---

[1] R.2, p. 77; cf. "Es giebt keine Empfindung die nicht fromm wäre"; R.2, p. 78.
[2] R.2, p. 60.
[3] *Ibid.*, p. 72.
[4] Cf. R.2, p. 77 "Euer Gefühl insofern es Euer und des Universum gemeinschaftliches Sein und Leben auf die beschriebene Weise ausdrükt, insofern Ihr die einzelnen Momente desselben habt als ein Wirken Gottes in Euch durch das Universum, dies ist Eure Frömmigkeit."

the most characteristic definition of Religion. In the *Reden* (1806) this definition had been omitted. "Anschauen des Universums" was no longer the definition of Religion, but "Gefühl" had taken its place. "Anschauung" had become only one aspect of the nature of Religion. When "Anschauung" was united with "Gefühl," "Wissen" was formed. "Anschauung" formed the objective side of "Wissen" and "Gefühl" the subjective side. "Anschauung," therefore, was replaced by "die Betrachtung."[1] "Die Betrachtung" observed the finite in the infinite, the temporal in the eternal, and the eternal in all change and variableness, that is, "in allem Thun und Leiden." "Die Betrachtung" located everything in God and God in everything ("the Finite in the Infinite and the Infinite in the Finite"). "Gefühl" became, therefore, the most significant expression for Religion in the *Reden* (1806). Feeling became the feeling of absolute dependence, that is, the sense of the individual's total relationship to the infinite. Therefore, Schleiermacher, in the *Reden* (1806), could note that Religion belonged "to the province of necessity" ("in dem Gebiet der Nothwendigkeit").[2] "Gefühl" was not simply the expression of a sense-experience, but a feeling which was elevated to the nature of community and rationality.[3]

In the *Reden* (1799), Schleiermacher defined Religion in terms of both the "Universum" and the Self. According to the *Reden* (1806), there were three factors which belong to Religion: the Self, God, and the World ("Universum"). The individual was related to the World only when he was related to God.[4] God was the original force which created the World. Therefore, Religion as "Gefühl" was "the immediate and original being of God in us through feeling" ("das unmittelbare und ursprüngliche Sein Gottes in uns durch das Gefühl").[5] God as such was given in immediate self-consciousness. Therefore, Religion was an immediate (in the sense of the primal) experience of God. The unity of the infinite, the eternal, the unchanging and the finite and the changing was experienced in feeling. This formed the

---

[1] "Freilich ist der Religion die Betrachtung wesentlich ... aber diese Betrachtung geht nicht auf das Wesen eines Endlichen im Gegensaz gegen das andere Endliche; sondern sie ist nur die unmittelbare Wahrnehmung von dem allgemeinen Sein alles Endlichen im Unendlichen und durch das Unendliche, alles Zeitlichen im Ewigen und durch das Ewige." R.2, p. 59.

[2] R.2, p. 62.

[3] R.1, p. 111.

[4] *Ibid.*

[5] *Ibid.*

true "essence" and the higher self-consciousness of the individual.[1] However, God was never to be identified with feeling. God was communicated through the World, and had to be overagainst man. At the same time, however, He was in relationship with man. Religion was the expression of the relationship between God and man, which was apprehended through feeling.

Religion was related in a transcendental way to "Wissenschaft" and "Praxis."[2] In relationship to this discussion, Schleiermacher dealt with three concepts: "the Thing – You" ("die Dinge – Ihr"); "Nature – Reason" ("die Natur – die Vernunft"); "the Finite – the Infinite" ("das Endliche – das Unendliche"). He asserted that "the eternal unity of Reason and Nature" ("die ewige Einheit der Vernunft und Natur") was identical to "the Universal Being of all Finitude in Infinity" ("das allgemeine Sein alles Endlichen im Unendlichen"). Therefore, Religion was "a taste for the Infinite" ("Geschmack für das Unendliche").

"Wissenschaft", however, without Religion was an empty concept. "Handeln" without Religion was a dead form, said Schleiermacher.[3] "Wissenschaft," based upon Religion, represented the finite in the infinite, as well as "Handeln," "Leben," and "Kunst," which were also based upon Religion, and were defined as the representation of the infinite in the finite. Both were possible only because of Religion, which formed "the unity of Reason and Nature" ("die ewige Einheit der Vernunft und Natur"),[4] and "the Universal Being of all Finitude in Infinity" ("das allgemeine Sein alles Endlichen im Unendlichen").[5] Religion as feeling was the transcendental presupposition for "Wissenschaft" and "Handeln." Only through Religion was it possible for "Wissenschaft" and "Handeln" to exist.[6]

---

[1] "Die welche ihn (Gott) so unabhängig vom Gefühl über Alles stellen, wollen auch etwas was ihr (die Religion) fremd ist." R.2, p. 174.

[2] "Wahre Wissenschaft ist vollendete Anschauung; wahre Praxis ist selbsterzeugte Bildung und Kunst; wahre Religion ist Empfindung und Geschmack für das Unendliche. Eine von jenen haben zu wollen ohne diese, oder sich dünken lassen man habe sie so, das ist eine verwegene übermüthige Täuschuung." R.2, p. 65.

[3] R.2, p. 66 ff., cf. R.1, p. 53.

[4] *Ibid.*

[5] *Ibid.*

[6] Cf. Dilthey, *Denkmale ...*, p. 134; "Physik und Ethik sind die beiden Wissenschaften, welche von der Elementarphilosophie ausgehen." cf. also, R.1, p. 66.

D. *The Essence of Religion and Christianity in Die Weihnachtsfeier – Ein Gespräch* (1806)

Die Weihnachtsfeier was a concrete illustration of Schleiermacher's conception of the relationship between Religion and Christianity.[1] In this work, Schleiermacher presented different points of view of the nature of Religion and Christianity, and in each of these there could be found an element of his own point of view.[2] The critical and analytical Leonhardt, the immediate and emotional Josef, were representative of different periods in Schleiermacher's development.

Schleiermacher began *Die Weihnachtsfeier* with the definition of Religion as "Feeling". In the celebration of Christmas there was a great deal of immediacy in one's feeling for life.[3] Josef expressed the meaning of Christmas as the feeling of happiness found in the communal form of the many celebrations associated with Christmas.[4] Feeling revealed that which was most original and immediate about man, that is, it revealed "the child in the Self."[5] Faith and love revealed the nature of the divine to children. As the religious dimension was added, Christmas became the celebration of the childhood of Jesus, which was the recognition of the unity of the child with God.[6] Josef's appreciation of Christmas was as the feeling which expressed "ein Sein

---

[1] In the second edition of Weih., Schleiermacher wrote that his purpose in writing the work was to show "wie die verschiedensten Auffassungeweisen des Christenthumes hier in einem mässigen Zimmer nicht etwa nur friedlich neben einander sind, weil sie sich gegenseitig ignoriren, sondern wie sie sich einander freundlich stellen zur vergleichenden Betrachtung." S.W. I:1, p. 464.

[2] Cf. G. Carstensen: *Individualitetatanken hos Schleiermacher*, p. 395. cf. H. Bleek, *Die Grundlagen der Christologie Schleiermachers* (Berlin: Reimer, 1898), p. 185 ff., also K. Beth, *Die Grundanschauungen Schleiermachers in seinem ersten Entwurf der philosophischen Sittenlehre* (Göttingen: Vanderhöck und Ruprecht, 1898), p. 65 ff.

[3] S.W. I:1, p. 465.

[4] "Ich bin nicht gekommen Reden zu halten, sondern mich zu freuen mit euch; und ihr kommt mir, dass ich es erlich sage, wunderlich und fast thöricht vor, dass ihr dergleichen treibt, wie schön es auch mag gewesen sein." This was in deference to "euer schlechtes Princip dieser Leonhardt, der denkende reflectirende dialektische überverständige Mensch." S.W. I:1, p. 465.

[5] "Die meinige kann wie ein Kind nur lächeln und jauchzen. Alle Menschen sind mir heute Kinder." S.W. I:1, p. 524. Different participants express the meaning of *Kindheit: Karoline:* "Eben dies, jede Stimmung und jedes Gefühl für sich hinnehmen und nur rein und ganz haben wollen," "der Kindersinn, ohne den man nicht ins Reich Gottes kommen kann." S.W. I:1, p. 491.
Agnes: "Und glaubst du denn, die Liebe geht auf das, wozu wir die Kinder bilden können? Was können wir bilden? Nein, sie geht auf das schöne und göttliche, was wir in ihnen schon glauben, was jede Mutter aufsucht in jeder Bewegung, sobald sich nur die Seele des Kindes äussert." S.W. I:1, p. 488.

[6] S.W. I:1, p. 493.

im Ganzen." Leonhardt[1] came closest to interpreting Christianity in such a way as to permit it to disappear in an indeterminate and "lyrical" feeling. Ernst introduced the general term "happiness" to express the meaning of Christmas, but related everything to the historical appearance of the Savior Jesus Christ. Eduard took his starting point in the Fourth Gospel, which he felt gave a better interpretation of the meaning of the Christ than any other source.[2]

Leonhardt was the representative who came closest to a rationalistic interpretation of Christianity.[3] The celebration of Christmas itself was the basis for faith in the historical Jesus Christ, who was a supernatural and eternal reality.[4]

Ernst demanded that the Christmas celebration had to be united with the historical appearance of Christ. He said that Christianity was a feeling of happiness which had been elevated to a universal experience[5] because of Christ's historical appearance. He referred, furthermore, to Christianity as "the original Nature" ("die ursprüngliche Natur"), in the sense of "der Kindersinn" or "Kindheit." Happiness revealed the unity of the divine and the human and could be seen most clearly in the child. Life is the opposition between "Appearance and

---

[1] Cf. Dav. Fried. Strauss, *Charakteristiken und Kritiken*, (Berlin: Reimer, 1839), p. 43; in which he asserted that Schleiermacher offered a speculative Christology in his *Weihnachtsfeier*.

[2] It seems clear that Schleiermacher was moving in the direction of a Christocentrism; cf. his later Christocentric standpoint in the *Glaubenslehre*.

[3] "Verherrlichen und preisen kann man jedes auf eine zwiefache Weise; einmal indem man es lobt, ich meine seine Art und innere Natur als gut anerkannt und darstellt, dann aber wiederum indem man es rühmt, das heisst seine Trefflichkeit und Vollkommenheit in seiner Art heraushebt." S.W. I:1, p. 508. Leonhardt accepts the second viewpoint: "Wenn man sagen wollte, das Andenken an die Geburt des Erlösers werde weit mehr durch die Schrift erhalten und durch den Unterricht im Christenthum überhaupt als durch das Fest: so möchte ich dieses läugnen." *Ibid.*

[4] "Was nämlich die auf ihm (Christus) beruhende Versöhnung unsers Geschlechtes betrifft, diese knüpfen wir ja alle erst an seinen Tod," however, "es gleich hiebei wie ich denke mehr auf einen ewigen Rathschluss Gottes ankommt. als auf eine bestimmte einzelne Thatsache, und wir deshalb diese Ideen lieber nicht an einen bestimmten Moment knüpfen, sondern sie über die zeitliche Geschichte des Erlösers hinaushaben und symbolisch halten sollten." S.W. I:1, p. 510 ff.

[5] "Was so allgemein ist, kann schon um deswillen nicht willkührlich ersonnen oder verabredet worden sein, sondern es muss einen gemeinschaftlichen inneren Grund haben ... Dieser innere Grund aber kann kein anderer sein, als dass die Er scheinung des Erlösers die Quelle aller andern Freude in der christlichen Welt ist ... Die Geburt des Erlösers bleibt das einzige allgemeine Freudenfest, weil es nämlich für uns kein anderes Princip der Freude giebt als die Erlösung." S.W. I:1, p. 517.

Being" ("die Erscheinung und das Wesen"), "Time and Eternity" ("die Zeit und die Ewigkeit"). In Christ, this opposition was removed,[1] and man was able to experience "das gesteigerte Dasein."

Eduard synthesized the rationalistic and the historical points of view[2] and constructed his own thinking upon the concept of "the original Nature" ("die ursprüngliche Natur"), ("die Kindheit") which was present in Christ as "a divine Child" ("ein göttliches Kind"). When flesh ("Fleisch"), the Word ("Wort"), and the Incarnation ("Fleischwerden") were defined, it was then possible to determine the meaning of Christ's birth.[3] These were then related to the historical and empirical life of Christ.[4] Man's need for salvation had its basis in the incongruity which existed between the "Mensch an sich," the ideal man, and the empirical man. Man recognized that he was separated from "Mensch an sich," and, thereby, from the human community. Salvation was effected only when the individual found himself in his individuality, that is, when the individual "considered himself in relationship to the Infinite."[5] The Church, too, had a task to perform in God's plan of salvation. The Church provided "the self-consciousness of Humanity" ("das Selbstbewusstsein der Menschheit").[6]

II. The Systematic Period (1806–1834)

A. *Religion in the Lectures on Ethics* (1806–1834)

The conception of Religion had become by this time the most fundamental element in Schleiermacher's entire theological system.

---

[1] S.W. I:1, p. 518, Ernst said to Leonhardt: "Und so komme ich dazu, Leonhardt, dich zu widerlagen eben indem ich dir beistimme ... mögen die historischen Spuren seines (Christus) Lebens, wenn man die Sache in einem niedrigeren Sinne kritisch betrachtet, noch so unzureichend sein: das Fest hängt nicht daran sondern wie an der Nothwendigkeit eines Erlösers, so an der Erfahrung eines gesteigerten Daseins, welches auf keinen andern Anfang als diesen zurükkzuführen ist." S.W. I:1, p. 518.

[2] Eduard says: "Ich will mich an den mystischen unter den vieren halten, bei dem gar wenig von einzelnen Begebenheiten vorkommt, ja auch kein Weihnachten äusserlich, in dessen Gemüth aber eine ewige kindliche Weihnachtsfreude herrscht. Dieser giebt uns die geistige und höhere Ansicht unseres Festes." S.W. I:1, p. 520 ff.

[3] Cf. S.W. I:1, p. 521.

[4] *Ibid.*

[5] S.W. I:1, p. 522; cf. this definition of religion with R.1 and R.2, in which religion is an intuition of the infinite in the finite. Salvation, according to *Weihnachtfeier* meant that the individual saw himself as "ein Gedanke des ewigen Seins."

[6] *Ibid.*

It was the formal principle around which every element of his thought revolved. Theology, too, became a positive science which had the task to describe the various historical expressions of the Christian faith.

Schleiermacher's works on ethics during this period included: Lectures on Ethics in 1812 (*Ethics* C), Lectures on Ethics sometime between the years 1812–1827 (possibly 1816) (*Ethics* D), Lectures on Ethics in 1827 (*Ethics* E), and the Lectures on Ethics in 1832 (*Ethics* F).[1]

The similarity in Schleiermacher's ethical thought between the years 1806 and 1834 and his earlier position is quite obvious. Ethics cannot exist by themselves, he said, but must be derived from a higher "Wissenschaft." Religion, as it was related to Ethics, was dealt with in two ways: first, Religion gave form to the "symbolizing" activity of the ethical life, and, second, Religion was "das hochste Wissenschaft." Religion became, therefore, for Schleiermacher, the transcendental presupposition for Ethics. Religion gave Ethics their rational character. In addition, Religion was identified with "die Gottheit."[2]

Religion, identified with the symbolizing activity of "Wissen" and "Erkennen," also had to be identified with Religion was an organizing activity.

"Das Erkennen" had "an objective and subjective side" ("eine objective und subjective Seite"), which corresponded to "Wahrnehmung" and "Gefühl." The objective side of "Erkennen" was universal knowledge (i.e., "dieselbe in Allen und als gültig für Alle"). "Gefühl" was defined as "das individuelle, eigenthümliche und subjective Erkennen." "Das subjective Erkennen" or "Gefühl" was identified with "das bestimmte Selbstbewusstsein," that is, it represented "ein Sein für sich." "Selbstbewusstsein" could also represent "ein Sein im ganzen," and therefore could be used as an expression for Religion.

"Gefühl" was further defined as, "die Einheit und Totalität der Vernunft."[3] Feeling became religious when it was elevated to the level of community, unity and totality.[4]

---

[1] See Alex. Schweizer: *Vorwort des Herausgebers*; S.W. III:5, p. XI ff. cf. *Einleitende Vorrede till Friedrich Schleiermachers Grundriss der philosophischen Ethik* (Berlin: Reimer, 1841) ed. A. Twesten, p. IV ff., who attempted to date these lectures.

[2] "alles Wissen," "das ethische und physische," "ist als Vernunftgehalt habend nur insofern Wissen, als es auch transcendental gewusst wird d.h. als es dialektisch und als es religiös ist." S.W. III:5, p. 223.

[3] *Ibid.*, p. 221.

[4] Cf. S.W. III:5, p. 254 ff.

The view of Religion in *Ethics* C was two-fold. First, Religion represented "die absolute Einheit," "die höchste Form im Wissen," the unity of Nature and Spirit. It formed the basis for "die Ethik" as well as for "die Physik." It was apriori, and could not be subsumed under ethics. Secondly, Religion was "Gefühl," a form of "Erkennen." Now it was a posteriori, and belonged to culture.[1]

Ethics D was so very similar to *Ethics* C that it indicated no real change from Schleiermacher's earlier position.[2] Religion was defined as feeling, and was included under the heading of the symbolizing activity.[3] It was also placed in relation to "Selbstbewusstsein" and "Selbstthätigkeit," which referred to "Empfänglichkeit" and "Bewusstsein der Dinge."

Ethics D recognized the transcendental character of Religion. This transcendental element was expressed as "man's striving for God"[4] which in turn was related to religious feeling.

Ethics E dealt at great lengths with the relationship of ethics to dialectics. "Das Wissen" and "das Sein" were considered to correspond to one another.[5] "Vernunft" and "Natur" formed an antithesis within "Sein." "Wissen" always corresponded to "ein Sein." "Wissenschaft" or "Vernunft" was, therefore, partly moral law ("Sittenlehre"), and partly historical knowledge ("Geschichtskunde").[6] The highest knowledge ("das höchste Wissen") and the highest Being ("das höchste Sein") were never found "immediate in our consciousness," but were present only as "the primary source of all of our knowledge."[7] God was not identified with "das höchste Wissen," but was the indentity of "das höchste Wissen" and "das höchste Sein." In this way, Schleiermacher preserved the transcendental character of God and the transcendental character of Religion. Religion became the ultimate a priori presupposition for life.

The Absolute "innere des Menschen" was always represented in a transcendental way.[8] However, this was expressed externally, which

---

[1] Cf. R.2, and the two definitions given to religion.

[2] Cf. S.W. III:5, p. 86 ff.

[3] "Die Weisheit des Gefühls als besteht darin, dass nichts in dem Menschen Lust und Unlust werde als nur vermöge seiner Beziehung auf das ideale." S.W. III:5, p. 35.

[4] S.W. III:5, p. 115; also as, "das schlechthin innere des Menschen." Note, however, "das Streben nach Gott bildet Gedanken und Empfindungen."

[5] S.W. III:5, p. 14.

[6] S.W. III:5, p. 38.

[7] S.W. III:5, p. 18; p. 16.

[8] S.W. III:5, p. 114 ff.

expression corresponded to the a posteriori character of Religion. In this way, Schleiermacher could present Religion as a form of "Wissen" in the sense, of "Gefühl." "Gefühl," therefore, was an expression of reason in Nature, which gave "itself to the unity of life."[1] This definition of Religion as "Gefühl" would be seen again in the *Glaubenslehre* as "immediate self-consciousness" ("unmittelbares Selbstbewusstsein").

Ethics F gave emphasis to Schleiermacher's definition of Religion as "the feeling of absolute dependence." This series of lectures also defined Religion as "Gefühl" and "unmittelbares Selbstbewusstsein," and represented Religion once again as the symbolizing activity.[2] The categories "Mannigfaltigkeit" and "Einheit," which were related to "das Mathematische" and "das Transcendente," were considered to be constitutive for "das Wissen."[3] Schleiermacher defined religious feeling as a form of human consciousness and, as such, a feeling of dependence.[4] The transcendental category appeared in the feeling of "dependence" ("Abhängigkeitsbewusstsein").[5] "Das Abhängigkeitsbewusstsein" was always conditioned by "the consciousness of change" ("Veränderlichkeitsbewusstsein").[6]

We can see, therefore, that Schleiermacher's conception of Religion had moved from the definition given in the *Reden* (1806) to that which is found in the *Glaubenslehre*, that is, Religion as "unmittelbares Selbstbewusstsein" and "Abhängigkeitsbewusstsein," the feeling of absolute dependence.

B. *The Conception of Religion in Schleiermacher's Lecture on Dialectics, 1811–1831*[7]

Schleiermacher did not define Dialectics in a singular way. When he dealt with the subject of Dialectics, he attempted to discover the

---

[1] S.W. III:5, p. 138; "Selbstbewusstsein ist jedes Gefühl ... aber auch nur immittelbares." S.W. III:5, p. 140.

[2] S.W. III:5, p. 243.

[3] *Ibid.*, p. 222; cf. p. 221.

[4] *Ibid.*, p. 243.

[5] *Ibid.*

[6] Both "das einzelne Veränderlichkeitsbewusstzein und das absolute Abhängigkeitsbewusstsein" are "die das einzelne Leben umfassenden Elemente des Selbstbewusstseins." *Ibid.*

[7] Schleiermacher never presented his dialectics in such a way that they could be printed from prepared manuscripts, cf. L. Jonas in *Vorwort* to S.W. III:4, 2, p. VIII, who said he wrote them down "kurz vor seinem Tod für den Druck." What we have is Schleiermacher's lecture notes, given in 1811, 1814, 1818, 1822,

transcendental basis and presupposition for the conscious life of man. We have already seen that Schleiermacher had defined Religion as the "transcendental basis for all of human and conscious life." Therefore, it was obvious that Schleiermacher's lectures on Dialectics during this period would employ his previous definition of Religion.[1] Religion, which had never lost its subjective character, possessed, at the same time, in Schleiermacher's view, an objective referrent. There was no contradiction in Schleiermacher's definition of Religion in the *Reden* (1799) as, "eine höchste Philosophie," or in 1802, as "die Elementars- philosophie." The transcendental presupposition for every experience, Schleiermacher asserted, was found in Religion. In his Lectures on Ethics, the relationship between Religion and Ethics was so defined that Religion became the a posteriori form of "das Wissen," as well as the a priori presupposition for Ethics. Religion could not be placed in relationship to an objective "Wissenschaft" as its necessary presup- position, if it did not possess at the same time an objective character. It was this relationship which formed the basis for Schleiermacher's Dialectics. In the lectures, he began with an investigation of "das Erkennen" (or "das Wissen"), and expanded this concept to include "das Wollen" and "das Gefühl."

In *Dial. A*, he investigated the nature of "das Wissen." His Dia- lectics appeared first as a "Wissenlehre." Schleiermacher accepted "das Wissen" as a positive and necessary category. All knowledge, he said, dealt with ideas and judgments. The syllogism could never pro- duce an independent kind of knowledge, but had to be related to the total knowing experience.[2] The idea represented that which was identical with itself, "das Sein als Einheit."[3] The judgment ("Das Urtheil")

1828, and 1831. For reference to all this material, cf. Jonas, *Vorwort*; cf. also Bruno Weiss, *Untersuchungen über Fr. Schleiermachers Dialektik – Erster Teil* of G. and H. J. Halpern, *Schleiermachers Dialektik* (Berlin: Reimer, 1903), which attempts "eine vollständige, geschlossene Gestalt der Dialektik in ihrer reifsten Ausbil- dung," *Ibid.*, p. XXXIII. For the sake of clarity, the following form shall be used: *Dial* A, lectures on dialectics from the year 1811; *Dial* 1814, lectures on dialectics from the year 1814; *Dial* C, lectures on dialectics from the year 1822; *Dial* E, lectures on dialectics from the year 1831, which includes the salient features of all the lectures on dialectics, usually designated by A, B, C, D, E, *Dial* 1814. Bruno Weiss has verified the dating of these lectures; cf. *Untersuchungen über Fr. Schleiermachers Dialektik*, Z. Philos. 73 Bd., 1878, p. 20 ff.

[1] Cf. what Bruno Weiss, in *Untersuchungen über ...* p. 5 said of the relationship of Schleiermacher's dialectic and his conception of religion.

[2] S.W. III:4, 2, p. 327.

[3] "In den wirklichen Begriffen (von den allgemeinen Dingen) ist nichts zu-

represented "empirical, historical knowledge" ("das empirische, historische Wissen"); "der Begriff," the philosophical ("das philosophische").[1] This meant that knowledge was perfected by that which belonged to both "das empirische" and "das philosophische". Schleiermacher discovered, therefore, the critical method, based upon the synthesis of the real and the ideal, and the empirical and the speculative. In this way, he felt, he had discovered the "transcendental presupposition" for all knowledge. The Absolute was not simply a formal category, but was a real category. The Absolute was, therefore, the highest synthesis of knowledge.

Schleiermacher spoke of the Absolute as "a formal element in all acts of knowledge" ("formelles Element aller Acte des Erkennens").[2] "Die Gottheit" was defined as "the formal principle of all knowledge" ("das formelle Princip alles Wissen").[3] But, we may also notice that the Absolute was not to be conceived as "an individual thing" ("ein einzelnes Ding"), but as "in thought" ("im Denken"), and as "the idea of the Absolute" ("die Idee des Absoluten"),[4] which was "a universal thing" ("ein allgemeines Ding"). The Absolute was, therefore, only the formal presupposition for knowledge, that is, it possessed an a priori quality.[5] The Absolute as the formal presupposition for knowledge, was "inconceivable" ("unbegreiflich"), but was the presupposition for "the knowledge of divinity." Schleiermacher spoke of the "knowledge of God" ("Wissen um Gott") in such a way that it was only possible through it for the Absolute to receive real content. Man possessed the idea of the Absolute within himself.[6] The Absolute was given in knowledge and was expressed in judgment.[7] Reason was always considered to be the principle of community. In the synthetic judgment, the particular was given as "the proper area of judgment" ("das eigentliche Gebiet der Urtheille"), and consisted of "the individual separate thing" ("die einzelnen besonderen Dinge").

---

fälliges und wechselndes, sondern nur das wesentliche und sich selbst gleich bleibende gesest." "Das eigentliche Gebiet der Urtheile sind die einzelnen besonderen Dinge." *Ibid.*, p. 323.

[1] *Ibid.*

[2] S.W. III:4, 2, p. 328.

[3] *Ibid.*

[4] S.W. III:4, 2, p. 330.

[5] "Die Gottheit ist eben so gewiss unbegreiflich, als ihre Erkenntniss die Basis aller Erkenntniss ist." S.W. III:4, 2, p. 322.

[6] "Wir haben ihn (der Begriff des absoluten) nicht als dies und jenes einzelne, sondern wir haben ihn als Vernunft." *Ibid.*, p. 328.

[7] *Ibid.*, p. 323.

The synthesis itself was thought to be Reason or the Absolute. Therefore, judgment became, for Schleiermacher, a form of "das Wissen." In this way, the Absolute received a real content.

Schleiermacher asserted that the Absolute was given in knowledge, although the Absolute could never be isolated in "ein einzelnes Ding."[1] He stressed that the idea of the Absolute (even in its religious sense) always appeared in thought.[2] In *Dial.* A, therefore, Religion corresponded to knowledge.[3]

Dial. 1814 dealt with "the principle of philosophy," and attempted to present "the interior relationship of all knowledge" ("den innern Zusammenhang alles Wissens"). "Das Wissen" as "Denken" appeared as both speculative and empirical knowledge.[4] The antithesis between speculative and empirical knowledge, however, was not absolute, for all knowledge was basically a synthesis of both.[5]

Schleiermacher next described the conditions which were necessary for real knowledge. Knowledge had to possess the characteristic of self-identity, and it had to be a synthesis of thought and being.[6] Self-consciousness was related intimately to Thought.[7] The synthetic unity of apperception was also a necessary condition for knowledge. In self-consciousness the Absolute appeared.

The two definitions of the Absolute as the identity of subject and object, and as the "Ding an sich" had been already given in Schleiermacher's youthful period, as he attempted to overcome the Kantian dualism between "Erscheinung" and the "Ding an sich." In *Dial.* 1814, Schleiermacher overcame this dualism by his assertion that they were "the same being" ("dasselbe Sein").[8] The Absolute in *Dial.* A

---

[1] *Ibid.*, p. 322.

[2] *Ibid.*, p. 330.

[3] "Das absolute ist nicht als einzelnes Ding zu denken... Es giebt keine isolirte Anschauung der Gottheit." "Es ist auch eben so auf der Seite des Gefühles." S.W. III:4, 2, p. 322. Also, "Anders als dass die Gottheit als transcendentes Sein das Princip alles Seins, und als transcendente Idee das formelle Princip alles Wissens ist, ist auf dem Gebiete des Wissens nichts von ihr zu sagen. Alles andere ist nur Bombast oder Einmischung des religiösen, welches als hierher nicht gehörig hier doch verderblich wirken muss." *Ibid.*, p. 328.

[4] S.W. III:4, 2, p. 2, 81, 130.

[5] *Ibid.*

[6] "Dasjenige Denken ist ein Wissen, welches a. vorgestellt wird mit der Nothwendigkeit, dass es von allen denkenefähigen auf dieselbe Weise producirt werde; und welches b. vergestellt wird als einem Sein, dem darin gedachten, entsprechend." S.W. III:4, 2, p. 43.

[7] *Ibid.*, p. 53.

[8] *Ibid.*, p. 99.

was "das formelle Princip alles Wissens." In *Dial*. 1814, the Absolute was identified with the world and was the presupposition for the content of real knowledge.[1] Real knowledge had to possess both the "intellektuelle" and "organische" activities. The ultimate principles of knowledge, "due Idee der Gottheit" and "die Idee der Welt," were intimately related to one another.[2] The transcendental presupposition for all knowledge, therefore, was found outside knowledge. "Die Idee der Gottheit" and "die Idee der Welt" were transcendentals, and were the bases for our knowledge.[3] Feeling expressed the Absolute as "die Gottheit" or as "die Welt." Feeling was, thereby, identical with Religion. All knowledge became religious on the basis of its ultimate relationships. Science had its transcendental ground in "die Idee der Welt,"[4] which was given only in Religion. In addition, the theoretical area as well as the volitional area, had their transcendental presuppositions in Religion.[5] The ideas of "die Gottheit" and "die Welt" were characteristic of "a transcendental knowledge" ("ein transcendentales Wissen"), and were comparable to Religion as "eine höchste Philosophie," or "die Elementarsphilosophie," or "die Wissenschaftslehre," or "die Wissenschaftswissenschaft." Religion as the transcendental presupposition for volition was called "Conscience" ("das Gewissen").[6] Schleiermacher could therefore say that "we have God in us" ("wir haben Gott in uns"). This meant for Schleiermacher that knowledge and will presupposed "the pure transcendental identity of the ideal and the real" ("die rein transcendentale Identität des idealen und realen"). The transcendental ground for knowledge and will was to be found only in "Gefühl."[7] Feeling formed, therefore, the "identity of thought and will" ("Identität des Denkens und Wollens"). The transcendental "ground" for all of conscious life was to be found "only in the relative identity of thought and will, that is, in feeling" ("nur in der relativen Identität des Denkens und Wollens,

---

[1] "Wie die Idee der Gottheit der transcendentale terminus a quo ist, und das Princip der Möglichkeit des Wissens an sich: so ist die Idee der Welt der transcendentale terminus seinem Werden." S.W. III:4, 2, p. 164.

[2] *Ibid.*, p. 99.

[3] *Ibid.*, p. 162 ff., cf. p. 60.

[4] *Ibid.*, p. 163.

[5] "Ausserhalb und gleichsam unterhalb des Begriffs steht das Empfinden, die Action der noch nicht objectiv gewordenen Receptivität; ausserhalb und gleichsam oberhalb des Urtheils steht das Wollen, die Action der schon objectiv werdenden Spontaneität." *Ibid.*, p. 61.

[6] S.W. III:4, 2, p. 151; cf. p. 156.

[7] S.W. III:4, 2, p. 151.

nämlich im Gefühl"). Therefore, "the feeling of God is religious" ("das Gefühl von Gott das religiöse ist").[1]

Dial. C gave Religion a more prominent and necessary place in the life of man than had *Dial.* A or *Dial.* 1814. The main task of *Dial.* C was given as "to find the transcendental task."[2] The two basic conditions for knowledge were repeated: 1) the identity of thought with itself, and 2) the agreement of thought with being.[3] These were correlated to "Vernunft" and "Organisation." The polarity within knowledge, between "Vernunft" and "Organisation", determined much of Schleiermacher's position in *Dial.* C.[4] The polarity within knowledge was defined as a tension between "die intellektuelle Function" and "die organische Function."[5] It was also defined as the antithesis between "das Sein" and "das Denken," and the real and the ideal. However, the Absolute, which was the presupposition for real knowledge, was indifferent to these antitheses.[6]

Schleiermacher arrived at a definition of the Absolute by means of an analysis of the relationship between Thought and Will.[7] Thought and Will were related to "our Being" ("unser Sein"), and as such were similar to "Gefühl" in the sense of "immediate self-consciousness" ("unmittelbares Selbstbewusstsein"). "Gefühl" as "unmittelbares Selbstbewusstsein" became "the transcendental Ground itself" ("der transcendente Grund selbst").[8] "Das transcendentale" was not "das Wissen," "das Denken," or "das Wollen," but was "das religiöse Gefühl" or "das unmittelbare Selbstbewusstsein."

Dial. E took for granted the relationship between "das Wissen," "das Wollen," and Religion. However, knowledge and will had to be the "consciousness of something" ("bewusstsein von etwas"), and in *Dial.* E they are the "consciousness of Nothing" ("bewusstsein von

---

[1] Cf. "Wenn nun das Gefühl von Gott das religiöse ist: so scheint deshalb die Religion über der Philosophie zu stehen, wie auch viele behaupten. Es ist aber nicht so. Wir sind hieher gekommen, ohne vom Gefühl ausgegangen zu sein, auf rein philosophischem Wege." *Ibid.*, p. 152. The contrast between Dial. A and Dial. 1814 is indicated by the fact that Schleiermacher believed that there wrs a philosophic road to God, and, as well, a religious road, which was more direct; cf. S.W. III:4, 2, p. 154 ff., p. 76, p. 35 ff., also Br. 1, p. 381.

[2] S.W. III:4, 2, p. 384.

[3] *Ibid.*

[4] S.W. III:4, 2, p. 388.

[5] *Ibid.*, p. 389.

[6] *Ibid.*, p. 399. "Das unbedingte Sein" was "Gottheit, höchstes Wesen, absolutes, auch Nichts."

[7] *Ibid.*, p. 426 ff.

[8] *Ibid.*, p. 429 ff.

Null"), and even in reference to God.[1] The transcendental presupposition found in self-consciousness was the primary condition for "the unity of our Being" ("die Einheit unseres Seins").[2] This meant finally that the God-consciousness was the necessary presupposition for self-consciousness.[3] There was no further discussion in *Dial. E* of the transcendental ground, other than a reference to immediate self-consciousness and religious feeling.

C. *The "Essence" of Religion and the Christian Faith in Der christliche Glaube*

The definition of the nature of Religion is dealt with in the introduction to *Der christliche Glaube*. Religion must be constructed as a "Lehnsäse aus der Ethik, aus der Religionsphilosophie und aus der Apologetik."[4] In this form, Religion developed in the closest relationship with the church. Religion, Schleiermacher wrote, could not be considered as "a knowledge" ("ein Wissen"), nor "an action" ("ein Thun"), but as "a determination of Feeling" ("eine Bestimmtheit des Gefühls") and "a determination of immediate selfconsciousness" ("eine Bestimmtheit des unmittelbaren Selbstbewusstseins").[5] In the *Reden* (1799), Schleiermacher's major interest was to delimit Religion from metaphysics and morals; in the *Reden* (1806), to demonstrate its relationship to knowledge and moral activity, and in both instances to demonstrate how Religion (defined as "Anschauung und Gefühl") was the basis for all of human life. In *Der christliche Glaube*, Schleiermacher defined Religion as "Gefühl" and "unmittelbares Selbstbewusstsein." He dealt with the relationship of Religion to "Wissen" and "Thun" in the following way:

1. "Unmittelbares Selbstbewusstsein" had to be added to the definition of Religion as "Gefühl." However, "Selbstbewusstsein," included in the definition of Religion, was never "ein Wissen" or "ein Thun." It was "ein unmittelbares Selbstbewusstsein."[6] Religion was therefore the most basic level of life and revealed and connected all of the other experiences of life. It was separate from and differentiated from all other experiences. It was, furthermore, the presupposition for "Wissen" and "Thun".

---

[1] S.W. III:4, 2, p. 523 ff.
[2] S.W. III:4, 2, p. 525.
[3] S.W. III:4, 2, p. 524 ff.
[4] Fr. Schleiermacher, *Der christliche Glaube*, Reimer edition, 1830.
[5] Gll. 1, Par. 8.
[6] Religion as *Gefühl* in the sense of "unmittelbares Selbstbewusstsein" is "die unmittelbare Gegenwart des ganzen ungetheilten Daseins." Gll. 2, Par. 3:2.

2. Life was "an exchange of consciousness and action" ("ein Wechsel von Insichbleiben und Aussichheraustreten des Subjects," that is, "ein Wechsel von Bewusstsein und Thun"). "Wissen" and "Gefühl" appeared as forms of "das Bewusstsein." Therefore, Religion as "Gefühl" in the sense of "unmittelbares Selbstbewusstsein," subsumed "das Wissen" under "das Bewusstsein." In this way, "das Wissen" and "das Gefühl" were separated from "das Thun."

3. However, although Religion and "Wissen" were related, they were not identical. "Das Gefühl" and "das Wissen" were both forms of "das Insichbleiben" ("das Bewusstsein"), and therefore stood in opposition to "das Thun" as "das Aussichheraustreten." However, "das Wissen" as "Erkannthaben," formed "ein Insichblieben" and, as such, corresponded to "das Gefühl." "Das Gefühl" became "ein Insichbleiben," because Religion, as "Gefühl," stood in opposition to "Wissen" and "Thun."

4. Religion, as feeling in the sense of "unmittelbares Selbstbewusstsein," united every particular moment, and had the capacity to determine "Wissen und Thun."[1] There was, therefore, a relationship between "Gefühl" and "Wissen" and "Thun." Nevertheless, Religion was not identified with them.[2]

5. Religion and the other experiences of man were related to "das Selbstbewusstsein."[3]

6. Religion as "an action generating Knowledge" ("ein Handlungen erzeugendes Wissen" and, "ein aus einen Wissen hervorgegangenes Thun"), did not relate "Thun" to "Wissen," without at the same time presupposing "an intervening determination of self-consciousness" ("eine dazwischentretende Bestimmtheit des Selbstbewusstseins").[4]

Up to this point Religion had been defined as "Gefühl" in the sense of "unmittelbares Selbstbewusstsein." This definition presupposed that Religion was something unique and distinct from all other experiences of man. However, Religion was not simply "Gefühl" or "unmittelbares Selbstbewusstsein," but "eine Bestimmtheit des Gefühls und des unmittelbaren Selbstbewusstsein." Feeling, which was

---

[1] "Ware es anders, so könnten sich ja die frommen Momente mit den übrigen nicht zu einem Leben verbinden, sondern die Frömmigkeit wäre etwas für sich ohne allen Einfluss auf die übrigen geistigen Lebensverrichtungen." Gll. 2, Par. 3:4.

[2] *Ibid.*

[3] Gll. 2, Par. 3:5.

[4] *Ibid.*

identified with Religion, had to be distinguished from every other feeling.

Religion defined as "Gefühl" or "Selbstbewusstsein" included "Bewusstsein." However, in consciousness one was not only aware of oneself, but also of the variable character of consciousness. The consciousness one has of oneself was "ein Sein" or "ein Sichselbst-sezen." The variable quality was "ein Sichselbstnichtsegesesthaben" or "ein Irgendwiesewordensein." It was apparent that the former represented the active element within man, ("Selbstthätigkeit"), and the latter, the passive element, ("Empfänglichkeit"). Man's relation-ship to another in community presupposed receptivity. Man was always related to another, who was not identical with himself. There was in the variableness of self-consciousness a factor which was con-tinuous throughout. It was expressed as, "we feel ourselves dependent" ("wir uns abhängig fühlen"). This feeling of dependence was the expression for that side of consciousness which included receptivity ("Afficirtsein"). The sense of freedom was the expression for that side of self-consciousness which was active ("Sichselbstsezen"). These two elements coincided with one another in self-consciousness in such a way that there was made possible the element of reciprocity between oneself and another. Man's self-consciousness was the consciousness he had of his relationship to the World. It consisted of his feeling of dependence and at the same time, his sense of freedom.

The feeling of absolute dependence ("schlechthiniges Abhängig-keitsgefühl") was always found in "das Selbstbewusstsein" as a con-tinuous element. Only in "das Abhängigkeitsgefühl" could one find the "schlechthinig". Religion, which Schleiermacher had defined as the feeling of "unmittelbares Selbstbewusstsein," had now become "the feeling of absolute dependence" ("das schlechthinige Abhängig-keitsgefühl").

"Gott" was that which was most original within the "unmittelbares Selbstbewusstsein," and was that which could not be identified with "die Welt." "Die Welt" was related to self-consciousness, but was not the element of continuity within self-consciousness. "Das schlecht-hinige Abhängigkeitsgefühl" was therefore similar to one's awareness of standing "in relationship to God" ("in Beziehung mit Gott").[1] Re-ligion meant that man was conscious of his absolute dependence (that is, "dass wir uns unsrer selbst als schlechthin abhängig, oder,

---

[1] Gll. 2, Par. 4:4.

was dasselbe sagen will, als in Beziehung mit Gott bewusst sind").[1]

Schleiermacher spoke of three levels of "Selbstbewusstsein: "the animal, the brutish" ("das animalische, das thierische"),[2] "the sensuous" ("das sinnliche"), and "the higher self-consciousness" ("das hohere Selbstbewusstsein"). Only the last was to be identified with the feeling of absolute dependence. The lowest level of consciousness was not "animalische Selbstbewusstsein," because that consisted only of a dreamlike awareness, which was described as located somewhere between sleeping and waking. The next level, the "sinnliche Selbstbewusstsein," consisted of the feeling of dependence and the feeling of freedom. It was at this level that "Gefühl" and "Anschauung" appeared, that is, it was at this level that there was consciousness of a subject and an object. This level was called, "sinnlich," even though feeling was not only "the selfish" ("die selbstischen"), but also "the social and moral feeling" ("die geselligen und sittlichen Gefühl"). It was at this level that man was conscious of his finitude. This level did not express that element of continuity which united every particular moment in the life of a man into some kind of meaningful whole. This continuity was to be found only at the highest level, which was the level where one was aware of "das schlechthinige Abhängigkeitsgefühl."[3] The feeling of Absolute dependence was a common possession of all mankind and characteristic of man's finitude. Man's consciousness of himself as a finite being introduced this higher self-consciousness, that is, the feeling of Absolute dependence. However, the awareness of finitude came at the level of the "sinnliches Selbstbewusstsein." This meant that the higher self-consciousness was related positively to the sense of finitude. However, the feeling of Absolute dependence, or "the relationship to God" ("die Beziehung mit Gott") was transcendent to the consciousness of finitude.

The feeling of Absolute dependence was immediate to self-consciousness. It was not derived from either "ein Wissen" or "ein Thun."[4] This higher self-consciousness was raised above all antitheses of subject and object. *Der christliche Glaube* defined Religion as a higher-

---

[1] Gll. 2, Par. 4; cf. Gll. 1, Par. 9.

[2] This level is characterized by "das gegenständliche und das in sich zurückkgehende, oder Gefühl und Anschauung, nicht gehörig auseinander treten, sondern noch unentwikkelt in einander verworren sind." Gll. 2, Par. 5:1.

[3] On this highest level, man is conscious of the meaningful life in the deepest sense of the term. Cf. Gll. 2, Par. 5:1.

[4] Gll. 2, Par. 5:2.

self-consciousness and as the feeling of Absolute dependence. It included the two-fold definition of the Absolute as immanent and transcendent. The higher self-consciousness referred always to the finite Self. The Absolute ("Gott") was related to the finite in such a way that the finite was dependent upon the Absolute for its existence.

The most characteristic aspect of the Christian religion was that the higher self-consciousness did not refer to the Absolute Self, which was identified with God, but to the finite Self. When this was raised to the higher Self-consciousness there was the recognition on the part of man that he was standing in the relationship of dependence upon the Absolute power of God. The consciousness of finitude was also the consciousness of one's relationship to God.

Religion, defined as the higher self-consciousness, was never an ideal or an a priori category, but was always real and a posteriori. The higher self-consciousness never existed without the empirical and the historical. If Religion was that which assured the element of continuity in consciousness, it was apparent that the higher self-consciousness could not exist except in relation to the empirical and historical.[1] This relationship permitted self-consciousness to be a concrete consciousness.[2]

The terms Religion and Christianity were used almost interchangeably in *Der christliche Glaube.* The religious a priori was defined as the presupposition or ground for all of the concrete and historical religions. It was that which was specifically religious in all of the real religions of mankind. Schleiermacher did not recognize any other type of Religion than the historical, that which was strongly characterized by "an individual Religion." Christianity, as a real and positive Religion, was not simply empirical, but was a realization and an "individualization" of the religious a priori. Within Christianity, the religious a priori had most perfectly been realized.

That which was most characteristic of a positive Religion was its specific "Grundanschauung." This was Schleiermacher's term for the

---

[1] Gll. 2, Par. 5:3.

[2] Schleiermacher's intention in R. 2 was to show "dass Ihr in eben der Gestalt der Religion welche Ihr so oft verachtet, im Christenthum, mit Eurem ganzen Wissen, Thun und Sein so eingewurzelt seid, dass Ihr gar nicht heraus könnt, und dass Ihr vergeblich versucht Euch seine Zerstörung vorzustellen, ohne zugleich die Vernichtung dessen was Euch das Liebste und Heiligste in der Welt ist, Eurer gesammten Bildung und Art des Daseins, ja Eurer Kunst und Wissenschaft mit zu beschliesen." R. 2, p. 364 ff.

religious a priori in a given Religion. It was also the principle of individuation by which Religion participated in concrete reality. By means of the "Grundanschauung" the realized religions received a positive, historical and necessary quality. Schleiermacher exemplified the realization of the religious a priori by reference to Christianity. The "Grundanschauung" of Christianity was historical even in the sense that its "Grundanschauung" was related to the historical and dramatic antithesis between the finite and the infinite. Man had removed himself from God, but God sought to overcome this animosity by means of the Mediator, who participated in both the finite and the infinite. The "Grundanschauung" of Christianity was charac-· terized by the necessary fulfillment of mediation. This "Grundanschauung" determined the form and content of Christianity. Every single statement of the faith of the Christian community had to be seen in relation to its "Grundanschauung."

Schleiermacher also defined the apologetic task of Christianity. This was a necessary task within the church because of the universal principle of "the irreligious" ("das Irreligiöse", "Die Irreligion," or "die Sunde"). Overagainst this, Religion was to provide "a continuum within man" ("ein Continuum im Menschen"). This was the task of the Christian Religion, as it was Christ's task as "Mittler" and "Erlöser."[1] Christ's divinity was seen in his consciousness of his work as Mediator.[2] He was not "the only Mediator" ("der einzige Mittler"), but there was the possibility that the consciousness of the task of mediation would be awakened in another individual as it was in Christ.[3] Christianity was an ethical and historical Religion, and, therefore, the principle of individuality had to be present.[4]

---

[1] Cf. R.w, p. 34 ff. Christ's task is not dependent upon "the purity of his ethical teachings" nor upon "the individuality of his character", rather "das wahrhaft Göttliche ist die herrliche Klarheit, zu welcher die grosse Idee, welche darzustellen er gekommen war, sich in seiner Seele ausbildete: die Idee dass Alles Endliche höherer Vermittlungen bedarf, um mit der Gottheit zusammenzuhängen, und dass für den von dem Endlichen und Besonderen ergriffenen Menschen... nur Heil zu finden ist in der Erlösung." R. 2, p. 350 ff.

[2] R. 2, p. 353.

[3] This follows the principle: "nichts ist unchristlicher als Einförmigkeit zu suchen in der Religion." R. 2, p. 360.

[4] This is the basis for Schleiermacher's separation of Roman Catholocism and Protestantism, cf. R. 2, p. 371; cf. also the relationship of R. 3 (1821) and R. 4 (1830), to R.1 and R.2, and finally to Gll. When Schleiermacher in Gll.2, Par. 11 defined Christianity as "eine der teleologischen Richtung der Frömmigkeit angehörige monotheistische Glaubensweise", which differentiates itself from every other because "alles in derselben bezogen wird auf die durch Jesum von Nazareth

Schleiermacher had also seen the necessity of relating Christianity to the culture of his time. The *Prolegomena* to the dogmatic task, which formed part of Schleiermacher's introduction to *Der christliche Glaube*, asserted that the Christian faith must be related to all of life. Christianity was to form the basis for all of cultural life.[1]

D. *The Nature of Christianity; Theology as a Positive Science in Kurze Darstellung des theologischen Studiums:*

In *Kurze Darstellung*, Schleiermacher presented "die theologische Encyklopädie."[2] However, he dealt first with the term "Wissenschaft." Theology was not related to the pure sciences but was a science "of another order." Theology was a positive science, and gathered its content from the expression of Religion in history. Theology, as a positive science, was a specific realization of the Religion of infinity, that is, Christianity. Theology was an "objective science" ("Gegenstandswissenschaft"), a practical science in the service of the Church.[3] Christianity received a positive "historical meaning and independence" ("geschichtliche Bedeutung und Selbständigkeit") first within the Church. Theology and the theological task had to be understood from the standpoint of the particular forms which the Christian faith took in history. Theology, therefore, had to follow the development and life of the Church. Christian dogma had to be placed in relationship to the life of the Christian community. The content of doctrine

---

vollbrachte Erlösung", there was here everything which was present in the earlier editions of *Reden*, R.1 and R.2; "Die monotheistische Glaubendweise" refers to the relationship of the finite to "Ein Höchstes und Unendliches". All of the characteristics of Christianity in Gll. are found already in *Reden*.

[1] Cf. Karl Barth, Die christliche Dogmatik I, (Basel; Zollikon, 1927), p. 11 ff, who recognized Schleiermacher's *Der christliche Glaube* as belonging to the "modern period".

[2] Fr. Schleiermacher, *Kurze Darstellung des theologischen Studiums*, krit. Ausgabe v. Heinr. Scholz, (Leipzig: 1910), *Quellenschriften zur Geschichte des Protestantismus*, 10 Hft. Lücke in Theologische Studien und Kritiken IV, 1834, reports: "Berlin bezeichnet, wie ein Jahrhundert früher Halle, eine neue Periode in der Theologie... Den geist der neuen Universität auf dem theologischen Gebiete bezeichnet bald nach der Stiftung Schleiermachers kurze Darstellung des theologischen Studiums zum Behuf einleitender Verlesungen 1811." p. 772. Schleiermacher was always interested in constructing "die theologische Encyklopädie", which was to be "ein rein deutsches Bedürfniss und Erzeugniss" (Lücke); cf. those works upon which Schleiermacher based his lectures: J. G. Planck, *Einleitung in die Theolog. Wissenschaften* I–II, 1794–95 and J. A. Nösselt, *Anweisung zur Bildung angehender Theologen* I–III, 1786–89. BrG., p. 2.

[3] K.D. 1, p. 1, Par. 2; cf. K.D. 2, Par. 2.

had to be contemporary and alive. Christianity, the Church, and the Christian life were the primary sources for theology. Theology, therefore, was a practical discipline which described the consciousness of the religious community, the Church. By means of the Church, religious content was brought to consciousness. However, the Christian faith and its expression was always developing and changing, and was dependent upon the intellectual milieu of the time.

Schleiermacher saved the scientific quality of theology by reference to the romantic concept of history. History was to be seen as the "continuous realization of an Idea," which was never lost in contingencies. History, therefore, was the realization of an Idea which possessed the Eternal and the Absolute. Every individual event in history possessed the character of Absoluteness. Therefore every individual form of Christianity, whether individual or communal, was a realization of the Christian faith's "Grund" or "Zentralanschauung." Theology had the task to demonstrate in what way the religious consciousness was an expression of this "Grundanschauung."[1]

Schleiermacher attempted to demonstrate the necessary relationship which existed between theology as a science and every other science. However, he maintained that every indication of the historical realization of the Religion of infinity was imperfect and therefore limited.[2] In *Kurze Darstellung des theologischen Studiums*, Schleiermacher asserted that Christianity could not be excluded from this characterization.

Philosophical Theology, for Schleiermacher, became Apologetics and Polemics.[3] Practical Theology corresponded to Philosophical Theology by its characterization as "Practice" ("Ausübung").[4] Historical Theology was different from them both by its characterization as "Betrachtung."[5] Philosophical Theology was related to "Die Ethik." Historical Theology was included within the historical

---

[1] Schleiermacher expressed the basic task of theology: "So wenig des eigentümliche Wesen des Christentums bloss empirisch kann aufgefasst werden, eben so wenig lässt es sich rein wissenschaftlich auf Idee, allein ableiten." K.D. 1, p. 11. Par. 1, cf. K.D. 2, Par. 2. "Es (das eigentümliche Wesen des Christentums) ist nur durch Gegeneinanderhalten des geschichtlich in ihm Gegebenen und des in der Idee der Religion und der Kirche als veränderliche Grösse Gesetzten zu bestimmen." K.D. 1, p. 11, Par. 2, cf. K.D. 2, Par. 32.

[2] This has already been expressed in R.1.

[3] K.D. 1, p. 15, Par. 19, cf. K.D. 2, Par. 39 ff.

[4] K.D. 1, p. 22, Par. 3, cf. K.D. 2, Par. 66.

[5] *Ibid.*

sciences.[1] Because Philosophical Theology was both Philosophy and Theology and was expressed in Apologetics and Polemics, Historical Theology had the task to examine the historical development of Religion and the Christian faith.[2] Historical Theology became, "the knowledge of the beginnings of Christianity" ("die Kenntnis von dem Anfang des Christentums" as well as, "die Kenntnis von seinem weiteren Verlauf" and also "die Kenntnis von seinem Zustand in dem gegenwärtigen Augenblick").[3] Historical Theology dealt with "the idea of doctrine" ("den Lehrbegriff" and "die Kirchenverfassung" The development of "Lehrbegriff" was to be treated, however, within the history of dogma. The expression of the "Lehrbegriff" of the church in every given moment in time became the essential task of Dogmatics.

Philosophical Theology presented the "norm" or "essence" of the Christian faith. Historical Theology discerned the nature of this norm, and Practical Theology presented the medium through which the church lived and expressed itself. Dogmatics became, therefore, a part of Historical Theology, and expressed basically, "die christliche Sittenlehre."[5] It was primarily "Gegenstandswissenschaft," but it was not to be considered definitive, fixed, or concluded. It had no perfect or absolute character, but was filled with imperfections. Dogmatic Theology was not "the expression of a so-called Biblical Theology" ("die Aufstellung einer sogenannten biblischen Theologie").[6] It was not the means by which orthodoxy was preserved or an ancient doctrine maintained. Dogmatic Theology had to be heterodox in the sense that it was open to every new form and representation of the "essence of Christianity."[7] However, this did not mean that it was conditioned by arbitrariness or capriciousness, or represented merely the subjective feeling of the individual.[8] Dogmatics was a part of Historical Theology, and thereby possessed the same necessary and given quality as the historical expression of the Christian faith within time. Doctrine had to express that which was permanent and fixed

---

[1] K.D. 1, p. 24, Par. 1, cf. K.D. 2, Par. 69.
[2] K.D. 1, p. 24, Par. 3, cf. K.D. 2, Par. 70.
[3] K.D. 1, p. 28, Par. 19, cf. K.D. 2, Par. 85.
[4] K.D. 1, p. 29, Par. 20, cf. K.D. 2, Par. 90, 95.
[5] K.D. 1, p. 62, Par. 31, cf. K.D. 2, Par. 230.
[6] K.D. 1, p. 57, Par. 4.
[7] K.D. 1, p. 58, Par. 11; cf. K.D. 2, Par. 203 ff.
[8] K.D. 2, p. 57, Par. 4.

within the Christian faith. Every expression of a specific doctrine of the Church was determined by that given period within the life of the Church.[1] Dogmatics did not attempt to conserve the past. Rather, it was located in the present, and was open to the future.[2]

---

[1] K.D. 1, p. 61, Par. 23; cf. K.D. 2, Par. 212, also R.2 p. 366.
[2] K.D. 1, p. 57, Par. 6, cf. K.D. 2, Par. 199, also K.D. 1, p. 59, Par. 19, cf. K.D. 2, Par. 202.

NYGREN'S CONCEPTION OF RELIGION

CHAPTER THREE

THE RELIGIOUS APRIORI

Anders Nygren constructed his *Religiöst Apriori* during a time when philosophers of religion and theologians were very much interested in the application of such a concept within their systems. The "Religious A Priori" literature is boundless.[1] Basically, the religious a priori is offered as a means of determining the truth and validity of religion and the religious experience. However, Nygren found that there was no consensus of opinion as to the nature and meaning of the religious a priori within different systems. Nygren saw as his own task to provide a unanimity! He wrote that if the religious a priori is going to be employed meaningfully in a scientific discussion, that is, if its content is to be freed from subjective and arbitrary interpretations, it must offer one clear and precise statement of its function.[2] This then was the task of his *Religiöst Apriori*, which Nygren published in 1921. Nygren did not want to present another religious a priori, but rather to validate the use of a religious a priori within the philosophy of religion.

Nygren dealt with the subject of the religious a priori in the following way:

A. *The Religious A Priori was a Transcendental A Priori; (Religion was, therefore, a "necessary and universal experience, inseparable from the nature of man")*

The task, at the outset, as Nygren explained,[3] was to deal with a philosophical concept. Theological consequences were derived after the philosophical concept of an a priori was made applicable to the religious experience. Nygren's methodology followed the following pattern:

1. A philosophical analysis of the a priori concept, in order to reveal the different types of the a priori which may be used in the construction of the specifically religious a priori;

---

[1] cf. Anders Nygren, *Religiöst Apriori*, (Lund: Gleerupska Universitets-Bokhandeln, 1921), pp. 23–91.

[2] *Ibid.*, p. 94. "Skall det emellertid med fördel kunna användas i den vetenskapliga diskussionen, så måste detta subjektiva godtycke vid dess innehållsbestämning upphöra, och det måste åsättas en tydlig, från alla synpunkter meningsfull prägel."

[3] *Ibid.*, pp. 94, 95.

2. The result of this analysis would present the manner in which this concept could be employed in a philosophical discussion;

3. An examination of the a priori concept to determine whether it could be employed in the scientific investigation of religion.

Nygren's basic problem therefore, was to determine if there was a religious apriori, and if so, to decide how best it might be used in a philosophical system. Nygren finally purposed to examine the content of the religious material itself (that is, the religious expression of a given, historical "Church") to determine if it was necessary on the basis of the religious expression of the Church to modify the philosophically conceived a priori concept.

As a result of this methodological proposal, Nygren, in his *Religiöst Apriori*, examined the literature of the a priori concept. His method was not a "historical-genetic" (nor a "logical-systematic") approach, but a "typological-classificatory" procedure. The following characteristic types of the a priori concept appeared in the literature:[1]

1. The Platonic a priori;
2. The Stoic-rationalistic a priori;
3. The Ontological a priori;
4. The a priori as "ideae innatae" (Descartes);
5. The a priori as a "representation" (Leibnitz);
6. The Transcendental a priori (Kant);
7. The a priori as "immediate rational knowledge" (Fries, Nelson);
8. The a priori as a "psychological function" (Simmel);
9. The a priori as an "epistemological fiction" (Vaihinger);
10. The a priori "expressive for universal value" (Lotze, Windelband, Rickert).

Nygren hesitated to speak of possessing the necessary critical measure by which to decide which of the above were legitimate to present the religious a priori. There were two viewpoints from which every theory of the religious a priori had to be examined, that is, the philosophical and the religious. The usual fault with the presentation of the religious a priori was that the content of the religious a priori was arbitrarily determined without a consideration of the philosophical presuppositions included in the concept of any a priori system. As a result, an erroneous content was given to the religious experience. Nygren asserted that it was necessary first to examine the idea of the religious a priori within the context of the general philosophical dis-

---

[1] *Ibid.*, cf. p. 128 ff.

cussion of an a priori. In this way, Nygren believed, the scientific character of the religious experience and the religious a priori could be assured.

Plato was the prototype of the thinker who dealt with the a priori in an incorrect manner. Plato had complicated the nature of the a priori by dividing it into two parts. On the one hand, the a priori was the "higher validity founded upon logic." On the other, it was the "higher validity, based upon its psychological and genetic character." However, Nygren believed that Plato had approached the problem of the validity of knowledge and experience in the correct manner. When Plato discovered that experience could never give him absolute validity, his only recourse was to the pre-existent world of ideas. Recollection, for Plato, was then necessary for validity to be present. Nygren stamped this attempt as metaphysical and hypothetical, and an abandonment of the critical method in which thought was placed in relationship to experience.[1] As well, Nygren discovered that every "logical" and "genetic" and "psychological" treatment of the a priori was unsuccessful. The same rejection of all contemporary a priori structures which were "logical," "genetic," and "psychological" can be seen in Nygren's later works.[2] Experience could not be explained psychologically or metaphysically. But it was Kant, the philosopher "par préférence," who did not employ a priori theories built upon a genetic and psychological or metaphysical basis. Instead, a priori knowledge meant for Kant that which was "necessary and universal," that which was "independent of experience." Nygren concluded therefore that, although there was a certain degree of unclarity in Kant's a priori system, fundamentally he was anti-psychologistic. This was apparent, Nygren explained, from the main problem he dealt with, which was, "How is a synthetic a priori judgment possible?" This question would have been meaningless if the presuppositions for the synthetic a priori were sought for. The synthetic a priori judgment was possible only when it was treated as logical and transcendental.

Nygren found that in all of the conceptions of the a priori there was a fundamental basis which united them all, and that was the concern for the validity of experience in all of its different forms, the theoretical,

---

[1] *Ibid.*, p. 130. "Platon är ett instruktivt exempel på huru filosofien liksom av sig själv kan glida över från den kritiska fråga, som tanken måste ställa inför erfarenhetens faktum, till en hypotetisk, metafysisk betraktelse."

[2] Cf. Anders Nygren, *Dogmatikens Vetenskapliga Grundläggning*, (Stockholm: SKD, 1922); also *Filosofisk och Kristen Etik*, (Lund: C.W.K. Gleerup, 1923).

the ethical, the esthetic, and the religious. Furthermore, Nygren found that every attempt to explain away the fundamental basis for the a priori resulted in failure.[1] Nygren maintained that Plato had not dealt with experience when he defined validity by reference to a metaphysical or preexistent world. Neither did the Stoics when they said that there were ideas which were valid by themselves. The "lumen aeternum" of the ontological a priori system was uncontrollable and could not contribute to the theory of validity. The a priori, which was understood as reason, whether as an "innate idea" or as a "representation," was tautologous, because the presupposition for logical thinking rested upon the presupposition that one had an ability to think logically. Fries' theory that within the nature of man there was a hidden and immediate knowledge of reason, rested upon a psychologism, said Nygren. Nygren also directed his criticism against Simmel's "psychologistic" a priori.

Nygren found that it was only the transcendental theory of the a priori which avoided the fallacies associated with the genetic, psychological, and metaphysical definitions, and which sought to place the problem of the validity of experience in the center of philosophical investigation. Nygren adopted the transcendental method at this point, because he found that it alone satisfied this requirement.[2]

However, Nygren said that a religious a priori could not be postulated, but it must be discovered in the factual historical religions of man. The a priori, in its transcendental sense, was never a psychological fact (as in Troeltsch and Otto) which could be compared to other psychological facts. It was the moment in experience upon which validity rested, that is, it was that moment which made "logical" experience ("factual" not "psychological") possible.[3] In order to extend the analysis of the a priori to religion it was necessary to employ a transcendental a priori. The question was asked by Nygren, whether the

---

[1] Nygren, *Religiöst Apriori*, p. 133. "Vi hava vidare funnit, *att de olika aprioriuppfattningarna, var och en på sitt sätt sökt giva psykologiskt-genetiska eller metafysiska begrundningar och förklaringar av detta grundfaktum, men att dessa förklaringar, som skulle intaga en tjänande ställning, så småningom förvandlandes till självständiga filosofemer, som lösgjorde sig från det ursprungliga sammanhanget med giltighetsproblemet och ställde detta i skuggan i stället för att bidraga till dess lösning.*"

[2] *Ibid.*, p. 134.

[3] *Ibid.*, p. 137, 138. "Apriori är ju i transcendental mening ingalunda ett psykologiskt faktum bredvid andra psykologiska fakta, utan det moment i erfarenheten, varpå dennas giltighet vilar, det varigenom erfarenheten "logiskt" sett (d.v.s. "sakligt", ej "psykologiskt") är "möjlig".

religious experience itself claimed to be universal and valid. If the answer was in the affirmative then the a priori which had to be employed had a transcendental character. Only then would the a priori be legitimate within the area of religion.

Nygren designated the critical philosophy of Kant as the proper and adequate methodological tool to investigate the validity of the different forms of human experience. Critical philosophy was concerned with that which was necessary and universal, and became therefore a general theory of experience. It related itself, as Kant described, to the empirical and sense experience.[1] Necessity and objective validity were constitutive for Kant's conception of experience, But only when an experience was not accidental could it be said to possess objective validity. Every experience which had more than a subjective character was the proper object for philosophy. Philosophy had to determine its "validity." Philosophy, therefore, was a theory of general experience, and it was critical philosophy which best satisfied this requirement. However, the concept of experience had to be seen in the widest possible connotation, as that which included the mathematical and natural sciences, the biological, the historical, the sociological, the practical, the ethical, as well as the religious experiences.[2] Nygren said that an experience was to be included if there was "an immediate feeling and conviction that a phenomenon was unconditionally valid."[3] Without an immediate recognition of an experience as such, there was no reason to investigate its foundation of validity. Critical philosophy, therefore, began with experience, and determined the logical basis for its validity. However, it had to concern itself always with the most general forms of experience. On the basis of critical philosophy, Nygren attempted to investigate the following claims of validity; the *theoretical* experience, which related validity to knowledge, in relationship to the two kinds of scientific knowledge, mathematical and historical; the *ethical* experience, which examined the nature of morality; the *asthetic* experience, which analyzed the characteristics of beauty; and finally, the *religious* experience, which

---

[1] "Empirische Urteile, sofern sie objektive Gültigkeit haben, sind Erfahrungsurteile; die aber, so nur subjektiv gültig sind, nenne ich bloss Wahrnehmungsurteile." Nygren, *Det Religionsfilosofiska Grundproblemet*, (Lund: Gleerupska Universits-bokhandeln, 1920), p. 55, from Kant, *Prologomena zu einer jeden Künftigen Metaphysik* (Leipzig: Redam, 1783), p. 77.

[2] Nygren, *Det Religionsfilosofiska Grundproblemet*, p. 36.

[3] *Ibid.*

asked the question of what was the basis for the claim of religion to be a valid experience.[1]

The transcendental a priori was relevant to the individual religious experience as well, for it was the philosophical formulation of the claim that it possessed trans-subjective validity.[2]

A problem arose when Nygren went to the "self witness of religion" and found (for example, in Jeremiah 20:7 and Amos 3:8), that religion and the religious experience could not be coerced. Religion, Nygren discovered, was the "actualization of a higher freedom," which was based primarily upon a positive and personal decision. It appeared, therefore, said Nygren, that religion must either be defined as an act of freedom or as the religious a priori. Nygren denied that there was such an alternative in the definition of religion, and said that it was a "psychological" definition, reached by an investigation of the religious experience alone. The experience which the a priori dealt with in religion was a transcendental experience. No arbitrary structure was set up, but rather it was an experience which could give meaning to our existence which was to be scrutinized.[3] There was nothing compulsive about the religious experience. Religion and the religious experience *necessarily* possessed the character of validity, because they were related to the transcendental a priori.

Nygren asked whether the transcendental necessity of religion could be compared to the claim of transcendental validity on the part of the other experiences? Was not the necessary quality of knowledge another kind of necessity than that which dominated the other areas? The logical law of contradiction would seem to be an absolute and coercive criterion. This law could never be denied, and, therefore, must be a purely "factual" necessity. In ethics, however, there was "personal" necessity, related to the consciousness and will of the individual. Logical validity could not be placed under the category of personal validity for this reason. Nygren averted the difficulties inherent in the structure of the categories by his insistence that when

---

[1] *Ibid.*, p. 58, 59.

[2] Nygren, *Religiöst Apriori*, p. 144. "*Aprioribegreppet, transcendentalt fattat, står tvärt om i bästa överensstämmelse med den religiösa upplevelsens karaktär och är blott den filosofiska formuleringen av denna upplevelses anspråk på att äga transsubjektiv giltighet.*"

[3] *Ibid.*, p. 146. "Den nödvändighet, som aprioriåskådningen vill finna i det religiösa, är ej en psykologisk, utan en transcendental nödvändighet, d.v.s. denna åskådning hävdar, att det icke är en godtycklig åtgärd, när vi ställa vår tillvaro under religiös synpunkt, utan en nödvändig åtgard, och detta till den grad, att om det religiösa bortfölle, tillika hela vår tillvaro förlorade sin betydelse."

one deal with purely formal and logical relationships, there must be the element of logical compulsion. But as soon as one turned to knowledge which has a definite content, the coercive character which belonged to the logical category disappeared. There was no logical necessity which forced us to assume that there was true knowledge. When the different conceptions of validity were placed parallel to one other, there was no agreement in the particular method which had to be employed to handle them. However, when they were treated as a unity, they were found to rest upon a common presupposition. Knowledge which was valid (with logical coerciveness) was the presupposition upon which all knowledge rested. This assertion could be understood only by reference to the transcendental character of knowledge. Without the validity of knowledge, no experience was possible. This same transcendental method, therefore, had to be used in the analysis of the validity of the presuppositions for *morality, art* and *religion*.[1]

Nygren insisted that there was a correspondence between the "self-witness of religion" and the transcendental a priori. This was demonstrated by the criteria which belonged to the nature of both religion and philosophy, that is, their claim to universality and necessity. Furthermore, religion itself made a claim to be universal and necessary in a transcendental way. Religion also claimed that its object was real in a transcendent way. Religion rested ultimately upon the reality of the object of its faith. Therefore, the *transcendental method* and the *religious a priori* were to be be employed in the demonstration of the universality and necessity of the religious experience.

Nygren asserted, therefore, that the philosophy of religion must employ the critical method, and not transform itself into a metaphysical, dogmatic "pseudo-philosophy." In reference to the claim of religion to be universal and necessary, the question of the transcendental a priori of religion must be asked.[2] This was the only way the philosophy of religion could be a valid philosophical enterprise.

---

[1] *Ibid.*, p. 149. "Här är det således ej för kunskapens vidkommande fråga om de enkla slutledningarna, som gälla med logiskt tvång, om blott premisserna på förhand stå fast, utan om de förutsättningar, varpå all kunskap vilar, vilka blott kunna rättfärdigas på transcendental väg genom påvisande av att utan deras giltighet erfarenheten överhuvud ej är möjlig. Samma transcendentala betraktelse måste användas, när fråga är om giltigheten hos sedlighetens, konstens och religionens översta förutsättningar, och häri allenast ligger den parallelitet, som måste upprätthållas mellan de olika giltighetsområdena."

[2] *Ibid.*, p. 150.

B. *The Religious A Priori Must Not Be Interpreted Psychologically or Metaphysically*

The a priori had philosophical significance only when treated in a transcendental way. The claim of the religious experience to be a valid experience could be maintained only when the religious a priori was a transcendental a priori. Therefore, every attempt to interpret the religious a priori psychologically or metaphysically a priori was doomed to failure.

Psychology never could be a methodological tool to demonstrate the religious a priori. Instead, psychology demonstrated what was the phenomenon with the soul. Nygren criticized Troeltsch and Otto for using the concept of the religious a priori in the wrong way; that is, in a psychological way. Troeltsch had attempted to assure the independence and validity of religion. He had done so by a reliance upon the pre-critical philosophical understanding of the a priori. This led him, therefore, to a psychological, a "philosophical-historical," and metaphysical interpretation of the religious experience.[1] Otto, who followed Fries' anthropological and psychological presuppositions, did the same, in order to derive the foundation of religious knowledge from "the hidden ground of reason."[2]

These misinterpretations of the religious a priori were summarized by Nygren in this way:

1. The religious a priori was identified with a "content-less tautology." The transcendental religious a priori was far superior because it did not presuppose something to explain the religious experience. Rather, it dealt with the factual religious experience itself. It submitted this experience to the transcendental analysis of its validity.

2. The religious a priori was defined as a "creative power." Nygren rejected this definition, too, because it did not relate itself to the critical method. It was an unsatisfactory attempt to explain validity primarily in psychological and metaphysical terms. Nygren criticized

---

[1] Cf. Ernst Troeltsch, *Die Absolutheit des Christentums* (Tübingen: J. C. B. Mohr (Paul Siebeck), 1912); *Psychologie und Erkenntnistheorie*, (Tübingen: J. C. B. Mohr (Paul Siebeck), 1905); and the following from *Gesammelte Schriften* II, (Tübingen: J. C. B. Mohr (Paul Siebeck), 1913), "Wesen der Religion und der Religionswissenschaft"; "Moderne Geschichtsphilosophie"; "Logos und Mythos in Theologie und Religionsphilosophie"; "Zur Frage des religiösen Apriori"; "Empirismus und Platonismus in der Religionsphilosophie."

[2] Cf. Rudolph Otto, *Kantisch-Fries'sche Religionsphilosophie* (Tübingen: J. C. B. Mohr (Paul Siebeck), 1921); *Das Heilige* (Breslau: Trewendt und Granier, 1922).

Lange, Troeltsch, Kalweit, and Bornhausen for using the a priori in this way.

3. The a priori was employed as the psychological foundation for the origin of the religious experience. This was also rejected by Nygren because the transcendental analysis could never be mixed or confused with a psychological analysis. In this reference, he rejected particularly the analyses of Troeltsch, Kalweit, Otto, and Rosen. The a priori experience must be determined by its necessity and validity. The contingent or factual aspects of experience were its empirical or a posteriori moments. The "psychologizing" of the a priori united the a priori with the a posteriori and called the combination of the two a priori. As a result, the transcendental method was confused with a psychological analysis. The transcendental method concerned itself only with the presentation of the validity of religion. The psychological method dealt with the psychological origins and character of religion. Furthermore, the psychological analysis dealt with experience in a given spatio-temporal area. The transcendental method questioned the possibility of all experience.

4. The religious a priori was interpreted in a metaphysical way. Nygren rejected any kind of metaphysical interpretation of the religious a priori. It was Troeltsch who was the object of his sharpest criticism here. Troeltsch, Nygren felt, had not been consistent in his use of the critical method. Troeltsch began with a critical analysis, and distinguished between the necessary and valid moment and the factual and empirical moment in experience. But Troeltsch then transformed validity into a metaphysical concept, and described it as an "emanation of the absolute and divine spirit." The transcendental a priori thereby yielded its analytical structure, and could no longer deal with the transcendental validity of religion, but had to seek to maintain religion as a metaphysical reality.

C. *The Religious A Priori Is a Formal A Priori*

Nygren dealt with the question of whether the religious a priori was to be defined in terms of its formal structure or in reference to its content. The theoretical a priori and the ethical a priori were indifferent to content. In this reference, Nygren used the causal law as an example, which, he said, was a formal a priori; that is, it proposed a necessary and universal relationship between cause and effect. It, however, did not determine what was a cause. The same condition existed with the categorical imperative. It was a purely formal category which employed the formal properties of a valid ethic, and never concerned itself with the content of the ethic. So must be the case for the religious a priori. The religious a priori had to be a formal category. It could not become a critical standard of value. Troeltsch's interest in the religious a priori centered about its availability as a standard of value to judge the other forms of religion. But he did this, said Nygren, by recourse to a metaphysical philosophy of religion, and, as Nygren indicated, he thereby abandoned the critical method. A formal a priori could never serve as a standard to evaluate the content of the different religions of man. It was impossible by means of the formal a priori to decide which particular experience possessed validity. The task of the a priori was to question the general presuppositions which belonged to the valid experience. The a priori investigated the forms of experience to see what were the basic presuppositions necessary for validity. Nygren rejected the following thinkers for their confusion on this point: Süskind, Kalweit, and Dunkmann.[1] As well, Nygren rebuked Kant for a similar error in terms of the ethical experience.

Therefore, if the religious a apriori was to correspond to the critical method, it had to be understood in a *formal* manner. It could never attempt to determine or construct the content of a valid experience. The religious a priori, therefore, was not the same as religion. It was only the "form of religion." It was that which was factually given. It could never be constructed, but must be given.[2] Religion was never the object of an investigation for this reason. Its validity and character as an experience had to be presented by the critical method.

The philosophical task, therefore, was to examine the religious experience and determine the nature of its validity. It had to examine the characteristics which made religion legitimate as a "necessary and universal form of the spiritual life." It, furthermore, had to investigate

---

[1] H. Süskind, "Die religiöse Apriori bei Schleiermacher," *Religion und Geistes-kultur*, 1914. P. Kalweit, "Das religiöse Apriori," *Theologische Studien und Kritiken*, 1908; "Religion und Allgemeingültigkeit," *Zeitschrift für Theologie und Kirche*, 1907. K. Dunkmann, *Das religiöse Apriori und die Geschichte*, (Berlin: Reimer, 1910); *Religionsphilosophie*, (Berlin: Reimer, 1917).

[2] Nygren, *Religiöst Apriori*, p. 164. "fatter man endast i överensstämmelse med kriticismens problemställning det religiösa apriori fullkomligt formalt, så bort-faller frestelsen, att därur söka härleda något innehållsligt. Men då det religiösa apriori ej är detsamma som religion, utan blott "religionens form," så inses lätt att religionens innehåll måste uppfattas såsom det faktiskt givna, som aldrig intellektuellt kan framkonstrueras, utan helt enkelt måste tagas såsom det är givet."

the logical conditions which were necessary so that all experience was possible, and to see if these conditions were satisfied in the given factual religions. It was only the first of these tasks, however, which belonged to the religious a priori.[1]

D. *The Religious A Priori was Realized, never Actualized*

Nygren had now come to the point in his analysis of religion where he could relate the religious a priori to religion itself. A religious a priori, he reminded us, had never been found in and of itself, but it was present only in the form of the factually given religions.[2]

Troeltsch defined mysticism as "the psychological actualization of the religious a priori." He found this to be the psychological explanation for the nature of religion. The religious a priori, for him, was one of the psychological factors necessary for real religion. But Nygren maintained, as he had done before, that this interpretation of the religious a priori was not faithful to the critical method, and therefore had to be rejected. Nygren spoke of "the realization of the religious a priori," and meant that when the religious a priori was demonstrated, religion was established as a universal and necessary experience. However, religion was never "actualized." The religious a priori was "realized" in the concrete forms of religion. The conditions for this realization had to be investigated within the framework of the critical method.

The religious experience, as "immediate and unified," was all that was given in reality. The validity of experience presupposed a "fictitious" separation of the *validity* moment and the *factual* moment into distinct aspects of experience. Validity referred to religion and knowledge and morality and art, only when they were given a factual quality. However, all that was given in reality was experience. The a priori and the a posteriori were "fictitious" categories, but they were nonetheless employed to question the validity of the religious experience. Therefore, Nygren said, the religious a priori had to be understood as a category which purposed to explain the validity and experiential character of religion. There was no longer a "Wiederaufeinanderbeziehung" (which was Troeltsch's term) by means of which the religious a priori category constructed the religious experience. There was no instance of the psychological actualization of the re-

---

[1] *Ibid.*, p. 165.
[2] *Ibid.*, p. 170.

ligious a priori, rather, there was a *realization* of the religious experience in history. The philosophy of religion, when it demonstrated the religious a priori in a given religious experience, was giving an answer to the question: "How is religion possible?" This method of analysis was faithful to the critical method which questioned the nature of the validity of experience. The result of the investigation of the a priori demonstrated the place religion occupied within the life of consciousness. The concrete reality which filled up the life of consciousness was religion as a historical fact. This was the religious a priori *realized*.

Nygren concluded by saying that the a priori understood psychologically resulted in the actualization of the religious a priori. The transcendental a priori, on the other hand, realized the religious a priori.[1]

The religious experience was passive in nature. Man was never the active participant in the religious experience. Instead he had to be passive and receptive. He never created and produced, but rather was created and became productive. Nygren criticized the notion of creativity as it was found in the religious a priori systems of Kalweit and Otto.[2] He denied the attempt to equate the prophetic power of religion with artistic creativity. The prophet did not possess the same sense of freedom and productivity as did the artist. Though the artist, "in a moment of highest inspiration," could experience something which resembled the sense of religious dependence and passivity (that which was an experience of "a higher power"), nevertheless, this could never be equated with the voice of the prophet when he said, "Thus saith the Lord." The artist and the prophet, Nygren concluded, had to be set over against each other. These experiences belonged to different dimensions of the human life. Finally, Nygren found that the psychological treatment of the religious a priori conflicted with the factual nature of the religious experience itself, because it predetermined what the character of the religious experience would be.

E. *The Religious Experience Possessed an A-theoretical Character*

Did the acceptance of a religious a priori lead to an intellectualizing and rationalizing of religion? Herrmann, Spranger, Traub, Kade,

---

[1] *Ibid.*, p. 175. "Utgår man från ett psykologistiskfattat religiöst apriori, så kommer man till problemet om det religiösa aprioris aktualisering; utgår man åter från ett transcendentalt fattat religiöst apriori, så föras man till problemet om det religiösa aprioris realisering."

[2] P. Kalweit, "Das religiöse Apriori," p. 147. R. Otto, *Das Heilige*, p. 188 ff.

Webbermin, and Wendland all said that it did.[1] Nygren answered that it did not! Religion could never be of a rational or of an intellectual nature. Therefore, the religious a priori, understood in a transcendental way, could never stand in opposition to the actual nature of religion. Religion was not to be defined as universal knowledge. The religious a priori simply gave expression to the claim that the religious experience was a valid experience.

Troeltsch, again, was the object of Nygren's criticism. Nygren found that his analysis of the a priori was rationalistic, particularly when he spoke of the search for the "truth" of religion. Nygren's critical method separated the a priori from the a posteriori "moments" of knowledge, but never assigned a lower value to the a posteriori moment. The a posteriori was never equated with the a priori. Both were necessary for knowledge. The a priori had no superior ability to determine the nature of validity. It was the formal moment, which guaranteed the universality and necessary character of knowledge. The a priori and the a posteriori, the necessary form and the factual content, presupposed one another and belonged to one another in a valid experience.

Nygren had shown earlier in his discussion of the necessity of asking the question of the religious a priori, that the transcendental religious a priori was in perfect agreement with the nature of religion, and that furthermore it did not involve any intellectualizing or rationalizing of religion. The use of the religious a priori as the basis for a rationalistic religion (Troeltsch, Otto) was a false interpretation of the religious a priori. The belief that the religious experience was a product of the "law of reason" (Troeltsch) or was a "predisposition of reason" (Otto) was a fallacious belief. A rationalistic religion was unavoidable, said Nygren, if the religious experience was defined in psychological terms. A rationalistic element, however, left its mark on all experience.[2] The attempt to neutralize the rational element with the use of an irrational moment in religion was not a sufficient so-

---

[1] W. Herrmann, *Religion och historia* (Lund: Gleerups, 1912). E. Spranger, *Ernst Troeltsch als Religionsphilosoph*, (Tübingen, J. C. B. Mohr (Paul Siebeck), 1906). F. Traub, *Theologie und Philosophie* (Göttingen; Vanderhöck und Ruprecht, 1910). R. Kade, *Rudolf Euckens neologische Methode in ihre Bedeutung für die Religionsphilosophie* (Göttingen; Vanderhöck und Ruprecht, 1912). G. Wobbermin, *Die religionspsychologische Methode* (Tübingen: J. C. B. Mohr (Paul Siebeck), 1913). J. Wendland, *Die Stellung der Religion im Geistesleben* (Tübingen: J. C. B. Mohr (Paul Siebeck), 1920).

[2] *Nygren, Religiöst Apriori*, p. 189.

lution. Nygren's transcendental a priori, therefore, consciously avoided all psychological constructions of the religious experience. It questioned in what manner the religious experience was valid and necessary. The a priori and a posteriori elements of the critical method were not psychological categories, but were two "moments" within the religious experience itself. It was this concentration upon the religious experience which kept the transcendental a priori from becoming a rational concept. The religious experience was an a-theoretical experience. However, the religious a priori could not be defined in a similar way. It could never be designated as a composite category containing rational and irrational elements. Validity itself was not a-theoretical, nor a combination of rational and irrational elements. It was, however, the valid *experience* which was a-theoretical and which included the rational and irrational moments. When the a priori was dealt with psychologically, it then possessed a theoretical and an a-theoretical element, as well as a rational and an irrational "moment."

F. *The Religious Experience as a Valid Form of Experience Was Given*

Nygren found from the above analysis that the a priori category still possessed a hypothetical character. He had discovered that the only task the religious a priori had in the philosophy of religion was to describe the validity of the religious experience. The religious a priori provided the philosophical means of saying that religion possessed the characteristics of universality and necessity. Nygren posed the following questions:

1. Were the conditions present for the acceptance of the religious a priori?

2. Was there any a priori as such?

1. All the conditions were present, Nygren said, to accept the religious a priori from the presupposition of religion because religion made a claim to represent a valid experience. But were there the conditions necessary which permitted us to accept the religious a priori? Could religion be considered an independent and individual experience? There could never be a specific religious a priori if religion was only "applied ethics" ("angewandte Ethik"), as in Kant. Kantian philosophy could never give religion a *sui generis* character.[1] Logic,

---

[1] H. Cohen, *Kants Theorie der Erfahrung* (2 Aufl.; Berlin: Bruno Cassirer, 1925); *Religion und Sittlichkeit* (Berlin: Bruno Cassirer, 1907); *Der Begriff der Religion im System der Philosophie* (Berlin: Bruno Cassirer, 1915).

ethics, and aesthetics comprised the valid areas of experience. The fact that religion formed a part of culture could never be the basis for its claim that it belonged to the transcendental structure of experience. Nygren questioned whether there was sufficient reason to deny the independent character of religion. Cohen was rejected by Nygren as "a champion of an outmoded psychologism."Windelband, who reported, "dass Religion kein eigenes Gebiet der Vernuftwerte besitzt,"[1] was also rejected. However, Nygren discovered that the denial of the independent character of religion was not based upon an analysis of the actual character of religion. Nygren found that the denial of the independent character of religion rested upon the "doubtful psychological division" within Kant's theory of experience. Nygren maintained that it was this division which had prompted later Kantians to deny the validity of the religious experience. Again, Nygren insisted that a psychological investigation of the origin of experience could say nothing about the validity of the experience itself. The real nature of religion would protest every attempt to be subsumed under another form of experience. Religion demanded the right to be considered as a valid form of experience just the same as every other form of experience. Nygren quoted from the writings of Rickert, who employed neo-Kantian categories to show that it was not necessary to deny the independent character of religion. Also Görland and Mehlis had come to the same conclusions as Rickert.[2]

Nygren identified religion as a particular form of experience which made a claim to validity. It was valid because of the individuality of the religious experience. Therefore, Nygren said, we have to speak of a *specific* religious a priori.[3] The presuppositions appeared to be present for the assertion of a *specific* religious a priori.

2. However, was such a religious a priori given? The Marburg school represented by Bornhausen, maintained that the "epistemological Apriori" determined the nature of religious faith.[4] The only

---

[1] W. Windelband, *Die Geschichte der neueren Philosophie I* (5 Aufl.; Freiburg, 1911), p. 149.

[2] H. Rickert, *Der Gegenstand der Erkenntnis* (3 Aufl.; Tübingen: J. C. B. Mohr (Paul Siebeck), 1913). G. Mehlis, *Einführung in ein System der Religionsphilosophie* (Tübingen: J. C. B. Mohr (Paul Siebeck) 1917). A. Görland, *Mein Weg zur Religion* (Göttingen: Vanderhöck und Ruprecht, 1910).

[3] Nygren, *Religiöst Apriori*, p. 197. "Då religionen såsom en särskild form av erfarenhet gör anspråk på giltighet, men då det sätt, varpå den gäller, tydligen får sin särskilda karaktär genom den religiösa erfarenhetens egenart, så hava vi att fråga efter ett specifikt religiöst apriori."

[4] K. Bornhausen, "Dass religiöse Apriori bei Ernst Troeltsch und Rudolf

a priori was this "epistemological Apriori." From a transcendental viewpoint, asserted Nygren, there was no reason to assert that the "epistemological Apriori" was the only a priori that could claim to possess validity. This, for Nygren, was another indication of a "psychologism." The religious a priori in the form described by Bornhausen and others (Günther, Köhler)[1] could never be a valid a priori, because the conditions for its existence were dependent upon whether or not it was real, that is, whether or not it existed. But, Nygren continued, *reality* and *existence* were categories which were useless to describe the transcendent a priori. The transcendental category was concerned with validity, and nothing more. The a priori neither was nor existed, it was only valid in terms of the characteristics of necessity and universality.

Kant never said that the a priori was real and existent. Neither did he describe a specific a priori such as the theoretical a priori, the ethical a priori, or the aesthetic a priori, but rather only a priori knowledge and the a priori judgment. Knowledge and judgment had an a priori validity, that is, they were valid with necessity and universality. Nygren insisted that to continue to use the Kantian transcendental method there had to be the inclusion of the religious experience in addition to the theoretical, ethical, and aesthetic experiences. Religion was an a priori form of experience, that is, the religious experience contained an a priori moment. The religious a priori, however, was never given as such, but the religious experience itself possessed a priori validity. Therefore the religious experience was a transcendentally necessary and universal experience.[2]

Finally, Nygren said that the transcendental a priori could only be demonstrated by means of the transcendental deduction. If the religious experience represented an a priori experience, that is, a universal and necessary form of experience, then the religious experience had to be included within the transcendental method. The proposal to make the religious experience a valid a priori experience could be accomplished in no other way.

Otto," *Zeitschrift für Philosophie und philosophische Kritik*, 1910, Band 139, p. 196 ff.

[1] W. Günther, *Die Grundlagen der Religionsphilosophie Ernst Troeltsch*, (Tübingen: J. C. B. Mohr (Paul Siebeck), 1914). R. Köhler, *Der Begriff a priori in der modernen Religionsphilosophie*, (Tübingen: J. C. B. Mohr (Paul Siebeck), 1920).

[2] Nygren, *Religiöst Apriori*, p. 200, 201.

G. *The Transcendental Deduction of Religion*[1]

Kant had employed the transcendental method, not only in reference to theoretical knowledge, but also in reference to the ethical and aesthetic areas of experience. A discussion of the a priori took a central place in all three of Kant's *Critiques*. But Kant, true to the tradition of the Enlightenment, could not find an independent place for religion within his system. It may have been a *universal* experience, but it was not an *independent* experience ("Moral führt unumgänglich zur Religion"). Religion was only a "modification" of the moral experience. Nygren accused Kant on the one hand of submitting to the spirit of his time, and on the other, of misunderstanding the nature of religion. Kant had not carried out the philosophical possibilities which belonged to his transcendental method. The possibilities were present – it remained for Nygren to employ them in the area of religion.

Nygren asserted that Schleiermacher introduced a new insight into the nature of the transcendental method which would permit its use in the area of religion. Therefore, at this point, Nygren turned from Kant to Schleiermacher. Schleiermacher was characterized by Nygren as the first thinker after Kant who attempted to carry through the transcendental deduction in the area of religion. Nygren found that Schleiermacher, concerned at all times to maintain the independent character of religion, was not satisfied with a definition of religion as a psychological phenomenon. The independent quality of religion could not, Schleiermacher maintained, be presumed on the basis of a psychological analysis. Religion had to be a necessary experience in the sense that if one were to take it away, there could never be possible any kind of experience. Nygren asserted that this was exactly the nature of the transcendental claim he wanted to make for religion. The necessary character of religion, expressed in Schleiermacher's "feeling of absolute dependence" asserted that if religion were absent, self-consciousness, in every form, would not be possible. Our self-consciousness, however, was made up of the feeling of absolute dependence. Therefore all of the activities of the self had to bear witness to this absolute dependence. The transcendental feeling of absolute dependence, Nygren held, was characteristic for religion; that is, one could equate "the relationship with God" with "the feeling of absolute

---

[1] Nygren had established already in *Det Religionsfilosofiska Grundproblemet*, that the task of a philosophy of religion was the transcendental deduction of religion's ground category.

dependence." The transcendental deduction of religion was carried out with reference to the feeling of absolute dependence, which was inseparable from self-consciousness and was a necessary and universal element in every moment of consciousness. Furthermore, this moment had been demonstrated to be the characteristic moment in religion.[1] This feeling of absolute dependence was not a psychological description of the nature of the religious subject's awareness of the religious object. It served to demonstrate that religion was a legitimate and valid experience found in the life of all men. Nygren was finally not satisfied with Schleiermacher's transcendental method and developed his own deduction of religion. He was dependent at this point upon Carl Stange, but criticized him, too, for not carrying out the full implications of the transcendental deduction of religion.[2] If the transcendental method was to be used in the area of religion, it was not sufficient merely to assert that the religious question was a necessary one, or that a stand had to be taken to the religious question. The transcendental method, which Nygren constructed, asserted the necessity of taking a stand in relation to religion, but, more than this, directed the course of this stand toward religion. The transcendental deduction would show that it was necessary to recognize the "basic values" of religion, and to relate oneself to religion, because religion was "the condition for the possibility of experience."[3] Stange failed to limit the transcendental method to experience in all of its dimensions, and this had caused him to attempt to define the "truth of religion." But Nygren wanted the transcendental method to be broadened to include all experience. If it could be demonstrated, he said, that some experience was valid with necessity and universality, then an attempt to demonstrate its objective reality was irrelevant. Necessity and universality had to be recognized as that which was the basis for all that validity meant. The transcendental deduction of religion required that the religious experience be of such a character that without it no experience at all was possible.[4] The transcendental

---

[1] Nygren, *Religiöst Apriori*, p. 223.

[2] Cf. Carl Stange, *Christentum und moderne Weltanschauung* I, (Das Problem der Religion), (Leipzig: A. Deichert, 1913); *Die Ethik Kants* (Leipzig: A. Seichert, 1920); *Einleitung in Die Ethik* (Leipzig: A. Deichert, 1900).

[3] Nygren, *Religiöst Apriori*, p. 229.

[4] *Ibid.*, p. 233. "Vid den transcendentala deduktionen av religionen erfordras, att vi kunna uppvisa ett moment i den religiösa erfarenheten, som är av den art, att det förutan ingen erfarenhet är möjlig, eller med andra ord att detta moment måste tillerkännas giltighet för att överhuvud något skall gälla."

deduction did not attempt to prove the validity of the religious experience as a whole, or for any particular concrete religion, but rather directed itself to the "validity moment" in the religious experience as such. It had to determine the "ground-category" or the "ground-value" of religion.

However, the transcendental deduction of religion possessed characteristics which did not belong to the other areas of experience. When the transcendental deduction was carried out in the theoretical area, that is, in reference to the question of which theoretical categories or most general principles of knowledge must be valid for anything to be valid, this validity was restricted and was content with the validity of knowledge alone. It did not seek for those principles which were the conditions for the possibility of any experience, but related itself only to the theoretical experience. It confined itself, therefore, to knowledge. The same tendency was found in ethics. The categorical imperative did not demonstrate that for all validity to be possible there had to be moral experience. The same was true with the aesthetic experience. But in religion, the situation was different. Religion was not limited to one area of experience. However, the other experiences could never be equated with the religious experience.

Nygren described the differences which existed between the theoretical, moral and aesthetic areas of experience on the one hand, and religion on the other. The first three could be described by the term, "culture forms." Religion could not be defined as a culture form in the same way. Culture possessed an active and productive nature. On the other hand, religion was passive. The transcendental deduction of religion, therefore, could not satisfy itself with a transcendental deduction of the forms of culture. The particular cultural forms were more easily determined as valid than the particular religious values because they stood in a necessary relationship to all of cultural life. Religion, however, did not. Nygren said that this could be easily demonstrated by reference to a negative formulation: those who deny the general cultural values exclude themselves from cultural communication. Those who deny general theoretical value, the value of truth, place themselves outside all intelligible communication. In the same way, those who deny the primary transcendental presuppositions of morality place themselves outside the society which can only exist if there is some positive meaning to ethical principles. When the transcendental deduction demonstrated that in the moral sphere certain ethical categories had to be recognized if there was to be any morality at all, it was justified in doing so. Those who did not recognize the values of morality excluded themselves from human interaction within a group. If this same deduction was applied to the area of religion, however, the same result followed, but only within the religious community. Those who denied the value of religion, excluded themselves, thereby, from the religious community. If one recognized religion as something *valuable*, this may be a valid conclusion. From a scientific point of view, however, this assertion had to be invalid. If there was no recognition of the religious "ground-category," which was the basis for the religious experience and for the religious community, the only thing that had been demonstrated was that the religious experience and the religious community had to be done away with.

From the above analysis, Nygren maintained that the transcendental deduction of religion had to assume a greater burden of proof than the transcendental deduction of the forms of culture allowed. The transcendental deduction of the forms of culture had no relevance to religion. Nygren said that it had to be shown that not only the religious experience was impossible, but far more, every experience would be impossible without the religious "ground-category." Nygren was saying, therefore, that there was no validity other than that which rested ultimately upon religious grounds. If this could be shown, the religious experience did not stand isolated from the other experiences of man.[1]

Before Nygren carried out this program, that is, to show that the religious ground category was the foundation for the validity of all the forms of experience, he had to clear away certain misunderstandings. First of all, he was not dealing with the reason for religious faith, but rather, with a demonstration of what entitled us to deal with religion as a necessary and universal form of life.

The universality and necessary character of religion could not be based upon a definition which located religion within a cultural system. Religion resisted every attempt to be treated as a form of culture. Nygren was not satisfied with a cultural analysis which de-

---

[1] *Ibid.*, p. 236. "Vi måste sålunda påvisa, icke blott att ingen religiös erfarenhet, utan fastmer att överhuvud ingen erfarenhet är möjlig utan den religiösa grund-kategorien, eller att det icke gives någon giltighet annat än på religiös grund. Om detta kan påvisas, så står icke längre den religiösa erfarenheten isolerad från de övriga erfarenhetsformerna."

monstrated that there was a vacant area in culture which only religion could fill, and from this, to postulate religion as a necessary and universal form of experience. Cultural systems were related to religion in such a way that culture itself had to rest upon those presuppositions which were only realized in religion.[1] Nygren wanted to show that the "ground-category" of the religious experience was also the necessary presupposition for every other experience.

To demonstrate this, Nygren felt that he had to go behind the different general cultural values and see what was the presupposition for their validity; that is, to determine what were the conditions which had to present something as *true*, *good*, or *beautiful*. The common factor in all of these forms of experience was that each of them made the claim to be valid. However, the idea of validity itself referred to something which was above sense experience. The assignment of value to something, whether it was knowledge, a direction of the will, a way of acting, raised it above the conditions of sense experience and over the limitations of time and space.[2] When something was designated as valid, it was valid for more than a particular point in time and space. It was valid without reference to time and space. That which is true today was also true yesterday, and it was also true before anyone knew about it. It, therefore, possessed validity even if it was not recognized as true by some specific individual consciousness.

Nygren concluded by saying that the presupposition that something was valid meant that we were justified in raising it above the sphere of time and space. However, this presupposition that something was valid when we could raise it above the sphere of time and space, and that upon which all culture was constructed, was of a religious nature.[3] Religion made the claim to raise human life above the given sensuous and transient sphere to the eternal sphere. This designation

---

[1] *Ibid.*, p. 237. "Om det således är omöjligt att statuera att nödvändigt förhållande mellan religionen och kultursystemet på så sätt, att religionen finner en nödvändig plats inom detsamma, så återstår blott den andra vägen, att påvisa, att religionen står i nödvändigt sammanhang med kultursystemet såtillvida som detta i sin helhet vilar på förutsättningar, som blott äro förverkligade i religionen."

[2] *Ibid.*, p. 238.

[3] *Ibid.*, p. 238, 239. "Förutsättningen för att överhuvud något skall gälla är alltså, att vi äro berättigade att på detta sätt höja något utöver det rumsligas och tidligas sfär. Men denna förutsättning, varpå hela kulturlivet bygger, men som ingen enstaka kulturform förmår begrunda lika litet som de skilda kulturformerna tillsammantagna, är av religiös art. Ty religionen gör just anspråk på att höja det mänskliga livet utöver den givna sinnliga, ändliga sfären. Den gör – för att uttrycka det på religionens eget sätt – anspråk på att höja över timlighetens till det evigas sfär."

of eternity was not cultural, but religious, in the truest sense of the term. Therefore, the category of eternity was the transcendental "ground-category" of religion. It was the a priori presupposition for the religious experience.

The category of eternity, if it was to be valid as the "ground category" of religion, could not in any way be subject to the conditions of finitude. From a philosophical standpoint, this was negatively described as, "an elevation above the limits of time and space." Positively, it included all that which was valid. From a religious standpoint, the eternal was that which "participated in the life of God." Every moment of life became equated, therefore, with the religious dimension of existence. All existence was placed, "sub species aeternitatis."

The religious man immediately recognized his relationship to the Eternal in the present moment. Nygren agreed with Schleiermacher on this point.[1] Stange was also correct, said Nygren, when he spoke of man being forced to make a decision in every moment of his life as to whether he accepted the world of sense experience for the whole of reality or not.

The transcendental deduction of religion had proven, said Nygren, that the category of eternity was valid as the a priori category of religion. As a result, Religion was firmly established within the life of consciousness, for all of the forms of culture built upon these presuppositions which were only realized in religion.[2] What the other a priori categories needed so as "not to float in the air," was given by religion. Religion was therefore not an accidental or arbitrary experience, nor did it force itself into the life of man. Religion was a necessary and universal experience, inseparable from the life of man.

Furthermore, the category of eternity had demonstrated itself to be a true "transcendental a priori," that is, a purely formal category which was the same as the other categories, but that category which was the presupposition for all of the other categories.

---

[1] "Je mehr nun in jedem Moment sinnlichen Selbstbewusstseins das Subject sich mit seiner theilweisen Freiheit und theilweisen Abhängigkeit zugleich schlechthin abhängig sezt, um desto frömmer ist es." Quoted by Nygren, *Religiöst Apriori*, p. 240, from Schleiermacher, *Der christliche Glaube* (2 Aufl.) Par. 5:3.

[2] Nygren, *Religiöst Apriori*, p. 241. "Den transcendentala deduktionen av religionen har ådagalagt, att evighetskategorien har att gälla såsom religionens aprioriska kategori, och att i kraft av denna religionen är fast förankrad i medvetenhetslivet, enär alla kulturformer bygga på en förutsättning, som endast i religionen finner sitt förverkligande."

H. *The Transcendent Character of Religion*

Nygren posed the question whether the transcendental a priori meant that the transcendent claim of religion had to be surrendered? Did it follow, therefore, that religion originated within man's consciousness?[1] Did the recognition of the transcendental necessity of religion deny its transcendent reality?

The category of religion, as the most necessary and most essential moment within the spiritual life, could be employed in a valuable way by theology, asserted Nygren. However, this did not imply that the religious a priori assured the reality of religion. The transcendental or critical method (Nygren used the terms interchangeably) had nothing to do with the reality claims of religion. It had to be recognized, said Nygren, that the concept of transcendence was an important concept for religion. However, one could maintain the existence of the concept of transcendence by a demonstration of the existence of the religious a priori.[2] The philosophy of religion, as well as philosophy in general, could not make a claim for the existence of something simply because it possessed a conceptual nature. Therefore, philosophy and the philosophy of religion could not demonstrate the nature of the transcendent object of religion. The basic problem of philosophy was not the problem of reality, but the problem of *validity*.[3] Philosophy had to leave the problem of reality alone, and question what was valid, and not what existed.[4] Furthermore, the validity of the religious experience could not be identified with the reality of the religious experience.

I. *The Truth of Religion*

Nygren differentiated between a philosophical and a theological demonstration of the truth of religion. He wanted to avoid the use of a philosophy of religion which dealt with the reality and transcendence of religion. This attempt was indicative, said Nygren, of "a philosophy of religion of a pre-Kantian, neo-Platonic period."

---

[1] Nygren refers to P. Natorp, *Religion innerhalb der Grenzen der Humanität* (2 Aufl.; Tübingen: J. C. B. Mohr (Paul Siebeck), 1908), p. 44 ff.

[2] Nygren, *Religiöst Apriori*, p. 244. "Först och främst måste härvid oförbehållsamt erkännas, å ena sidan att transcendenstanken är en för religionen väsentlig tanke, å andra sidan att man från transcendental-kritisk utgångspunkt aldrig kan nå from till denna tanke eller till något bevis för sanningen i religionens transcendensanspråk."

[3] *Ibid.*, p. 245.

[4] *Ibid.*

Nygren's indictment was against the philosopher of religion who attempted to demonstrate the "truth" of Christianity. The religious a priori never referred to a specific religion or religious faith. It dealt only with the truth of religious value or with the "ground category" of religion.[1] The philosophy of religion was a philosophical discipline and, as such, its claims of universality had to be respected. Therefore, the "truth" of the Christian faith could never be demonstrated by the religious a priori. The philosophy of religion acknowledged only the *validity* of religious value. Its transcendent character validated the truth of religious value, not the "truth" of Christianity.

Nygren then discussed the relationship of the philosophy of religion to theology in reference to the matter of the truth of religion:

1. The philosophy of religion, by means of the a priori category, had revealed the transcendental necessity of religion.

2. The historical realization of the religious a priori revealed further that religion could be realized only in a historical form. For this reason, the problem of the truth of religion concerned the validity of the different forms of the historical religions. Because of this fact, the answer to the problem of the truth of religion could not be found within the historical religions themselves. Theology came into the picture at this point, and began its work by an examination of the values and experiences of a specific historical religion.

3. For this reason, Christian theology had to deal both with the problem of the truth of religion as well as with the truth of Christianity. There could not be a philosophical construction of the Christian experience of value. Christian values and experiences served as the starting point for the theological demonstration of truth. The Christian built his certainty upon his experience of faith in a transcendent reality. Only then did the reality of religion have any significance. The realization of religious value was present only in the form of the historically given religions.[2] However, as religion was found in all stages of history, and in all cultures, the form it took necessarily changed with the times, as did the concept of the eternal within religion itself.

This relationship between the philosophy of religion and theology was only possible, maintained Nygren, because of the critical character of the philosophy of religion. The critical method limited the philosophy of religion to the transcendental apriori of religion. The

---

[1] *Ibid.*, p. 246.
[2] *Ibid.*, p. 248.

result was that the philosophy of religion was freed from a "metaphysical" starting point, and a harmonious relationship between the philosophy of religion and theology was established.[1]

J. *Religion and Culture*

We have seen, said Nygren, that the theoretical, ethical, aesthetic, and religious experiences are all a priori experience forms. They are independent and autonomous; as well, they are independent of one another. However, the significance of religion is destroyed if religion is judged solely on the basis of its meaning for the other forms of experience. As well, it would also have been a violation of these other forms of experience if they were evaluated from the basis of their significance for religion alone.[2]

Nygren asked whether any cultural life could be maintained other than on a religious basis? To find an answer, Nygren asked whether knowledge and morality were able to exist without reference to religion. This he found extremely doubtful.[3] The religious "Weltanschauung," he said, preceded every other "Weltanschauung", because it was orientated about experience. A "Weltanschauung" which was constructed without reference to the religious experience surrendered the only relationship it had to an organic totality. It isolated itself from experience and received an arbitrary character as a result. The religious "Weltanschauung," on the other hand, avoided this danger by relating itself to experience; that is, the religious experience.[4]

The same structure held true for morality. Morality could not be meaningful unless it was related positively to religion.[5]

Next, Nygren asked whether there could be culture without religion? It was possible, he said, that knowledge was fragmentary, and that a "Weltanschauung" was developed only to satisfy the demands of knowledge. In the same way, therefore, it was possible that there could be a culture without religion. However, this possibility was excluded by the transcendental universality and necessity of religion.[6]

---

[1] *Ibid.*, p. 249.

[2] *Ibid.*, p. 51. cf. Anders Nygren, *Det Religionsfilosofiska Grundproblemet*, p. 28 ff.

[3] Nygren, *Religiöst Apriori*, p. 252, 253. "... den religiösa erfarenheten är den enda erfarenhetsform, som möjliggör en sådan avslutande total överblick, som bildandet av en världsåskådning kräver."

[4] *Ibid.*, p. 253.

[5] *Ibid.*, p. 254.

[6] *Ibid.*, p. 255. "Då varje i kultursystemet ingående erfarenhetsform i sista hand

All cultural life had to rest upon religion. Religion was the "ground value" for all of cultural life.

K. *Religion and Obligation*

A religious experience was defined in terms of the individual's commitment to a transcendent reality. However, the existence of Christian obligation had to be independent of the religious experience itself. There was no claim for normativeness within religious faith, nor was there any certainty that the religious experience would ever be present.[2] The obligation of faith, from a transcendental viewpoint, meant simply that religious faith was a fundamental moment in human life. Anyone who participated in faith was entitled to take a positive stand in relationship to religion. The transcendent character of religion had indicated that the religious "ground category" was the transcendental presupposition for all of experience. On the basis of this discovery, the religious experience could be present in every moment of experience.

The concept of the "obligation of faith" was not an ethical predicate, however. It was the expression of the belief that religion was a normal and indispensable moment in every human life, and, therefore, that it made a claim to possess the characteristics of universality and necessity. At the same time it did not *assert* the fact of its universality.[3] The "obligation of faith" meant that it was an indispensable duty for everyone to consider the presuppositions for his life, which ultimately rested, Nygren claimed, upon religious grounds.[4]

The "obligation of faith" made a claim for religious faith in general, but not for a specific kind of faith. The primary task of theology was,

---

för sin giltighet är hänvisad på sammanhangt med det allmänna religiösa grund-värdet, så utgör egentligen varje kulturmoment vederläggningen av kulturlivets påstädda indifferens gentemot religionen. Att denna sistnämnda tanke likväl så ofta möter, vinner sin förklaring endast däruti, att man ej gör klart för sig de sista förutsättningar, varpå allt kulturliv vilar."

[2] *Ibid.*

[3] *Ibid.*, p. 258. "Har religionen en sådan betydelse i människolivet, att den i själva verket transcendentalt ligger till grund för allt vad erfarenhet heter, så kan det och uppställas såsom en oundgänglig plikt för var och en att besinna sig på denna sitt livs djupaste förutsättning."

[4] Nygren can agree perfectly with Heinzelmann's statement; "Religion wird immer nur gefunden unter der Form höchsten Sollens, und dieses Sollen wird in der Religion selbst erkannt als verbindlich für alle." Quoted in *Religiöst Apriori* p. 258.

therefore, to recognize that religion offered an answer to the basic questions of man's life. On this basis, man could be directed to the Christian faith.[1] But, again, there was never the element of coerciveness attached to this involvement in the Christian faith.

L. *Religion and Mysticism*

The religious experience was different from every other form of experience because of its relationship to the eternal. Nygren's definition of the religious experience was, therefore, broad enough to include every kind of experience which had a religious nature. It was also narrow enough to exclude everything which was foreign to religion. Nygren had found that the category of eternity was the most satisfactory category for this definition of the religious experience.

The experience of the mystic could not be identified with the kind of religious experience Nygren was referring to, however. Nonetheless, the religious a priori often appeared in association with the mystic's experience, because both were attempts to overcome a narrow and confining view of history. Mysticism asserted that the basic element in religion was not at all related to history. The transcendental a priori, on the other hand, showed that religion, as a necessary and universal experience, gained its content and realization only in reference to the historical dimension.[2]

---

[1] *Ibid.*, p. 259.
[2] *Ibid.*, p. 262.

APPLICATION OF THE RELIGIOUS APRIORI
TO ETHICS AND DOGMATICS

CHAPTER FOUR

I. PHILOSOPHICAL AND CHRISTIAN ETHICS

Anders Nygren's major work in ethics, *Filosofisk och kristen etik*, which appeared in 1923, was an attempt to define methodologically the nature of theological and philosophical ethics. Nygren's treatment of this subject must be related, from the outset, to Schleiermacher's discussion of the same subject. Nygren believed that Schleiermacher had presented certain basic methodological principles, which he himself did not develop fully.

Nygren's own position developed during a period in which there was a particularly strong criticism of the claim that Systematic Theology was a science.[1] Nygren proposed to demonstrate that Christianity could be both a "positive Christianity" and a "strict science."[2]

Nygren found in Schleiermacher's *Der christliche Glaube* and also in *Grundlinien einer Kritik der bisherigen Sittenlehre* the basic presuppositions for his own conception of the task of Systematic Theology and Ethics. In principle, Nygren believed, Schleiermacher had located his methodological starting point in "the critical method," that is, in Kant's critical philosophy, and had dealt with all of the problems Nygren wished to work with.[3] He was especially impressed with

---

[1] Cf. Anders Nygren, *Dogmatikens vetenskapliga grundläggning* (Stockholm: Svenska Kyrkans Diakonistyrelses Bokförlag, 1922), p. 2 ff, 5 ff, 8 ff.

[2] *Ibid.*, p. 10 ff. "Om dogmatiken skall kunna övervinna den kris, i vilken den råkat genom den kritiska filosofiens uppvisande av omöjligheten av en vetenskap om det transcendenta, så måste den uppgiva sitt anspråk på att vara en 'doctrina de deo et rebus divinis'; men på samma gång måste den vara positivt kristlig och strängt vetenskaplig. Intet av de här framställda trenne kraven får åsidosättas."

[3] Schleiermacher's position contains: "i princip den syntes, efter vilken vi ännu alltjämst söka. Men visserligen också blott i princip, ty i utförandet har han ofta icke lyckats förverkliga, vad hans principer lovade. Redan hos Schleiermacher själv kan man iakttaga, huru den från början riktigt fattade tanken under utredningens gång så småningom ombőjes och lämnar rum för främmande motiv. Måhända ligger häri förklaringen till att det gångna århundradets dogmatik, även där den velat lära av Schleiermacher, dock nästen undantaglöst anknutit vid helt andra sidor..." *Ibid.*, p. 10 ff, p. 14. Cf. A. Nygren, *Filosofisk och kristen etik* (2 Ed.; Lund: Håkan Ohlssons Boktryckeri, 1932); "Att det stannat vid en ansats är påtagligt", p. 83.

Schleiermacher's treatment of the Kantian critique of knowledge.[1] This had shown him the relevancy of Kant's *Critiques* for religion in general and for the philosophy of religion in specific. Kant himself did not fully realize the implications of his critical method.[2] Although Schleiermacher did not demonstrate the transcendental universality and necessity of religion, nevertheless, he moved in this direction, asserted Nygren.[3] His contribution to contemporary religious philosophy was to direct its attention to the universality and necessity of the religious experience.[4] It was religion which elevated human life above sense-experience and the finite sphere. The "ground category" of religion was, as Nygren had discovered, the category of eternity.[5] Religion was, therefore, an essential and necessary part of all cultural life. However, the philosophy of religion could only demonstrate that the religious "ground category" was a universal and necessary category. On the basis of this starting point, the historically given religions could be examined.[6]

The transcendental method, which was the "method *par excellence*"

---

[1] Cf. Nygren, *Religiöst Apriori*, p. 10; "Kriticismen är icke blott ett utvecklingsstadium i filosofiens historia, utan, en gång, funnen är den filosofiens metod par préférence."

[2] *Ibid.*, p. 215 ff, the section entitled "Saknaden av transcendental metod i Kants religionsfilosofi", and also "Schleiermachers transcendentala deduktion av religion", p. 218 ff. In DVG, 1922, the section "Schleiermacher och Kant", p. 58 ff.

[3] Nygren, *Religiöst Apriori*, p. 10, "frågen om den religiösa erfarenhetens allmängiltighet och nödvändighet eller om religionen som en oundgänglig och integrerande del i andelivet."

[4] Cf. Nygren, *Religiöst Apriori*, p. 205 ff., particularly p. 224 ff., in which the transcendental deduction of the ground category of religion takes place; cf. also DVG, p. 116. The classic expression of this has already been given: "Vid den transcendentala deduktionen av religionen erfordras, att vi kunna uppvisa ett moment i den religiösa erfarenheten, som är av den art, att det förutan ingen erfarenhet är möjlig, eller med andra ord att detta moment måste tillerkännas giltighet för att överhuvud något skall gälla.

[5] Eternity "icke i dess vulgära betydelse såsom förlängning av tiden i riktning bakåt och framåt, utan i dess på samma gång rent filosofiska och rent religiösa betydelse såsom den tillvarelseform, som ej är underkastad ändlighetens villkor"; Cf. also, in reference to the relation of the category of eternity to the whole of cultural life, "När vi tillskriva något giltighet, det så vara en kunskap, en viljeriktning, ett handlingssätt eller vad annat som helst, så höja vi det därmed upp över den sinnliga erfarenhetens betingelser att överhuvud något skall gälla är alltså, att vi är berättigade att på detta sätt höja något över det rumsligas och tidligas sfär. Men denna förutsättning, varpå hela kulturlivet bygger, men som ingen kulturform förmår begrunda lika litet som de skilda kulturformerna sammantagna, är av religiös art." *Religiöst Apriori*, p. 238.

[6] "Om den kritiska religionsfilosofien skall kunna konsekvent genomföras, så måste den historiska religionen uppfattas såsom religionskategoriens realisering." DVG, p. 131.

for the philosophy of religion, enabled Nygren to define Systematic Theology in terms of its descriptive function within the life of a particular historical religion. Nygren employed the concept of the "ground motif" to refer to the task of the systematic theologian. The systematic theologian had to attempt to find "the essence of Christianity." Systematic Theology, therefore, became Dogmatics, and its task was to locate the "ground motif" of the Christian faith as it expressed itself in history.[1] The transcendental method in the philosophy of religion and the dogmatic task of theology complemented one another.[2]

Nygren's philosophical methodology developed into a philosophy of culture,[3] and was the presupposition for his conception of philosophic and Christian ethics. The most general presupposition for Nygren's ethical theory was the affirmation of what he called the "universal value of culture."[4] Nygren denied, from the outset, all forms of skepticism, whether in reference to the claim to validity of the theoretical judgment, or in reference to the Kantian theory of value as a whole.[5] He constructed his system on the basis of the separate and distinct experiences of man, which, as we have seen, did not interfere with one another.[6]

---

[1] Cf. FM, p. 73 ff., also "Det religionsfilosofiska grundproblemet", p. 71.

[2] DVG, p. 159; "Den transcendentala metoden går up på att legitimera de allmänna principerna, och dess kriterium lyder; såsom allmän princip gäller det, genom vars bestridande och upphävande man tillika skulle upphäva erfarenheten överhuvud. Den dogmatiska metoden går ut på att legitimera enskilda trosomdömens kristna karaktär, och dess kriterium lyder: såsom kristet trosomdöme har det trosomdöme att gälla, genom vare upphävande man tillika skulle upphäva kristendomens centrum."

[3] cf. the structure of *Det religionsfilosofiska grundproblemet*, p. 71. Nygren compares the theory of religious experience to a religious theory of culture. He differentiates in the latter between 1) the universal relationship between religion and culture; 2) religion and specific forms of culture.

[4] FM, p. 29. It is "för den transcendentala analysen karaktäristiskt, att det som skall tjäna som utgångspunkt för densamma, näste vara något allmänt erkänt, något vars giltighet ej är utsatt för tvivel. Endast in så fall kan det nämligen tjäna som grundval för påvisande av principernas riktighet". cf. p. 32, p. 37; "Den kritiska kunskapsteorien frågar icke, om kunskap över huvud är möjlig; fastmer utgår den från den faktiskt föreliggande kunskapen såsom ett erkänt faktum, och frägar blott huru och under vilka förutsättningar denna kunskap är möjlig". cf. also, Anders Nygren, *Religiositet och kristendomen* (Uppsala: J. Lindblads, 1926), p. 59 ff.

[5] Nygren, *Religiöst Apriori*, p. 208 ff., "Den transcendentala deduktionens ide hos Kant", also p. 210; cf. also *Det religionsfilosofiska grundproblemet*, p. 66 ff.

[6] Cf. "Teologiens objektivitet", Anders Nygren, *Filosofi och Motivforskning* (Stockholm: SKD, 1940), p. 163 ff; Nygren constructs his system: "Teologien

Nygren dealt with "the historical realization of religion," and it was in this context that he examined the expression of a religious idea in terms of the different stages of its development in history.[1] In this way, Nygren could distinguish different "ground motifs" and their expression within a given historical religion. This was the answer Nygren gave to the questions posed by the philosophy of religion.

In the area of "Philosophical and Christian Ethics," Nygren questioned whether a theological ethic could possess knowledge.[2] Ethics belonged to that area of experience which could be examined philosophically, and which was paralleled by the other areas of experience, the theoretical, the aesthetic, and the religious experiences. However, the theological ethic claimed particular priority in the area of ethics. It could be questioned, however, whether the theological ethic could be legitimately included within the area of philosophical investigation.[3] To answer this question, Nygren undertook to investigate critically both the philosophical and the Christian ethic.[4]

Nygren discussed the philosophical ethic from the standpoint of the

ingår som ett nödvändigt led i en hel kedja av nödvändigheter, vilka gripa in i varandra utan att på någon punkt lämna rum för något godtycke. Begynnelsen till denna kedja vinnes därigenom, att religionsfilosofien förankrar religionen i andelivet överhuvud, i det den uppvisar att andelivet endast är möjligt på religionens grundval och att religionen sålunda har att gälla såsom dess oundgänglig förutsättning. Är religionens nödvändighet på detta sätt säkerställd, så visar religionsfilosofien för det andra, att religionen med nödvändighet måste vara realiserad i historisk form."

[1] Cf. Anders Nygren, *Den kristna kärlekstanken genom tiderna*, I, (2: a uppl.; Stockholm: SKD, 1939), p. 23 ff.

[2] "Vetenskapsteoretiskt sett hör det etiska problemet helt naturligt inom filosofiens område och är alldeles parallellt med filosofiens övriga huvudfrågor, det kunskapsteoretiska, estetiska och religionsfilosofiska problemet. Bevisskyldigheten åligger fördenskull uteslutande den teologiska etiken, då den framträder med anspråket på att få ha ett ord med i laget vid den etiska frågens behandlande. Dess eget vara eller icke vara såsom vetenskap beror på, om den kan giva en tillfredsställande förklaring för detta anspråk." FKE, p. 9.

[3] "Se vi nämligen på den enskilda vetenskapliga uppgiften idees förhållande till vetenskapen som totalitet, så äro vi berättigade att uppställa den fordran, å ena sidan att varje vetenskap måste hava sin specifika uppgift, strängt avgränsad från alla andra, så att densamma icke erhåller sin behandling och lösning inom någon annan vetenskap, å andra sidan att den sålunda henne allena tillkommande uppgiften i vetenskapens totalsammanhang visar sig vara en nödvändig uppgift." FKE, p. 2.

[4] "Det enda riktiga tillvägsgångssättet är att göra såväl den filosofiska som den kristna etikens uppgift till problem, var och en i sitt sammanhang. Det gäller alltså att uppställa frågan, huruvida det finnes något skäl att i filosofiens sammanhang behandla etiska problem, och att, om så är fallet, visa, huru det etiska problemet på detta område måste formuleras, samt huru långt man med användande av filosofiska metoder kan komma." FKE, p. 98 ff.

scientific character of philosophy.[1] Philosophy, as metaphysics, could not make the claim to comprehend all the sciences; that is, it could not extend the area of the sciences to effect a scientific "Weltanschauung."[2] The only way to maintain the scientific character of philosophy was to define philosophy as Critical Philosophy, that is, philosophy as a theory of universal experience and universal value.[3] Critical philosophy preserved the three basic characteristics of philosophy, that is, its universality, its scientific character, and its relationship to experience. It had done so in such a way that it had related them to one another and to philosophy as a whole.

Just as philosophy investigated the nature of validity, so a philosophical ethic must do the same.[4] Parallel to the validity which belonged to the theoretical and religious areas, the ethical experience had to be examined to determine what were the presuppositions necessary to make it a valid experience. Allied to the philosophical and critical ethic were distinct sciences which described the problems in ethics from different standpoints, that is, psychology, sociology, and the history of Ethics.[5] These, however, only described the ethical experience, and could not deal with the *validity* of the ethical experience.

Nygren distinguished between the metaphysical ethic and the critical ethic within the philosophical ethic. The metaphysical ethic was an aspect of a philosophy of "Weltanschauung." Nygren would,

---

[1] "Varken inom den nuvarande eller inom en utvidgad erfarenhet finnes något specialområde övrigt för filosofien." FKE, p. 104.

[2] Metaphysics, in FM, p. 14, follows "the law of participation"; "den griper ut något ur erfarenheten och identifierar detta med den sökta principen... eller annorlunda uttryckt, den besvarar frågan om vad verklighet är med att peka på något visst verkligt". This is Axel Hägerström's usual interpretation.

[3] In FM, p. 16 ff, Nygren defines philosophy as "principvetenskap ej specialvetenskap"; it shall "kritiskt undersöka erfarenhetens allmänna principen", which is "de ofrånkomliga logiska förutsättningar, som ligga inneslutna i all kunskap och giltighet överhuvud". cf. also "Såsom allmän erfarenhetsteori eller allmän giltighetsteori visar sig den kritiska filosofien vara den rätte arvtagaren till filosofiens stora tradition. Den har bevarat de trenne för filosofien karaktäriska dragen, dess universalitet, dess vetenskaplighet och dess erfarenhetsrelation och sammangjutit dem så, att såväl deras inbördes förhållande som ock filosofiens förhållande utåt till specialvetenskaperna blir harmoniskt." FKE, p. 109.

[4] "När nu filosofien såsom allmän erfarenhetsteori ställer som sin uppgift att undersöka de omfattande erfarenhetsformernas giltighet, så kan den självfallet ej gå förbi den etiska upplevelsens giltighetsanspråk utan att upptaga den till prövning. Liksom kunskapsteorien prövar den teoretiska och religionsfilosofien den religiösa erfarenheten med hänsyn till deras giltighet, så har den filosofiska etiken att pröva den etiska upplevelsen och se till under vilka förutsättningar den kan prövas såsom en giltig erfarenhet." FKE, p. 113 ff.

[5] FKE, p. 109 ff.

therefore, retain only the critical ethic. Under the concept "scientific ethic," Nygren included the descriptive ethic. Nygren could diagram this relationship in the following way:[1]

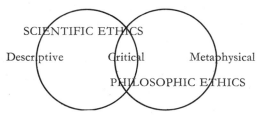

SCIENTIFIC ETHICS

Descriptive   Critical   Metaphysical

PHILOSOPHIC ETHICS

The normative ethic was associated with the metaphysical ethic, and had the task "to form and legitimatize rules and prescriptions in order for our relationships to be called ethical relationships."[2] It was not a scientific task, however, to present and judge the different ideals which belonged to the ethical life. The scientific endeavor had to be based upon an objective observation, and not a subjective evaluation.[3]

The task of the philosophical ethic was to define "the validity of the ethical experience," that is, the primary validity associated with the ethical predicates, "good," and "evil." These predicates, Nygren found, were the presuppositions for a meaningful ethical judgment.[4] Primary validity was therefore parallel to that validity which was the presupposition upon which the meaningful character of the theoretical, the aesthetic, and the religious proposition rested. It was a validity which was basic and necessary and the presupposition for all validity.

To examine the nature of this primary validity, the critical ethic had to employ the transcendental method. The transcendental method sought to legitimatize the validity of the highest ethical principle by demonstrating that everything which was valid had to be based upon it.[5] The primary validity of ethics was identical with "the validity of the proposition," "the validity of the a priori," which could also be termed "transcendental validity." This primary validity was the presupposition upon which anything which was valid had to be based.[6] The ethical categories possessed, therefore, "transcendental validity," but not "ethical validity." Only an ethical proposition could

---

[1] FKE, p. 116.

[2] *Ibid.*, p. 125.

[3] *Ibid.*, p. 126. Nygren also forbids the formation of ethical norms on an intellectual basis, cf. p. 129 ff.

[4] Cf. Anders Nygren, *Etiska grundfrågor* (Stockholm: SKD, 1926), p. 10 ff.

[5] FKE, p. 146.

[6] *Ibid.*, p. 148.

possess this validity. Nygren attempted to demonstrate that the ethical categories possessed transcendental validity. If this could be demonstrated, he said, then the ethical experience had been shown to be a universal, independent, and autonomous experience. It became, thereby, the "ground value" for all ethical activity as well as the specifically ethical validity.[1]

The task of the critical ethic was to answer two questions. The first was the question of the authority of the ethical judgment, and the relationship of the ethical judgment to the ethical alternatives of good and evil. The answer to this question was not given in reference to the authority of the ethical judgment itself, but instead with reference to the transcendental deduction of the ethical category.[2] The second question asked, "which universal ethical category had to be found in order for all ethical judgment to be possible?" Nygren proceeded to investigate that area in which the critical ethic sought its primary validity. He attempted to discover "what in a true sense could be judged good and evil by the ethical predicates."[3] In a section of *Filosofisk och kristen etik*, which was entitled "Purposive ethics, Legalistic ethics, and Dispositional ethics," Nygren discussed this problem. With reference to Kant's distinction between legality and morality, Nygren rejected the legalistic ethic. He also rejected the purposive ethic, on the basis that the purposive ethic legalized the ethical proposition.[4] Furthermore, the concept "purpose" could not, by itself, be primarily ethical. There was a confusion at this point, he found, between the concepts of good and evil. Neither did the purposive ethic maintain the distinction which had to be made between the ethical area and the scientific area.[5] For example, scientific, artistic, and religious values, constructed in such a way that they were primarily "purposive," confused the nature of ethical and transcendental

---

[1] *Ibid.*, p. 149.
[2] Cf. the obvious similarity between this and the transcendental deduction of religion in *Religiöst Apriori*.
[3] FKE, p. 160.
[4] Nygren expresses it by saying "ändamålet helgar medlen".
[5] "Antingen tillskriver man etiken från denna ståndpunkt uppgiften att på vetenskaplig väg fastställa på vilket ändamål det mänskliga handlandet i sista hand bör isriktas och sett omöjligheten av denna uppgift, om man insett att vetenskapen till följd av sin natur aldrig kan åtaga sig att uppställa ändamål för vårt praktiska förhållande – befriar man etiken från varje befattning med och uppställandet av ett slutmål, vilket fastmer tänkes vunnet på ovetenskaplig väg, men tillskriver den i stället den tekniska uppgiften att uppvisa genom vilka medel detta redan på förhand faststående slutmål kan bliva förverkligat." FKE, p. 181.

validity.[1] Therefore, the dispositional ethic was the only legitimate ethic. However, activity and the objective of ethical activity had to characterize the ethical disposition.[2] There was a positive relationship between a disposition and the objective of ethical activity. The specifically ethical, for Nygren, was therefore the *dispositional* ethic.

Finally, the philosophical ethic presented the formal categories for the ethical experience itself. The categories (for example, community, duty) were given a content by distinct ethical ideals, which were historically realized.[3]

The Christian ethic concerned Nygren next. His examination of the Christian ethic began by asking definite questions about the nature of the Christian faith.[4] Had the Christian faith formed a specifically Christian "ethos" which created a specific Christian ethic? Was the Christian faith so constructed that it necessarily asked ethical questions? Was there an ethical ideal within the Christian faith itself? From an ethical standpoint, could Christianity be dealt with so that it became a creative force in life? Before Nygren answered these and other questions, he found it necessary to define the Christian ethic. It was a dispositional ethic which was most appropriate to the Christian faith.[5] The most striking characteristic of the Christian ethic Nygren found to be "the requirement for the disposition of love."[6] The correct understanding of the Christian faith came only when faith was related to "the essence of Christianity," "to that which was centrally Christian," which was the requirement of love.[7] This immediately brought Nygren to another problem; that is, what was the essence of religion? Nygren had to define the essence of religion if he was to obtain an objective answer to the question of what was the "essence of Christianity." This was obtained only when one investigated the

---

[1] *Ibid.*

[2] "Det gives intet etiskt sinnelag, som ej har tendensen att omsätta sig i handling och intet handlande, som ej går ut på att förverkliga ett ändamål." *Ibid.*, p. 182.

[3] "Kulman när dess undersökning, då den uppvisar vissa rent formala etiska kategorier och angiver grunden för deras giltighet." *Ibid.*, p. 190.

[4] "Har kristendomen utbildat ett särskilt kristet ethos, en specifikt sedlig livsföring, som motiverar uppställandet av en särskild kristen etik? Är den kristna trön så beskaffad, att man, då densamma underkastas vetenskaplig betraktelse, med nödvändighet kommer in på vissa etiska problem? För den kristna tron med nödvändighet till ett på visst sätt beskaffat etiskt förhållande? Finnes det något med kristendomen sammanhängande etiskt ideal? Är kristendomen att betrakta såsom en från etisk synpunkt skapande faktor?" FKE, p. 192 ff.

[5] FKE, p. 207 ff.

[6] *Ibid.*, p. 228 ff.

[7] *Ibid.*, p. 235.

religious experience in relationship to the other experiences of life.[1] We were therefore once again, said Nygren, within the area of the philosophy of religion. Nygren referred his reader once again to his work, *Religiöst Apriori*. The philosophy of religion demonstrated that religion was a universal form of experience and was characterized by the fact that everything in religion had to be dealt with under the category of eternity. From this point of orientation, the essence of religion could be defined. Religion was the "revelation of eternity," or the "judgment of eternity." Religion would "effect the reconciliation of the temporal and the eternal, the human and the divine." Religion would locate the life of man within the life of eternity. Christianity, and the essence of Christianity, could be defined in the following way: "Christianity was the religion which found the essence of religion totally realized in Jesus Christ."[1] The person of Jesus had significance for revelation. His person was the locus for his own experience of eternity. Christ's experience of eternity was also a judgment upon human life, for in Christ there was the reconciliation of man to God: "The exclusive relationship between God and man was thereby suspended."[2]

Now Nygren could discuss the nature of the specifically Christian ethic. Christian ethics investigated the "essence of Christianity," to determine if there was included within Christianity a particular ethical position. Christian ethics had to examine the nature of Christianity in reference to its ethical ideal.[3] In reference to the above definition of religion, Nygren attempted to state precisely what was the Christian ethic. Christ, who had communicated to man the revelation of eternity, enlarged the concept of community. This concept had great significance for the ethical ideal.[4] Eternity had definite consequences for the self and its relationship to the community, "*sub specie aeternitatis*."[5] The role of mediation and reconciliation indicated that the Christian community was realized in Jesus Christ.[6] The inter-penetration of eternity into the life of man revealed that the Christian community had been realized *in love*.[7]

---

[1] *Ibid.*, p. 237.
[1] *Ibid.*, p. 238.
[2] *Ibid.*, p. 239.
[3] *Ibid.*, p. 240.
[4] FKE, p. 241, and the whole section "Kristendomens vidgade gemenskapsbegrepp".
[5] *Ibid.*, cf. also p. 252 ff.
[6] *Ibid.*, p. 276 ff. "Den kristna gudsgemenskapens förverkligande."
[7] *Ibid.*, p. 288 ff.

Nygren then discussed the relationships which existed between philosophical and Christian ethics. Both the philosophical and the Christian ethic had legitimate functions to perform.[1] The philosophical ethic was an integral part of experience. Christianity had demonstrated itself to be the creative factor in the ethical life. Christianity, furthermore, possessed its own independent ideal, which could develop only in accordance with the religious "ground value" or presupposition. This, however, could not be constructed philosophically. It could be expressed properly only within the area of theological investigation. Nygren asserted, however, that these two ethical systems were never exclusive of one another. The critical ethic did not offer any final or universal knowledge of the ethical ideal. It was Christianity which presented the ethical ideal. However, the ethical ideal of Christianity was not superior to any other ethical ideal. The "essence" of the ideal was non-demonstrable, and could never assert its priority by attempting to be demonstrable. Its priority was demonstrated only by virtue of its attractiveness.[2] On the basis of this, Nygren asserted the authority of the Christian ethic, because of the characteristic it possessed of "immediate experience."[3] The Christian ethic was, "the superior ethic" because it offered the possibility for the formal categories of ethics to receive a real content.[4] If the philosophical or critical ethic had a "need for completion," the Christian ethic could perform this function. The critical ethic, however, demanded that its formal categories be given a content. It demanded an ethical reality which rested upon the ground of validity. The Christian ethic offered such a content. However, the Christian ethic was also in need of the philosophical ethic, for it could not do without the "ground of validity" which the philosophical ethic offered. There was ultimately no conflict between the philosophical and Christian ethic.[5]

---

[1] "Det har visar sig, att den filosofiska etiken är en integrerande del i det filosofiska systemet, så att detta skulle bliva oavslutat och från en väsentlig sida förete en lucka, om man avstoda från etikens filosofiska behandling, liksom å andra sidan erfarenheten själv därigenom att den uppträder med anspråk på överindividuell giltighet, uppfordrar till en undersökning som blott kan utföras med filosofiska medel. Men det har ock visat sig, att kristendomen är en från etisk synpunkt skapande faktor, att den äger sitt egen, självständiga ideal, som blott kan uppväxa på dess religiösa grundval, men som däremot är filosofiskt okonstruerbart, och att detta kristendomens etiska ideal följaktligen endast kan komma till sin rätt i en ursprungligen teologiskt inriktad undersökning." FKE, p. 316 ff.

[2] FKE, p. 322.

[3] *Ibid.*, p. 232 ff.

[4] *Ibid.*, p. 324.

[5] The Christian ethic "kräver en innehållslig komplettering till sitt formala

II. THE SCIENTIFIC FOUNDATION OR DOGMATIC THEOLOGY

Nygren, who was dependent a great deal upon Schleiermacher's *Der christliche Glaube* for his conception of Dogmatics, described what he called "the transcendental necessity of religion."[1] *Der christliche Glaube* had become, Nygren maintained, the basic work for the contemporary dogmatician. Dogmatics in the 1930's had found itself in a critical period. The attempt to describe Dogmatics as a form of speculative theology had failed. This was so, primarily, because there was no universally recognized speculative system which could serve as the foundation for a dogmatic theology. Also, Nygren asserted, when Dogmatics began with a speculative position, there could never be any real Christian Dogmatics. The only other alternatives, asserted Nygren, were Biblicism on the one hand and the Theology of Experience on the other. The former alternative began with a historic document, which it absolutized; the latter, with the consciousness of the Christian, psychologically given, which it made normative for all of Christian experience. Both of these approaches to Dogmatics lacked *scientific* stature.[2] The Biblical approach had to be accompanied by a constant re-interpretation and modernization. The approach from experience was deficient because it was relevant solely to the individual. In order for the experience to become objective, it had to be related to the experience of the Christian community. The Christian church and the consciousness it had of itself was only relatively constant. Every attempt to base a Dogmatics upon a subjective interpretation of experience was not worthy of the designation scientific.[3]

Nygren saw, furthermore, that the confusion over the methodology which Dogmatics was to use was only symptomatic of a deeper problem for Dogmatics. The following questions were relevant for the problem of theological methodology:

---

kategorischema, den kräver en etisk realitet, som kan vila på dess giltighetsfundament, och håller därmed platsen fri för den kristna etiken, som just erbjuder en sådan, real, innehållslig komplettering. Men även den kristna etiken är i behov av den filosofiska etikens komplettering; den kan ej undvara det av denna lagda giltighetsfundamentet." FKE, p. 326 ff. cf. also FM, p. 42 ff.

[1] DVG, p. 117.

[2] *Ibid.*, p. 3, 4.

[3] *Ibid.*, p. 4; Nygren says, furthermore, that a speculative Dogmatics or an experiential Dogmatics is impossible. The speculative approach leads only to metaphysics. Biblicism cannot lead to anything other than an Old and New Testament theology, which is no more than biblical exegesis, and not Dogmatics.

1. Why should one undertake the dogmatic task?;
2. Was the dogmatic task based primarily upon a practical and religious interest or was there also a scientific reason?;
3. Did Dogmatics have any place within a scientific system?;
4. Was Dogmatics a normative or a descriptive science?

The reason for the confusion of the task of Dogmatics was the misunderstanding of the scientific character of dogmatics. "Early Protestantism" recognized the nature of the Dogmatic task within the Church. A modern dogmatician, however, could not presuppose that Dogmatics was universally recognized as a science.[1] Rather, it had first to legitimatize itself as a real science, thereby liberating itself from a subjective characterization.[2]

Kant's critical philosophy made it impossible to deal with Dogmatics in the way in which it was dealt with in the period of "Early Protestantism." Dogmatics, at that time, said Nygren, claimed to be "a science of God and divine beings," ("doctrina de deo et rebus divinis.") This definition paralleled the metaphysical type of the philosophy of religion, which often made the same claim. Dogmatics, during this period, differentiated itself from the metaphysical type of the philosophy of religion by its practical and religious interests, and attempted to discover the ultimate and absolute basis for existence. Dogmatics made use of the Holy Scriptures and Divine Revelation and constructed a scientific system from these. Reason, on the other hand, was the only tool employed by the philosophy of religion. Reason was the formal and material principle for religious truth.[3] Dogmatics, consequently, could make the claim that every one of its propositions had a rational character.

However, all of this was eradicated by Kant's critique of reason. Dogmatics could depend no longer upon the philosophy of religion for its scientific character. The critical method denied that it was possible to have a "knowledge of God and divine beings." Dogmatics, thereupon, entered a period in which there was a denial of the basic methodological assertions of theology.[4] Dogmatics, denied an

---

[1] DVG, p. 6.
[2] *Ibid.* "Fastmer måste den själv tillkämpa sig detta erkännade, visserligen i första rummet genom betydelsen av dess vetenskapliga produktion, så att den genom sitt eget arbete har att legitimera sig såsom en verklig vetenskap; men därför får icke det rent teoretiska klarläggandet av dess vetenskapliga karaktär och betydelse försummas."
[3] DVG, p. 7.
[4] *Ibid.*, p. 6.

independent object for its investigation, relegated itself to the history of dogma, or related religion to contemporary scientific thought. Dogmatics became thereby a problem for the philosophy of religion.[1] Dogmatics was, thereafter, degraded to a non-scientific and practical status, whose only existence depended upon its association with the character and message of the Christian church.

"Early Protestantism" had insisted that Dogmatics was both scientific and Christian. Nygren felt that it was now impossible to develop a Dogmatics which was similar to that of the older period. A new methodological starting point for Dogmatics had to be found.[2] Kant had shown the impossibility of knowledge of the transcendentals. A Dogmatics, therefore, which was a "doctrina de deo et rebus divinis," was wholly irrelevant. However, Nygren insisted, if there was to be Dogmatics, it had to be, "positively Christian and rigorously scientific."[3]

Nygren then attempted to find a new starting point for Dogmatics by relating Dogmatics to the critical method. Dogmatics did not have any characteristics, he said, which were antithetical to the critical method.[4] Dogmatics had to acknowledge the consequences of Kant's criticism,[5] that is, that no knowledge of the object of faith was possible. Even more, it had to assert that the task of Dogmatics was not to achieve immediate communion with the transcendent object of faith. The relationship of the individual Christian to his Church included a relationship to the divine, but always within the context of the faith of the Church. Dogmatics was a "branch of science." As a science, it could not have any immediate knowledge of the transcendent object.[6] Nygren asserted that only by limiting the scope of Dogmatics could the confusion between the Christian faith and theology and religion and science be overcome.

The other requirement for Dogmatics was that it possess a positive Christian character. This requirement did not deny the possibility of Dogmatics being a science, but it did remove Dogmatics from all

---

[1] *Ibid.*, p. 9, 10.
[2] *Ibid.*, p. 10, 11; "om dogmatiken skall kunna övervinna den kris, i vilken den råkat genom den kritiska filosofiens uppvisande av omöjligheten av en vetenskap om det transcendenta, så måste den uppgive sitt anspråk på att vara en 'doctrina de deo et rebus divinis'; men på samma gång måste den vara positivt kristlig och strängt vetenskaplig".
[3] DVG, p. 10, 11.
[4] *Ibid.*, p. 11.
[5] *Ibid.*
[6] *Ibid.*, p. 11, 12.

quasi-metaphysical speculations. As a science, Dogmatics had to begin with the factually given experience of religious faith, which was related to a historically given religion. Within such a context, the Christian faith could then be dealt with.[1] Nygren wrote, "If Dogmatics is a science, then it can be related to only one of the historical religions, which for us, is the Christian faith."[2]

Nygren had now proposed the new methodological starting point for Dogmatics. Dogmatics had to employ the critical method, and maintain its Christian character, but at the same time, it could not lose its scientific quality. Nygren believed that a perfect example of a Dogmatics which satisfied all of these requirements was Schleiermacher's *Der christliche Glaube*.[3] Schleiermacher had insisted that his Dogmatics possessed a "critical, Christian, and scientific character."[4] What Schleiermacher had accomplished in his Dogmatics, said Nygren, had to become the prototype for the contemporary dogmatician.[5]

Nygren demonstrated that Dogmatics was a "positive" science by specific reference to Schleiermacher's *Der christliche Glaube*.[6] Nygren began his discussion by referring to what Schleiermacher had called a "positive science."[7] Theology, for Schleiermacher, was a positive

---

[1] Nygren asserts that the demand for the scientific character of Dogmatics presupposes its Christian character; cf. DVG, p. 12, 13: "Det visar sig alltså, att det är så långt ifrån att kravet på dogmatikens vetenskaplighet skulle förutsätta dess emanciperande från kristendomen, att det fastmer leder fram till kravet på dess kristliga gestaltning. Vi äro alltså berättigade att uppställa satsen: från de metafysiska spekulationernas tomma lek kan den vetenskapliga dogmatiken lösgöra sig endast därigenom, att den avgjort och medvetet ställer sig på kristendomens mark."

[2] DVG, p. 13.

[3] Nygren continually quotes Schleiermacher to indicate the requirements he has set up for Dogmatics; cf. DVG, p. 13, 14.

[4] Cf. Schleiermacher's statement: "Wenn überall wissenschaftlicher Geist und religiöse Erregung gleichen Schritt halten müssen in theologischen Produktionen, so glaube ich zwar mir das Zeugnis geben zu können, dass an meinem Buche, sofern ich es als Tat, als Handlung ansehen kann, das eine soviel Anteil hat als das andere." Quoted from S.W. I, 2, p. 611 by Nygren in DVG, p. 14.

[5] Nygren believes he can demonstrate the scientific nature of Dogmatics without reference to Schleiermacher's *Der christliche Glaube*. DVG, p. 14.

[6] Nygren also makes reference to Schleiermacher's *Kurze Darstellung des Theologischen Studiums*, DVG, p. 18. "A positive science" is "ein solcher Inbegriff wissenschaftlicher Elemente, welche ihre Zusammengehörigkeit nicht haben, als ob sie einen vermöge der Idee der Wissenschaft notwendigen Bestandteil der wissenschaftlichen Organisation bildeten, sondern nur, sofern sie zur lösung einer praktischen Aufgabe erforderlich sind." *Ibid.*; it is questionable if this definition of science corresponds with that of *Der christliche Glaube*.

[7] Cf. DVG, p. 21; a positive science is "vermöge der Idee der Wissenschaft notwendiger Bestandteil der wissenschaftlichen Organisation."

science in the sense that it gathered together all the material common to Christianity, in order to examine it in an objective way.[1] Theology had the task to look at Christianity in the light of its origins and historical development, and at the same time comprehend its "organic expression" and conception of life.[2] Dogmatics, for Schleiermacher, was a positive science, in the sense that it recognized the "value of Christianity."[3] Schleiermacher, Nygren discovered, had employed the scientific method in order to present theologically what was the content of the Christian faith.[4]

Nygren asserted that to compare the major historical religions of the world to one another would never convince anyone of the superior nature of Christianity. However, Nygren said, "no one can prevent the Christian from seeing in Christianity the highest values of realized religion."[5] In this way, Nygren wanted to preserve the objective character of the scientific investigation of religion. The conception of religion had to be identical with every other universal idea, in the sense that it, too, was indifferent to value. It was apparent, said Nygren, that when a comparison was made of the value of one religion over against another, there was often confusion of the *value* of a religion with the *ideal* of a religion. It was obvious that the *ideal* of the Christian religion was different from that of the Buddhist religion. However, one could not construct a religious *ideal* upon the basis of these different types of religion.[6] From a scientific standpoint, religion could be investigated in terms of its objective expression in history,

---

[1] Cf. Nygren's analysis of "positive science," DVG, p. 22 ff.

[2] DVG, p. 26.

[3] *Ibid.*, p. 27: "Dogmatiken är alltså enligt Schleiermacher en positiv vetenskap, så tillvida som den har att utgå från erkännandet av kristendomens värde. Utifrån denna utgångspunkt har den att i rent vetenskapligt och uteslutande teoretiskt intresse framställa, vad som är innehållet i den kristna tron."

[4] Ernst Troeltsch has criticized this interpretation of Schleiermacher, cf. *Gesammelte Schriften* II, 1913, p. 200 ff; "Schleiermacher und die Kirche," in *Schleiermacher der Philosoph des Glaubens*, 1910. "Die Hauptfrage aber nach der Geltung des Christentums selbst ist keine rein historische, sondern eine geschichtsphilosophische oder religionsphilosophische, die in wissenschaftlichem Sinne nur von einer allgemeinen Theorie der Religion und einer Theoria ihrer geschichtsphilosophischen Abstufungen aus angefasst werden kann," *Gesammelte Schriften* II, p. 223. Nygren himself distinguishes between the scientific character of Christianity, which is "theoretical," and the personal and "practical" relation of the individual to Christianity. DVG. p. 37 ff.

[5] DVG, p. 39. cf. also Nygren's *Det religionsfilosofiska grundproblemet*, p. 51.

[6] DVG, p. 40: "Varje försök att med vetenskapliga medel legitimera, att de eller de momenten böra upptagas i religionsidealet med uteslutande av andra, är dömt att misslyckas."

nothing more.[1] Schleiermacher had demonstrated very clearly that
theology had to be a "scientific" discipline, which did nothing more
than examine, "the internal fundamental data of Christian piety" ("die
innere Grundtatsache der christliche Frömmigkeit.")[2] In this way,
Schleiermacher had related the dogmatic task to the historical fact of
Christianity.[3] He began with the universal concept of religion, "the
feeling of absolute dependence," and from this concept, dealt with
the entire content of Dogmatics.[4]

Schleiermacher, too, Nygren reminded us, had demonstrated the
transcendental necessity of religion by reference to "Lehnsatze zur
Ethik," the necessity of the realization of the historical religions by
reference to "Lehnsatze zur Religionsphilosophie;" and the necessity
of Christianity (as a special kind of "realized" religion) by reference to
"Lehnsatze zur Apologetik." Ethics, for Schleiermacher, was the
"science of the activity of the Human."[5] When this activity was expressed in history, ethics became "the science of the principles of history."[6] Ethics presented the principles which were constitutive for
man's activity in nature. Ethics became, therefore, a parallel discipline
to the natural sciences.[7] Schleiermacher's philosophy of religion was

---

[1] DVG, p. 40, 41. Nygren concludes that this is what Schleiermacher has done;
cf. GL 2, Par. 28, "Diejenigen Behandlungsweisen der christlichen Lehre, welche
unter dem Namen praktische Dogmatik oder populäre Dogmatik seit längerer
Zeit aufgekommen sind (scheinen freilich die Notwendigkeit einer wissenschaftlichen Gestaltung nicht anzuerkennen), weisen allerdings teils die dialektische
Sprache teils die systematische Anerkennung zurück; allein sie liegen auch ausser
dem Kreise, dem wir den Namen Dogmatik aneignen. Sie sind teils Mitteldinge
zwischen einem Lehrgebäude und einem Katechismus, teils schon Bearbeitungen
der Dogmatik für die Homiletik. Jene haben wohl grossenteils die Absicht, die
Resultate dogmatischer Entwicklungen auch denen in einem gewissen Zusammenhange mitzuteilen, die einem wissenschaftlichen Gange nicht leicht folgen würden;
allein wie die Absicht selbst ziemlich willkührlich ist (indem man sich damit von
dem wissenschaftlichen Gebiete entfernte), so scheint auch durch das Unternehmen mehr Verwirrung angerichtet und Oberflächlichkeit befördert worden zu
sein, als dass ein wahrer Nutzen erzielt wäre.", which Nygren quotes, DVG, p. 43.
[2] Fr. Schleiermacher, Gl. 1, Par. 31:2; Gl. 3, Par. 28:2, cf. Gl. 1, Par. 31:3, also
KD. 2, Par. 28 and 97; cf. also Gl. 2, Par. 26:2 ff.
[3] Cf. Gl. 2, Par. 27:4, where Schleiermacher speaks about "Scientific Dogmatics," quoted by Nygren, DVG, p. 46.
[4] "für die christliche Glaubenslehre ist die Darstellung zugleich die Begründung; denn alles in derselben lässt sich nur dadurch begründen, dass es als richtige
Aussage des christlichen Selbstbewusstseins dargestellt wird," quoted by Nygren
from Fr. Schleiermacher, S.W. I, 2, p. 638. DVG, p. 47.
[5] Cf. KD. 2, Par. 21, quoted by Nygren, DVG, p. 51.
[6] Cf. KD. 1, Par. 37, p. 9, also p. 12, Par. 6, quoted by Nygren DVG, p. 51.
[7] Therefore, ethics is "die der Naturwissenschaft gleichlaufende speculative

oriented to the problem of the *validity* of the religious experience. He dealt with religion from the standpoint of "the activity of the Human." The philosophy of religion therefore demonstrated that the concept of religion had been expressed in the different historical religions of the world.[1] Apologetics, for Schleiermacher, was not a discipline which defended Christianity against the non-Christian religions of the world, but rather, "the science of the 'essence' of Christianity."[2]

Nygren acknowledged his dependence upon Schleiermacher for the delineation of the scientific character of Dogmatics. He proposed, therefore, to do the following:[3]

1. To demonstrate that religion was a necessary and universal form of experience, which was an indispensable part of the life of man. The concept of religion had to be shown not to be a subjective or arbitrary concept. Furthermore, it had to be demonstrated that religion was not dependent upon culture.

2. To indicate in what way religion was realized in a historical and a positive form. Every investigation of religion, therefore, had to refer to the fact of the historical religions of the world.

3. To define what was the "essence of Christianity."[4]

Nygren began by stating that "if religion is a necessary and indispensable form of life which no one can justifiably deny, and if it cannot exist in any other form than in a positive and historical form, and if Christianity is such a realization of the religious experience, then the scientific basis for Dogmatics is assured."[5] When the "essence" of Christianity was recognized and defined, the task of Dogmatics became to describe in a systematic way what belonged to the

---

Darstellung der Vernunft in ihrer Gesamtwirksamkeit." Gl. 2, Par. 2. Quoted by Nygren, DVG, p. 52.

[1] Cf. Nygren, *Det religionsfilosifska grundproblemet*, as well as *Die Gültigkeit der religiösen Erfahrung* (Lund: Gleerups, 1922), particularly the chapter "Wass heisst Religionsphilosophie?" Schleiermacher has found the relationship of ethics and the philosophy of religion to be: "Alles in der Ethik Construierte enthält die Möglichkeit einer unendlichen Menge von Erscheinungen. Ausser dem empirischen Auffassen der letzteren entsteht noch das Bedürfnis einer nähern Verbindung des Empirischen mit der speculativen Darstellung, nämlich zu beurteilen, wie sie sich die einzelnen Erscheinungen als Darstellungen der Idee sowohl dem Grade als der eigentümlichen Beschränktheit nach verhalten. Dies ist das Wesen der Kritik, und es gibt daher einen Cyclus kritischer Disziplinen, welche sich an die Ethik anschlissen." Quoted by Nygren, DVG, p. 52.

[2] KD. 2, Par. 44, Par. 66, 68; Quoted by Nygren, DVG, p. 55.

[3] DVG, p. 52, 54.

[4] *Ibid.*, p. 54.

[5] *Ibid.*

Christian faith. Dogmatics therefore, had the task to demonstrate that every expression of the Christian faith in history had its common origin in the "essence" of Christianity. These historical expressions of the Christian faith stood in a necessary and organic relationship to the central affirmation of faith itself.[1]

Nygren had demonstrated that the religious experience was a universal and necessary experience, and he did this by employing the transcendental (critical) method.[2] All of this, Nygren had learned from Schleiermacher. Schleiermacher identified religion with the transcendental category of religion. From the concept of "Religion überhaupt," Schleiermacher dealt with the concrete historical religions. Real religion must be positively and historically expressed, he said.[3] Religion in its "essence" had to have within itself a principle of individuation which permitted the multiplicity of the religions known to man.[4] By the concept of "Religion überhaupt," Schleiermacher referred to the transcendental nature of religion, which was the presupposition for these real religions.[5]

When Schleiermacher dealt with the relationship of the religious categories ("die Anschauung des Universums, das schlechthinige Abhängigkeitsgefühl") to the historical religions, he did not attempt to

---

[1] "... att dogmatikens uppgift mindre är att i detalj framställa den kristna trosåskådningen än att uppvisa dess lagmässiga sammanhang," DVG, p. 55, and in relation to Schleiermacher's system, Nygren says, "Först här har dogmatiken blivit en verklig vetenskap. Dess uppgift är att i rent teoretiskt intresse framställa den kristna trons innehåll utifrån dess eget centrum och i det sammanhang, som dikteras av dess eget väsen. Det rent teoretiska intresset ställer dogmatiken på samma linje med övriga vetenskaper." DVG, p. 56.

[2] Cf. DVG, pp. 69–121.

[3] "Ich will Euch die Religion zeigen, wie sie sich ihrer Unendlichkeit entäussert hat und in oft dürftiger Gestalt unter den Menschen erschienen ist; in den Religionen sollt Ihr die Religion entdecken, in dem, was irdisch und verunreinigt vor Euch steht, die einzelnen Züge derselben himmlischen Schönheit aufsuchen, deren Gestalt ich nachzubilden versucht habe." Reden 3, p. 120 ff., quoted by Nygren, DVG, p. 119.

[4] "Die Religion ist ihrem Begriff und ihrem Wesen nach auch für den Verstand ein Unendliches und Unermessliches; sie muss also sein Prinzip, sich zu individualisieren, in sich haben, weil sie sonst garnicht dasein und wahrgenommen werden könnte." R.3, p. 122, quoted by Nygren, DVG, p. 120.

[5] "Die sogenannte natürliche Religion ist gewöhnlich so abgeschliffen und hat so philosophische und moralische Manieren, dass sie wenig von dem eigentümlichen Charakter der Religion durchschimmern lässt; dagegen jede positive Religion gar starke Züge und eine sehr markierte Physiognomie hat, so dass sie bei jeder Bewegung, welche sie macht, und bei jedem Blick, den man auf sie wirft, unfehlbar an das erinnert, was sie eigentlich ist...", R.3, p. 123 ff., quoted by Nygren, DVG, p. 121.

demonstrate the *truth* of religion. Rather, he dealt solely with the *validity* of the religious experience, which was relevant to all concrete religions. But this validity, that is, the validity of the religious experience, was the necessary presupposition for all of validity.[1] When the validity of the religious experience was established, then religion could make the claim that it was a valid experience. Schleiermacher was conscious of the fact, however, that the religious category could not exist without an experiencing subject. The religious experience was given, and could only become a valid experience when the "ground category" of religion was discovered. Once it was discovered, it necessarily expressed itself in the historical religions of man. In this way, the religious category was realized.[2]

It was, however, impossible to know beforehand what form the religious category would take. To know this, one had to refer to the factually given and empirically observable forms of religion. The critical method, we have seen, oriented itself to the category of religion and to the historically given religions.[3]

The Christian faith, according to Schleiermacher, had one apologetic task, and that was the presentation of the "essence" of the faith.[4] Schleiermacher defined Christianity as a monotheistic religion, teleological in nature, and individualistic in terms of its founder, Jesus Christ. The Christian faith was initiated by the feeling of absolute dependence, to which Jesus gave concrete expression in his life. Christianity was the historical religion in which the God-consciousness was perfectly expressed in the person of Jesus Christ. Man could now relate himself in a dependent way to God, all of which had been illustrated by the

---

[1] Cf. Nygren's discussion on this point, DVG, p. 122.

[2] Nygren very carefully distinguishes between the *realization* and *actualization* of the religious category; cf. *Religiöst Apriori*, pp. 165–175, DVG, pp. 125–131. The "actualization" of religion would treat religion as a psychological function and not as a transcendental function. Nygren parallels this assertion with a transcendental investigation of the theoretical area. He questions, "...vilka allmännaste kategorier ... måste erkännas, för att det överhuvud skall kunna givas någon kunskap," DVG, p. 126. The valid category which is found is not a category filled with content, but the category which is the presupposition for all knowledge.

[3] The critical method of Schleiermacher, which deals with the religious category and places it in relation to the empirically given religions, is called "Religionsphilosophie". cf. DVG, p. 132.

[4] Cf. DVG, p. 141; Schleiermacher describes it as, "Darstellung des Christentums seinem eigentümlichen Wesen nach".; also the reference in the well-known 11 paragraph of Gll.2, "Das Christentum ist eine der teleologischen Richtung der Frömmigkeit angehörige monotheistische Glaubensweise, und unterscheidet sich von andern solchen wesentlich dadurch, dass alles in derselben bezogen wird auf die durch Jesum von Nazareth vollbrachte Erlösung."

life of Jesus Christ. Christianity was therefore a religion of redemption, in which deliverance came from the person of Jesus. Christianity distinguished itself from all of the other historical religions. (all of which possessed some kind of feeling of absolute dependence, which Schleiermacher believed was central to the Christian faith) by placing the act of redemption in the center of religion,[1] through Jesus Christ.

The presuppositions for Nygren's Dogmatics have now all been given. Nygren could now define Dogmatics as the "scientific presentation of the Christian faith."[2] The location of religion within the life and experience of man had been validated by means of the transcendental "ground category" of religion. The religious category had been realized in every real religion. In this way, the essence of religion had been found, and this concept was indispensable for the concept of the "essence of Christianity." The essence of Christianity had, therefore, to take the form of the manner in which the Christian faith expressed itself in history. The scientific character of Dogmatics presupposed this representation of the "essence" of Christianity. The only legitimate way to maintain the scientific character of Dogmatics was to investigate the "chain of necessity" which began with the transcendental necessity of religion and concluded with the necessity of the dogmatic proposition.[3] The task of Dogmatics was, therefore, to describe, in a systematic way, the historically given expressions of faith of the Christian community.[4]

---

[1] Nygren is careful to emphasize the uniqueness of Christianity, and quotes Schleiermacher: "Das wird aus dem Gesagten folgen, dass wenn wir uns religiöse Momente denken sollten, in welchen alle Beziehung auf die Erlösung aufgeheben wäre, und das Bild des Erlösers gar nicht darin vergegenwärtigt, man von diesen würde sagen müssen, sie gehören dem Christentum nicht näher an als irgend einer andern monotheistischen Glaubenweise," Gl. 2, Par. 11:3; Nygren, DVG, p. 142–143.

[2] DVG, p. 142 "Dogmatikens vetenskapliga och kristna karaktär." Nygren criticizes Schleiermacher for reducing Christianity to the feeling of absolute dependence and permitting the religion of redemption to be only an appendix to it. DVG, p. 147 ff.

[3] DVG, p. 151.

[4] Schleiermacher expressed it this way: "Dogmatische Theologie ist die Wissenschaft von dem Zusammenhange der in einer christlichen Kirchengesellschaft zu einer gegebenen Zeit geltenden Lehre.", Gl.2, Par. 19, and, "Christliche Glaubenssätze sind Auffassungen der christlich frommen Gemützustände in der Rede dargestellt.", Gl.2, Par. 15; and Nygren this way: "Dogmatikens uppgift är icke någon annan än att systematiskt explicera, vad som ligger i detta centrala "kristna medvetande." Kristendomen är absolut avhängighetskänsla; det blir därför första delens uppgift att undersöka vad som ligger däri. Här är platsen för trosutsagorna om skapelsen och uppehållelsen, vilka blott äro uttryck för det förhållandet, att världen består i absolut avhängighet av Gud.", DVG, p. 156, and "Den transcen-

In a later work, *Filosofi och Motivforskning*, Nygren dealt with the same subject, the nature of Dogmatics, but did so in such a way that he related it to "motif interpretation" ("motivforskning").[1] Nygren differentiated between two contrasting points of view as to what was the task of Systematic Theology; that is, the speculative and the religio-positive tasks. The speculative task of Systematic Theology attempted to present what was the most universal religious experience; that is, to present the idea of eternity, which is religious, to free it from all of the contingencies of time, and to examine it as it appeared within the different historically expressed religions of mankind. This kind of Systematic Theology had necessarily to employ a philosophy of religion oriented to metaphysics.[2] In contrast, the religio-positive approach permitted Dogmatics to present the expression of the faith of a specific religious community. There was no attempt to propose a universal religious experience. Dogmatics had to begin with the basic conception of religious faith within a religious community, and attempt to describe it in as systematic a way as was possible. Systematic Theology was therefore identified with Historical Theology; that is, Systematic Theology reported what was the factual expression of the faith of a religious community.[3]

The primary task of Dogmatics, therefore, had to be the scientific task. This immediately removed the speculative approach to theology from further consideration. Instead of a scientific investigation of the historical religions, "speculative" theology attempted to discover what were the universal ideas of religion. This was a "philosophically composed religion,"[4] said Nygren, and did not result in an accurate definition of the meaning of religious faith. Nygren, therefore, asserted the priority of the "religio-positive" approach to Dogmatics, which dealt only with the factual object of a given religion. However,

---

dentala methoden går ut på att legitimera de allmänna principerna, och dess kriterium lyder: såsom allmän princip gäller det, genom vars bestridande och upphävande man tillika skulle upphäva erfarenheten överhuvud. Den dogmatiska metoden går ut på att legitimera enskilda trosomdömens kristna karaktär, och dess kriterium lyder: såsom kristet trosomdöme har det omdöme att gälla, genom vara upphävande man tillika skulle upphäva kristendomens centrum.", DVG, p. 159.

[1] *Filosofi och motivforskning*, particularly Chapters "Hür är filosofi som vetenskap möjlig?"; "Motivforskning som filosofiskt och historiskt problem"; "Atomism eller sammanhang i historiesynen"; and "Systematisk teologi och motivforskning", pp. 1–89.

[2] FM, p. 73.

[3] *Ibid.*, p. 74.

[4] *Ibid.*

he questioned if there was any reason to give a systematic investigation to every conception of religious faith. Religion, as it was dealt with in a historical way, did not necessarily mean that the dogmatic theologian had to elucidate the expression of every religious faith as it expressed itself in history. Rather, he could limit himself to his own religious community.

The normative character of Dogmatics developed from the above methodology. The function of Systematic Theology was to present what ought to be believed by the religious community. The speculative function of Systematic Theology presented what ought to be believed as universal religious truth. On the other hand, the religio-positive function presented what ought to be believed within a definite community; that is, the presentation of the normative conception of faith within a specific religious grouping.

Systematic Theology, in order to be a scientific discipline, first had to seek to understand and describe the Christian faith in "its characteristic uniqueness."[1] In this way, Systematic Theology could be identified with the scientific task which attempted to understand and elucidate the nature of its object. It had to present the unique assertions of the Christian faith in their relationship to one another, and to that which was in the "center" of the Christian faith. This would allow the Christian faith to appear in terms of its internal organic structure.[2] However, Nygren realized that the function of Systematic Theology presupposed that "the Christian faith" was a perfectly unified entity, which, of course, it was not. The Christian faith had been expressed in many different ways in its historical development. What, therefore, asked Nygren, had to be the goal of Systematic Theology? As long as we related ourselves to a particular interpretation to the Christian faith, Nygren said, there was no real difficulty in presenting the meaning of the Christian faith. A simple and objective answer had been given to the question, "What is the Christian faith?", by Tertullian, Augustine, Thomas Aquinas, Luther, and many others. However, Nygren asked, what was the relationship of these concrete expressions of the Christian faith to the Christian faith in general? It was obvious that the Christian faith was subject to many different and arbitrary interpretations. The more assertive Christian theologian would identify his view of the Christian faith with the Christian faith

---

[1] *Ibid.*, p. 76.
[2] *Ibid.*

in its entirety. Nygren questioned, furthermore, if it were possible to describe anything more than a particular given form of Christianity. Was there anything which one could call the "essence of Christianity," in the same way as one could define the "essence of religion?" The solution to these problems was found in Nygren's discovery of the "motif." "Motif research" became, therefore, "an objective way to determine the uniqueness of the Christian faith."[1] Nygren identified motif research with typological research or structural research. Religion could not be understood by reference to the generic structures of religion. Religion could only be understood in terms of an analysis of the "ground motifs" which belonged to its structure.[2] Nygren assigned a peripheral role to the history of religion and the history of dogma, for he maintained that these do not present the real meaning of the Christian faith. To understand religion and the Christian faith, one had to go back to its fundamental motif. Dogmatics had to search for the "Christian ground motif," which determined the structure and content of the Christian's relation to God.[3]

All real religion, Nygren said, was some form of communion with God. If Christianity, as a representative of "real religion" was only a collection of religious doctrines, then a doctrine could provide a proper definition of the Christian faith. However, the Christian faith was more than a display of religious doctrine, it was "communion with God." This was most characteristic for the Christian faith. This was its basic structure. This was the "ground motif" of the Christian faith. The Christian "ground motif" was not an arbitrary concept, but it was, "that which *alone* characterizes the Christian's communion with God."

There could be no question as to what the Christian "ground motif" was, asserted Nygren. From the very beginning, Christianity had been *evangelium*; the "glad tidings of divine love which was given to mankind in Christ Jesus."[4] The Christian's communion with God was

---

[1] FM, p. 78: "På denna punkt träder nu motivforskningen in, och dess betydelse för den systematiska teologien består just däri, att den anvisar en objektiv väg för bestämmandet av den kristna trons egenart."

[2] Cf. Nygren's classic work *Den kristna kärlekstanken genom tiderna* I, p. 12 ff., in which he discusses the nature of "grundmotiv och motivforskning", "motivforskning och värdering"; cf. also *Urkristendom och reformation* (Stockholm: SKD, 1932), p. 7 ff. cf. also G. Aulen, "Motiv och föreställning inom teologien" in STK, 1930, p. 249 ff.

[3] FM, p. 80.

[4] FM, pp. 81, 82: "Kristendomen möter alltifrån begynnelsen såsom ett evangelium, såsom glädjebudskapet om den gudomliga kärleken, som i Kristus har sänkt sig ned till oss och som utgiver sig själv för att rädda det förlorade. Den kristna gudsgemenskapen får sin prägel därav att det är Gud själv, som i sin

initiated by God's action. It was God who, in love and grace, created the relationship between God and man. Divine love was unmotivated. God loved because He Himself was love. Love created communion with God. God was *AGAPE*. This was the Christian "ground motif." Christianity would lose its uniqueness without it.

The Christian ground-motif appeared in its clearest form, said Nygren, when it was compared with the other, oftentimes conflicting ground-motifs, which also claimed to be an expression of "communion with God." Nygren found that there were two motifs other than *agape* that claimed to be the ground-motifs for the Christian faith. They were the motifs of *nomos* and *eros*. Christianity had been influenced by them a great deal throughout its history, and they could make a legitimate claim to being fundamental motifs. The *nomos*-motif was found first in the antecedent of Christianity, Judaism. Communion with God, in Judaism, said Nygren, was principally characterized by the law. It was against this background that the words of Jesus had to be understood: "I have not come to call the righteous, but to save sinners." The *eros*-motif was introduced into Christianity during the period of its life in the Greek world. The *eros*-motif was characterized by the attempt of man to reach the divine. The communion with God effected was the identification of man's desire to reach God with the *summum bonum*.

The long history of Christianity presented the constant challenge of these foreign motifs to the *agape* motif. Christian history revealed a perpetual alternation between the synthesis of conflicting motifs and the subsequent reformation of the *agape* motif between the attempt to assimilate foreign groundmotifs and the attempt to expel them from the Christian faith.[1] Motif-research was not concerned to sanction dogma, but rather to describe the types of Christian expression which were possible. When a dogmatic statement was made, motif-research did not look for its derivatives, but rather for its "ground-motif," that which was unique about a specific expression of the Christian faith.

---

kärlek och nåd upprätter den. Intet hos människan själv kan anföras som motivering för gudsgemenskapen. Den gudomliga kärleken är i denna mening 'omotiverad'. Gud älskar därför att han själv är kärleken. Gud söker gemenskap med människan, icke därför att människan äger det eller det värdet – detta motsäges därav att människan inför Gud alltid står såsom syndare – utan därför att kärleken är gemenskapsstiftande. Gud är agape." It is quite obvious that Nygren receives his Christian heritage from Luther and not from Thomas Aquinas; cf. the discussion in FM, p. 52 ff.

[1] Cf. *Urkristendom och reformation*, p. 147 ff, the chapter entitled "Syntes eller reformation?"

Nygren, by his use of the method of "motif research," had ess tablished the uniqueness of the Christian faith. He had found thi- uniqueness by reference to the historical development of Christianity. In the challenge of the Christian ground-motif to foreign motifs, the uniqueness of the Christian faith was found. The dogmatician (or systematic theologian) now knew how to fulfill his role within the Christian church.[1] Nygren needed, therefore, only to clarify two further problems:

1. How could one be so sure that the *agape*-motif was the "ground-motif" of Christianity?

2. Could the Christian "ground-motif" serve as the starting point for Dogmatics?

The first problem was a problem only when the Christian faith was dealt with on a general and abstract plane, and not factually and his- torically. There could never be any arbitrary interpretation of the Christian faith in this way. The motif which was accepted was the one which more than any other was faithful to the given material. When an interpreter presented something as the Christian "ground-motif", he was presenting something which had to be verified by reference to the historical material itself.[2] The hypothesis that the *nomos* or the *eros* motif was the ground motif had to be verified by reference to the historical development of Christianity. Nygren had gone to great lengths in his classic work *Agape and Eros* to de- monstrate that this was not possible![3]

The second problem as to whether Dogmatics could be satisfied with a perpetually changing structure was answered very simply. Faith was always relating itself to absolute truth and certainty, but the scien- tific reflection upon faith did not permit the same kind of absoluteness. The scientific treatment of religious material provided a method by which the historical expression of religious faith could be described.[4]

---

[1] Nygren diagrams the relationship this way:

Motif Research

History of Ideas   Systematization

History   Characterization

Chronicle   Caricature

Chaos

[2] Nygren displays his apologetic interest by the following words: "Den som känner kristendomens inre utvecklingsgång torde icke kunna vara blind för agapemotivets ovan omtalade kamp med såväl nomos-som erosmotivet.", FM, p. 87.

[3] Cf. his classic *Den kristna kärlekstanken genom tiderna*.

[4] FM, p. 89.

CHAPTER FIVE

THE RELATIONSHIP OF NYGREN'S
RELIGIÖST APRIORI TO SCHLEIERMACHER'S
CONCEPTION OF RELIGION: CONCLUSION

I. NYGREN'S USE OF SCHLEIERMACHER'S CONCEPTION OF RELIGION
FOR THE DESCRIPTION OF RELIGION AS "A NECESSARY AND
UNIVERSAL EXPERIENCE, INSEPARABLE FROM THE NATURE OF MAN."

A. Schleiermacher provided the methodological starting point for
Nygren's transcendental deduction of the religious category. It was
Schleiermacher who had described the value of religion within human
consciousness, and who had demonstrated religion as a necessary and
integrating part of the life of every man.

Nygren found that Schleiermacher had remained primarily within
the Kantian philosophical tradition, although he had carried out the
implications of Kant's *Kritik der reinen Vernunft* to their logical conclusions. Both Kant and Schleiermacher had employed the categories
of universality and necessity and had made them constitutive for the
structure of reality.[1] However, Nygren found that Schleiermacher's
"philosophy of identity" had led him to describe metaphysics in a
different way from Kant.

Schleiermacher, furthermore, said Nygren, had overcome the difficulty within Kant's ethical theory by his conception of the highest
good as "the totality of all realized moral goods." Kant had constructed an ethical theory on the basis of the opposition which existed between the highest good (virtue) and happiness. Schleiermacher, on
the other hand, asserted that the moral law should be related to the
highest good, as "an algebraic equation is related to a geometrical
structure." Schleiermacher affirmed that the highest good, and not the
moral law, was the controlling principle of morality.

Schleiermacher criticized Kant's conception of freedom in his
Über die Freiheit des Menschen. He also attempted in this book to solve
the problems which resulted from the Kantian dualism between the
absolute necessity within the phenomenal world and the freedom
within the intelligible world. Schleiermacher also attempted to free

---

[1] A. Nygren, *Dogmatikens Vetenskapliga Grundläggning*, p. 61. For the same discussion in a later publication, See *Filosofi och Motivforskning*, article "Religionen
såsom Anschauung des Universums hos Schleiermacher," pp. 197–207.

himself from the Kantian dualism between the world of sense-experience and the world of reason. Kant maintained that a causal relationship existed within the phenomenal world, while moral freedom existed within the practical world. Schleiermacher dealt with this dualism by asking the following questions:

1. Is absolute necessity compatible with the moral life?
2. Is transcendental freedom compatible with a real event?

Schleiermacher answered the first question affirmatively. He concluded that necessity pervaded the practical area of experience just as it did the theoretical area. He proposed a conception of moral responsibility on the basis of the following principles:

1. the existence of a "moral impulse;"
2. the moral impulse equated with the determinative principle within man's moral decisions;
3. the moral impulse located within the Self.

Schleiermacher believed that the cause of moral action had to lie "within the totality of present impressions," or within the Self related to these impressions.[1] Schleiermacher was not satisfied with Kant's purely rationalistic ethic, but demanded that there be an emotional element in ethical decision. The purely rationalistic ethic could not be put into practice, he said, nor could it ever be realized. Schleiermacher's ethical determinism was not built upon a subjective starting point, but upon what he felt was the actual content of ethical action.

The second question was also answered in the affirmative. Transcendental freedom for Kant was not something negative such as "Abwesenheit einer Nöthigung" but was positive: "das Vermögen eine Reihe von selbst anzufangen." Schleiermacher denied freedom in the practical area of experience and maintained an ethical determinism. He referred the question of transcendental freedom to the theoretical sphere, and presupposed that there was an *Absolute* presupposed for a real event. At the same time he maintained that the question of freedom and necessity was answered from the viewpoint of both the theoretical and the practical areas of experience. Schleiermacher's solution to the dualism between necessity and freedom lay in the synthesis of absolute necessity with freedom. This conception was also of fundamental significance for his ethical system. He introduced, as we have seen earlier, the conception of spontaneity and growth in his discussion of the life of the human organism. Schleiermacher gave

---

[1] Cf. the analysis in Horace L. Friess, *Schleiermacher's Soliloquies*, (Chicago: The Open Court Publ. Co., 1926), p. xxxiff.

a place to transcendental freedom in his definition of a real event. He dealt not only with causal phenomena in the real event but also with its absolute presupposition, an Absolute, a thing-in-itself.

Kant's dualism included a separation between the thing-in-itself, the "Ding an sich," and the thing-in-phenomena, the "Die Erscheinung." The thing-in-itself was the necessary presupposition for "die Erscheinung," the thing-in-phenomenon. It was, therefore, *never* the object of our knowledge. Because the senses were bound to the a priori subjective forms of time and space, the object given to man in intuition was not the "Ding an sich" but "Erscheinungen," that is, the "Ding an sich" in relationship to the subject's mode of intuition. The thing-in-itself had reality in intuition only as phenomenon. It had to be thought of as non-empirical, similar to the "Noumenon," that is, it was never an object of one's intuition. But simply because something could be described as phenomenon, there had to be the possibility of thinking of the thing-in-itself. This was, however, never an object for our experience.

The Noumenon which could never be the object of knowledge because all experience was determined by the senses, led Kant to define the intuitive aspect of knowledge. In thought the object was given. This fact made knowledge of "das Noumenon" possible. Kant posed the problem of how one knew he belonged to the intelligible world, that is, how one could have objective knowledge of himself. The recognition of the "Ding an sich" required intellectual intuition, he said. When one defined himself as pure thought, he could never conclude that he was an object in himself, but only as one's own thought of himself as a self-active being. One knew himself as a self-active being, as intelligence, through pure self-consciousness, but because of the lack of intuition one could not come to an objective knowledge of oneself.

This then was Kant's dualism between "das Ding an sich" and "die Erscheinung," the latter receiving an objective quality from the former. The question then arose for Kant, if the thing-in-itself was never an object of our knowledge, but only a thing in intuition (the thing-in-itself in its relation to the subject's way of intuiting, "Die Erscheinung"), how could the thing in intuition represent a real object? Did it become therefore merely an illusion? For Kant the thing-in-itself, in its relation to the subject's way of intuiting, corresponded only to a real object when it was structured by the apriori categories of time and space, and ultimately by the "unity of conscious-

ness." "Das ding an sich" was defined therefore as the objective corre-
late to sense receptivity. The empirical intuition was determined by
"das Ding an sich," on the one hand, and on the other hand by the
"pure synthetic unity of apperception." It was this deeper dualism
between the "pure synthetic unity of apperception" and "das Ding an
sich" which was the background for the dualism between "die Erscheinung" and "das Ding an sich."

As we have seen, Schleiermacher began his study of Spinoza in
order to find a solution to the Kantian dualism. In *Kurze Darstellung
des spinozistischen System*, he revealed that he was in basic agreement
with Spinoza. For Spinoza, the Infinite was similar to the Unlimited,
and the Finite to the Limited. For Schleiermacher, this corresponded
to Kant's designation of "die Noumena" and "die Phänomene."
Schleiermacher found that Spinoza had overcome for him the Kantian
dualism between "die Noumena" and "die Phänomene." The Noumenon was at the same time the cause of Phenomenon (Kant) as the Infinite was the cause of the Finite (Spinoza). All of this meant that the
phenomenal world was included within the eternal (noumenal) world.
Now there was no possibility of a causal relationship between Noumena and Phenomena because causality was only valid within the phenomenal world. *Identity* was determinative for the relationship between
the Noumenal and the Phenomenal worlds, and as well, for the relationship between "das Ding an sich" and "die Erscheinung," the thing-
in-itself and the thing-in-intuition, the objective and the subjective.

In this way, Schleiermacher defined the principle of identity, or the
identification of subject and object. The Absolute was no longer the
thing-in-itself, because the objective had been included within the
subjective. The Absolute was instead this identity of subject and
object. The Kantian conception of the "Ding an sich" was rejected.

Schleiermacher's philosophy of identity was not the only foundation for his subsequent philosophical development, however.
Spinoza had enabled Schleiermacher to overcome the dualism in Kant
between "das Ding an sich" and "die Erscheinung" by means of the
philosophy of identity. The Kantian "Ding an sich" remained to help
Schleiermacher interpret Spinoza's *substance* as an irrational and
transcendental category, and not merely as a rational and immanental
category.

Kant, however, in his discussion of religion, was representative of
the Enlightenment and could find no unique place for religion in
man's experience. Religion became only an appendage to his moral

system. Schleiermacher, on the other hand, found a "necessary, independent, and universal" place for religion, and denied every attempt to base religion upon morality. Religion for Kant was not an autonomous experience. Schleiermacher considered autonomy to be the primary characteristic of religion. Kant could accept any real religious experience; Schleiermacher, on the other hand, based religion upon the experience of Absolute Reality. Kant conceived of natural religion as the ideal religion; positive religion was only an epiphenomenon. Schleiermacher did not recognize any natural or ideal religion. It was only the positive historical religions which had any meaning for him.[1]

Schleiermacher's philosophy of religion employed basically the critical method, observed Nygren. The philosophy of religion, therefore, had no other task than to investigate the religious experience in reference to its validity. Philosophy and the philosophy of religion had to become, "a critical theory of experience." Every phenomenon which appeared or made a claim to be a "valid experience" was the proper material for a critical philosophy. Its task was to investigate the "basis for the validity of every form of experience." Philosophy had to have a criterion by which it could distinguish between that which was valid and that which was not valid.[2] One had to have a sufficient and intimate knowledge of religion in order to be able to recognize its claim to be an autonomous experience. Religion had to be considered to be an independent entity, and it had to make a claim to be a universal experience.[3]

---

[1] Cf. Nygren's discussion in *Dogmatikens Vetenskapliga Grundläggning*, p. 62 ff. "Vill man verkligen komma till grunden med frågan, vad Kant betytt för Schleiermacher, och å andra sidan, vilken betydelse Schleiermacher har i den kritiska filosofiens sammanhang, kan svaret icke bliva något annat än detta: Schleiermacher står principiellt på kriticismens mark; han är enig med Kant, när denne anvisar en ny riktning åt filosofien och söker förvandla den från en dogmatisk till en kritisk disciplin, det vill med andra ord säga, när han avkläder filosofien dess gamla ontologisk-metafysiska syftning och i stället tillskriver den den kritiska uppgiften att undersöka den givna erfarenheten i alla dess olika former med hänsyn till deras giltighet."

[2] "... den måste vara i besittning av en måttstock, efter vilken varje företeelse, som höjer giltighetsanspråk, kan prövas, en metod, som är allmän och omfattande nog för att ej utesluta någon dylik företeelse från prövningen, men som å andra sidan är bestämd nog för att det som kan legitimeras enligt denna metod måste erkännas såsom giltig erfarenhetsform." DVG, p. 64.

[3] "Om han, såsom så ofta i religionsfilosofiens historia skett, utgår ifrån att religionen ej äger någon självständighet, att den icke är något sui generis, utan restlös kan återföras på andra erfarenhetsformer, vare sig den uppfattas såsom en avart av den metafysiska kunskapen eller etiken eller den betraktas såsom ett kombinationsfenomen, som saknar ursprunglig struktur, så finns det i intetdera fallet någon anledning att uppkasta frågan om religionens giltighet." DVG, p. 64.

Kant could not employ his critical philosophy in the area of religion. Religion, for Kant, was never a specific and independent form of experience, but was rather a derivative experience: an "appendage to morals." Therefore, if, in terms of Kant's point of view, religion did not possess an independent status, then the problem of the validity of an independent religious experience could never present itself. Religion was, therefore, only a modification or derivative of morals, and was never an independent *valid* experience.[1]

However, it was Schleiermacher in the history of thought, who introduced the conception that religion possessed an independent quality which was different from all of the other forms of experience. Nygren referred constantly to the *Reden* to support his claim that religion was an autonomous experience.[2]

Nygren had seen that Schleiermacher insisted upon religion's claim to be an independent and autonomous experience. Religion was, therefore, for Nygren, "an *original* and *independent* spiritual whole, which was governed by its own laws and which did not receive its existence from any other source, but which had its value in and of itself..." Nygren, of course, could make this statement because of Schleiermacher's influence upon his thinking.

Nygren observed also that Schleiermacher, in the *Reden*, emphasized the character of necessity and universality which belonged to

---

[1] Cf. also DVG, p. 68: "Hos Kant kunde det ej komma till någon kritisk religionsfilosofi, utan han måste på detta område stanna vid en kompromiss med upplysningstidens religionsfilosofi. Väl funnos hos honom den kritiska religionsfilosofiens två första premisser, den som rör den allmänfilosofiska kritiska problemställningen och den transcendental-kritiska problemlösningen." See also *Religiöst Apriori*, p. 218: "Kant, som för upplysningstidens talan; Schleiermacher, som i romantiken finner möjlighet till en ny ställning till religionen; Kant, som icke vill höra talas om religiös upplevelas och i varje sådan upplevelse spårar mysticismens faror; Schleiermacher, för vilken den religiösa upplevelsen träder i centrum; Kant, som ännu i grund och botten hyllar den naturliga religionen såsom den ena sanna religionen, som blott dunkelt kan spåras bakom de positiva religionernas omklädnad, och med rätta bords undantränga dessa; Schleiermacher, som icke vet av någon naturlig religion, utan hävdar, att all verklig religion är positiv."

[2] "Ihr Wesen ist weder Denken noch Handeln, sondern Anschauung und Gefühl. So behauptet sie ihr eigenes Gebiet und ihren eigenen Charakter nur dadurch, dass sie aus der der Spekulation sowohl als aus dem der Praxis gänzlich herausgeht, und indem sie sich neben beide hinstellt, wird erst das gemeinschaftliche Feld vollkommen ausgefüllt und die menschliche Natur von dieser Seite vollendet. Sie zeigt sich Euch als das notwendige und unentbehrliche Dritte zu jenen beiden, als natürliches Gegenstück, nicht geringer an Würde und Herrlichkeit." DVG, p. 66.

the religious experience.¹ Religion, for Schleiermacher, Nygren observed, became, in addition, an integrating factor in the life of man.²

Nygren concluded, therefore, that Kant had given philosophy the critical method, but that Schleiermacher had carried out the ramifications of the critical method in the philosophy of religion. "Kant is the father of critical philosophy, Schleiermacher the critical philosopher of religion par préférence."³

B. *Schleiermacher Carried Through Kant's Transcendental Method in the Area of Religion; that is, A Transcendental Deduction of the Religious Category was Effected.*

Nygren called Schleiermacher the first philosopher to attempt to carry out the implications of the transcendental method within the religious area.⁴ Schleiermacher's importance to the history of thought was his attempt to give religion an independent place within the life of man. This was the task Nygren assigned to the *Reden*.⁵ Religion possessed furthermore the characteristic of necessity.⁶ In the religious experience there was the feeling of necessity and compulsion, the consciousness of one's own passivity and, at the same time, of

---

¹ "Blott om religionen uppfattas såsom ett självständigt tredje vid sidan av metafysik och moral, så att den ej kan återföras på någon av dem, är det möjligt att påstå, att den är "das *notwendige und unendbehrliche* Dritte zu jenen beiden"." *Ibid.*, p. 67.

² "Spekulation und Praxis haben zu wollen ohne Religion, ist verwegener Übermut." Nygren can say in relation to this: "Religionen är ett så grundläggande moment i andelivet, att om den skulle bortfalla, andelivet självt vore omöjligt och måste prisgivas, och att i så fall icke heller något moment överhuvud i andelivet kan upprätthållas." DVG, p. 67.

³ "Vad Kant urfört på filosofiens övriga områden, det har Schleiermacher genomfört i religionsfilosofien. Kant är den kritiska filosofiens fader, men i religionsfilosofien är han ännu fången i den förkritiska åskådningen. Schleiermacher är den kritiske religionsfilosofen par préférence." DVG., p. 69.

⁴ Nygren quotes Carl Stange on this point: "Die epochemachende Bedeutung dieser Gedanken Schleiermachers besteht darin, dass er das methodische Prinzip des Kantischen Kritizismus nicht als ein bequemes Mittel zu apologetischen Zwecken in Anspruch nimmt, dass er vielmehr das erkenntnistheoretische Verfahren zu einer wissenschaftlichen Theorie von der religiösen Begriffsbildung ausgestaltet." *Religiöst Apriori*, p. 219.

⁵ "Dass sie aus dem Inneren jeder besseren Seele notwendig von selbst entspringt, dass ihr eine eigne Provinz im Gemüte angehört, in welcher sie unumschränkt herrscht, dass sie es würdig ist, durch ihre innerste Kraft die Edelsten und Vortrefflichsten zu bewegen und von ihnen ihrem innersten Wesen nach gekannt zu werden." Fr. Schleiermacher, *Reden über die Religion*, (1799), p. 37.

⁶ "Dass alles weiss ich und bin von einer innern und unwiderstehlichen Notwendigkeit, die mich göttlich beherrscht, gedrungen zu reden." *Ibid.*, p. 3.

being grasped from above.[1] Man's religious experience, Schleiermacher said, was his consciousness of the immediate influence of the universe upon him.[2] "Die Menschheit" was no longer an ethical category, but became a stage in the development to the Infinite.[3]

Schleiermacher spoke of those ideas which belonged to religion as the expression of that which was most truly human in life. The religious subject was a passive being in relationship to the Absolute.[4] Revelation became "every new and original intuition of the Universe" ("jede ursprüngliche und neue Anschauung des Universums").[5] Inspiration ("Einigung") was only the religious term for freedom.[6]

Prophecy ("die Weissagung") was related to the intuition of the universe.[7] The activity of Grace ("die Gnadenwirkungen") was expressed in a similar way to the activity of the universe and the passivity of the religious subject.[8] These religious concepts were characterized by:

1. They proceeded from the religious self-consciousness;

2. They were expressions for that which was specifically religious, the religious subject's sense of being grasped, his passivity, his dependence upon a higher transcendent Absolute;

3. They have the character of religious universality.[9]

---

[1] "Dass ich rede, rührt nicht her aus einem vernünftigen Entschlusse, auch nicht aus Hoffnung oder Furcht, noch geschieht es einem Endzwecke gemäss oder aus irgendeinem willkürlichen oder zufälligen Grunde: es ist die innere unwiderstehliche Notwendigkeit meiner Natur, es ist ein göttlicher Beruf, es ist das, was meine Stelle im Universum bestimmt, und mich zu dem Wesen macht, welches ich bin." *Ibid.*, p. 5.

[2] "... ist seiner Gefühle als unmittelbarer Einwirkungen des Universums bewusst." *Ibid.*, p. 120.

[3] "Sie ist nur ein Mittelglied zwischen dem einzelnen und dem einen, ein Ruheplatz auf dem Wege zum Unendlichen, und es müsste noch ein höherer Charakter gefunden werden im Menschen als seine Menschheit, um ihn und seine Erscheinung unmittelbar aufs Universum zu beziehen." *Ibid.*, p. 105; cf. also, p. 125.

[4] *Ibid.*, p. 120.

[5] *Ibid.*, p. 118.

[6] "... ist nur der religiöse Name für Freiheit. Jede freie Handlung, die eine religiöse Tat wird, jedes Wiedergeben einer religiösen Anschauung, jeder Ausdruck eines religiösen Gefühls, der sich wirklich mitteilt, so dass auch auf andre die Anschauung des Universums übergeht, war auf Eingebung geschehen; denn es war ein Handeln des Universums durch den einen auf die andern." *Ibid.*, p. 119.

[7] "Jedes Antizipieren der andern Hälfte einer religiösen Begebenheit, wenn die eine gegeben ist, ist eine Weissagung." *Ibid.*

[8] "Alle religiösen Gefühle sind übernatürlich, denn sie sind nur insofern religiös, als sie durchs Universum unmittelbar gewirkt sind, und ob sie religiös sind in jemand, das muss er doch am besten beurteilen." *Ibid.*

[9] *Ibid.*, p. 120.

The insight gained from the religious self-consciousness led to self-communication.[1] This communication created the religious community, the Church.

Religion was related in a negative way to metaphysics and morals. Ethics understood the Absolute as immanent in terms of the feeling of freedom. The transcendent conception of the Absolute was based upon the knowledge of the Absolute as a metaphysical reality. Therefore, religion had to be kept separate from metaphysics and morals.[2]

Religion was sharply separated from metaphysics and morals.[3] Even if religion had the same object as metaphysics and morals, that is, "the universe and man's relationship to it," religion had to deal with this object in an entirely different way from metaphysics.[4] Religion was never an objective knowledge of the universe. Religion was immediate experience.[5] Events in the world were manifestations of God.[6]

Religion was sharply differentiated from the Kantian-Fichtean system of morality, in which morality was "a system of duties which ordered and prohibited action with unlimited power." This ethic effected "the uniform repetition of a highest Ideal" ("die einförmige Wiederholung eines höchsten Ideals").[7] Kant's system of morality had always placed sense-experience in opposition to reason. Religion,

---

[1] "Wie sollte er gerade die Einwirkungen des Universums für sich behalten, die ihm als das grösste und unwiderstehlichste erscheinen? Wie sollte er gerade das in sich festhalten wollen, was ihn am stärksten aus sich heraustreibt, und ihm nichts so sehr einprägt als dieses, dass er sich selbst aus sich allein nicht erkennen kann? Sein erstes Bestreben ist es vielmehr, wenn eine religiöse Ansicht ihm klar geworden ist oder ein frommes Gefühl seine Seele durchdringt, auf den Gegenstand auch andere hinzuweisen und die Schwingungen seines Gemüts womöglich auf die fortzupflanzen." *Ibid.*, p. 178.

[2] "Ihr Wesen ist weder Denken noch Handeln, sondern Anschauung und Gefühl;" *Ibid.*, p. 50; "So behauptet sie ihr eigenes Gebiet und ihren eigenen Charakter nur dadurch, dass sie aus dem der Spekulation sowohl, als aus dem der Praxis gänzlich herausgeht, und indem sie sich neben beide hinstellt, wird erst das gemeinschaftliche Feld vollkommen ausgefüllt und die menschliche Natur von dieser Seite vollendet." *Ibid.*, p. 52.

[3] *Ibid.* cf. Schleiermacher's discussion of religion and metaphysics, p. 34, 58, 145 ff.; morals, p. 31, 34, 63, 68 ff., 107, 219, 222.

[4] "...diesen Stoff ganz anders behandeln, ein anderes Verhältnis der Menschen zu demselben ausdrücken oder bearbeiten, eine andere Verfahrungsart oder ein anderes Ziel haben;". *Reden* (1799), p. 42.

[5] "Anschauen will sie das Universum, in seinen eigenen Darstellungen und Handlungen will sie es andächtig belauschen, von seinen unmittelbaren Einflüssen will sie sich in kindlicher Passivität ergreifen und erfüllen lassen." *Ibid.*, p. 50.

[6] "Alle Begebenheiten in der Welt als Handlungen eines Gottes verstellen, das ist Religion." *Ibid.*, p. 57.

[7] *Ibid.*, p. 92.

Schleiermacher insisted, had nothing in common with this.[1] Religion, instead, asserted that man was a unity. Therefore, the ethical system which had relevance for religion included the positive freedom which unified sense-experiences and reason, and the Self and Nature.[2]

But if religion was not to be identified with metaphysics and morals, what then was its nature? Schleiermacher's idea of religion, as we have seen, centered about the conception of "Anschauen des Universums," which was "die allgemeinste und höchste Formel der Religion."[3] Religion as "Auschauen des Universums" expressed the absolute unity (that is, Kant's "Ding an sich" and the unity of consciousness) as *subjective;* that is, immanent in consciousness, and *objective;* that is, transcendent to the given thing. Religion was the synthesis of this double aspect of man's consciousness. As we have seen, however, religion was also defined as "Gefühl."[4] "Anschauung" was the presupposition for "Gefühl," and "Gefühl" the presupposition for "Anschauung."[5]

Religion, furthermore, was a *necessary* experience.[6] Schleiermacher's conception of religion was not related to a psychological interpretation of religion, although the starting point for a definition of religion was the religious experience itself. The necessary character of religion had been indicated already by its negative relationship to metaphysics and morals. Religion was, for Schleiermacher, "something unique" ("etwas Eigenes").[7] Religion was "an other way of proceeding" in relation to metaphysics and morals. Metaphysics concerned itself with the ultimate nature of man ("geht aus von der endlichen Natur des Menschen"),[8] morals with the consciousness of freedom ("geht vom Bewusstsein der Freiheit aus"),[9] religion with the ability to see the infinite in all particularity and finitude

---

[1] Schleiermacher said: "Ich aber setze hinzu, dass es auch die grösste Verachtung gegen die Religion beweiset, sie in ein anderes Gebiet verpflanzen zu wollen, dass sie da diene und arbeite. Auch herrschen möchte sie nicht in einem fremden Reiche;". *Ibid.*, p. 35.

[2] *Ibid.*, p. 15.

[3] *Ibid.*, p. 55 ff., 86.

[4] "... bei denen das Universum der eine, und auf irgendeine Art euer eignes Ich der andere von den Punkten ist, zwischen denen das Gemüt schwebt." *Ibid.*, p. 111.

[5] "Nur die Anschauungen und Gefühle kann ich euch vergegenwärtigen, die sich aus solchen Momenten entwickeln." *Ibid.*, p. 108 ff., pp. 74–75.

[6] *Ibid.*, p. 75.

[7] *Ibid.*, p. 47.

[8] *Ibid.*, p. 52.

[9] *Ibid.*, p. 51.

("will im Menschen nicht weniger als in allen andern Einzelnen und Endlichen das Unendliche sehen").[1]

Religion was designated as "eine hochste Philosophie,"[2] and was the presupposition for the different aspects which made up man's spiritual life. Schleiermacher called his listeners to share in the fullest expression of the cultural life by means of religion.[3] However, religion was not only related to the spiritual life, but was also the necessary presupposition for metaphysics and morals.[4] In the positive relationship to metaphysics and morals, there could be found the transcendental deduction of religion. Religion became, therefore, the transcendental presupposition for metaphysics and morals.

In *Der christliche Glaube*, Nygren observed that Schleiermacher had accentuated the fact that the character of religion was a *necessary* form of experience. He found this most clearly expressed in Schleiermacher's designation of "Lehnsäze aus der Ethik."[5] Schleiermacher assigned to consciousness the specific area in which religion was to be located. Religion was not knowledge or action but a condition of Feeling, or the "sense of immediate self-consciousness."

Religion, however, was not to be defined simply as "Gefühl," but as "unmittelbares Selbstbewusstsein." The "Selbstbewusstsein" which was religiously oriented could not be mediated by knowledge or action or by any other kind of activity. Self-consciousness was always "unmittelbares Selbstbewusstsein." Therefore, religion formed the deepest layer of the Self and supported all of the different moments of the Self.

Immediate self-consciousness, which was equated with religion, was defined by Schleiermacher in such a way that it was distinct from all other possible experience.[6] However, if the feeling of dependence

---

[1] *Ibid.*

[2] *Ibid.*, p. 45.

[3] "Aber ich bitte euch, wendet ihr euch dann zu ihnen, wenn ihr den innersten Zusammenhang und den höchsten Grund jener Heiligtümer der Menschheit aufdecken wollt, wenn der Begriff und das Gefühl, das Gesetz und die Tat bis zu ihrer gemeinschaftlichen Quelle sollen verfolgt und das Wirkliche als ewig und im Wesen der Menschheit notwendig gegründet soll dargestellt werden." *Ibid.*, p. 19.

[4] "Spekulation und Praxis haben zu wollen ohne Religion, ist verwegener Übermut, es ist freche Feindschaft gegen die Götter, es ist der unheilige Sinn des Prometheus, der feigherzig stahl, was er in ruhiger Sicherheit hätte fordern und erwarten können." *Ibid.*, p. 52.

[5] Fr. Schleiermacher, *Der christliche Glaube*, (1830), Par. 2:3.

[6] Schleiermacher said: "In jedem Selbstbewusstsein sind zwei Elemente, ein um so zu sagem – Sichselbstsezen und ein Sichselbstnichtsogeszthaben, oder ein Sein und ein Irgendwiegewordensein." *Ibid.*, Par. 4:1.

were to disappear, self-consciousness in all of the forms in which we know it would disappear.[1]

As the feeling of dependence was the expression for the receptive side of self-consciousness, so the feeling of freedom was the expression for the active side of self-consciousness. Both of these were necessary for our consciousness of the world.

Schleiermacher had demonstrated that there could be no feeling of absolute freedom, but only the feeling of dependence which showed itself to be Absolute.[2] Therefore, Schleiermacher had deduced the feeling of absolute dependence as that which was most characteristic for Religion. This feeling of absolute dependence was equated with the consciousness of standing "in the relationship with God."[3] The transcendental deduction was now completed.[4]

Nygren had seen that Schleiermacher's conception of the feeling of absolute dependence had demonstrated the valid religious experience.[5] Nygren found that the nature of the valid religious experience was expressed in an extremely cogent manner in *Der christliche Glaube*.[6]

---

[1] "Könnten wir uns das Zusammensein mit anderem wegdenken, uns selbst aber übrigens so wie wir sind: so wäre kein Selbstbewusstsein möglich, welches überwiegend ein Afficirtsein der Empfänglichkeit aussagte, sondern dann könnte jedes nur Selbstthätigkeit aussagen, welche aber auch, auf keinen Gegenstand bezogen, nur ein Hervortretenwollen, eine unbestimmte Agilität ohne Gestalt und Farbe wäre ... Zu diesen Säzen kann die Zustimmung unbedingt gefordert werden." *Ibid.*

[2] "... eben das unsere gesamte Selbstthätigkeit, also auch, weil diese niemals Null ist, unser ganzes Dasein begleitende, schlechthinige Freiheit verneinende, Selbstbewusstsein ist schon an und für sich ein Bewusstsein schlechthiniger Abhängigkeit, denn es ist das Bewusstsein, dass unsere ganze Selbstthätigkeit eben so von anderwärtzher ist, wie dasjenige ganz von uns her sein musste, in Bezug worauf wir ein schlechthiniges Freiheitsgefühl haben zollten." *Ibid.*, Par. 4:3.

[3] "dass sich schlechthin abhängig fühlen und sich seiner selbst als in Beziehung mit Gott bewisst Sein." *Ibid.*, Par. 4:4.

[4] "När sålunda den absoluta avhängighetskänslan såsom oskiljaktig från självmedvetandet och såsom ett i varje dess akt tillika innehållet moment är ådagalagd såsom nödvändig och allmängiltig, och när vidare just detta moment är uppvisat såsom det för religionen karaktäristiska momentet, så är härmed den transcendentala deduktionen slutförd." *Religiöst Apriori*, p. 223.

[5] "Schleiermacher så klart som möjligt giver tillkänna, att den absoluta avhängighetskänslan icke blott skall tjäna som psykologisk omskrivning för religionens väsen och på så sätt tjäna såsom legitimation och giltighetsbevis för religionen." *Religiöst Apriori*, p. 223.

[6] "Die Anerkennung, dass dieses schlechthinige Abhängigkeitsgefühl nicht etwas zufälliges ist noch auch etwas persönlich verschiedenes, sondern ein allgemeines Lebenselement, ersezt für die Glaubenslehre vollständig alle sogenannten Beweise für das Dasein Gottes.... Man kann nicht das postulirte Selbstbewusstsein in dem beschriebenen Inhalt zugeben, und doch behaupten wollen dass es etwas

In Schleiermacher's *Dialektik*, Nygren found the same basic presuppositions for religion expressed. Dialectics had to distinguish those ideas which possessed validity from the great multitude of psychologically oriented ideas. But Dialectics had to concern itself primarily with the principles of knowledge and its highest presuppositions.[1] Schleiermacher's Dialectics had the same starting point, observed Nygren, as critical philosophy.[2] Schleiermacher, however, had already observed this, Nygren acknowledged.[3] Similar to a philosophy of Identity, Schleiermacher selected the "Absolute" as the highest principle of knowledge. The Absolute united thought and being, the ideal and the real.[4] The method Schleiermacher employed to perform the task of uniting these distinct concepts was the transcendental method. Nygren concluded that Schleiermacher had demonstrated that without this "original knowledge" ("die jedem Wissen notwendig einwohnende Form des Wissens"), there could not be any knowledge.[5]

Schleiermacher, according to Nygren, had thereby demonstrated the usefulness of the transcendental deduction of religion for the philosophy of religion. Schleiermacher believed that he could show that without the recognition of the religious presupposition as a necessary presupposition there could be no such thing as knowledge.[6]

---

unwesentliches sei d.h. dass es in einem menschlichen Dasein vorkommen könne und auch nicht, je nachdem der Mensch im Verlauf seines Lebens mit diesem oder mit jenem zusammentrifft... Dass aber das schlechthinige Abhängigkeitsgefühl an und für sich auch in Allen dasselbe ist, und nicht in dem Einen so in dem Andern anders, folgt schon daraus, dass es nicht auf irgend einer bestimmten Modification des menschlichen Daseins beruht, sondern auf dem schlechthin gemeinsamen Wesen des Menschen, welches die Möglichkeit aller jener Differenzen in sich schliesst, durch welche der besondere Gehalt der einzelnen Persönlichkeit bestimmt wird." *Religiöst Apriori*, p. 223; quoted from *Der christliche Glaube*, Par. 33.

[1] "Dialektik muss irgend wie die Prinzipien des Philosophierens enthalten." *Dialektik*, p. 2.

[2] Nygren observes "fastmer vill han pröva de förutsättningar, varpå de olika systemen vila, och överhuvud undersöka, på vilka väg, under vilka förutsättningar och inom vilka gränser man kan nå fram till något verkligt vetande." DVG, p. 75.

[3] "Es wäre daher gut, das Unternehmen, das Wissen als System aufzustellen, noch ruhn zu lassen. Diesem gegenüber tritt das Andere, eine Kunstlehre desselben aufzustellen, d.h. Methode, wie im Denken verfahren werden muss, damit es ausserhalb des Streites falle oder in der Richtung zur Auflösung des Streites liege." DVG., p. 75, quoted from *Dialektik*, p. 22.

[4] DVG., p. 77.

[5] *Ibid.*, p. 78.

[6] Nygren poses this question, "Vad måste alltså den, som sin plikt likmätigt vill vetandet, förutsätta med avseende på tänkandet? Han måste i sista hand förutsätta det absoluta, det religiösa gudsmedvetandet." *Ibid.*, p. 79.

Schleiermacher's *Dialectics* made this point very clearly.[1] Therefore, Nygren concluded that religion was the "ground category," and the presupposition for all knowledge. Schleiermacher did not include only knowledge within this designation, but also the functions of the will, "which lead back to the same transcendental religious presupposition." The idea of God was the transcendental presupposition for knowledge and will, which was realized only in religion.[2] It was at this point, said Nygren, that *Dialektik* pointed to *Der christliche Glaube*. When philosophy had performed the task of demonstrating the necessary and transcendental character of the "ground category" of religion, the next task was the theological one; that is, to demonstrate how the "ground category" was realized in religion.[3]

Nygren summarized the *Dialektik* by saying that it demonstrated

---

[1] "Das philosophische Bestreben will das Bewusstsein Gottes rein für sich haben, und es genügt ihm, sich desselben an und für sich als einer notwendigen Voraussetzung bewusst zu sein, so dass es jedem nachweisen kann so gewiss man wissen wolle, so gewiss bedürfe man dieser Voraussetzung des Absoluten, in welcher allein das Wissen begründet und aus welcher allein die Regeln für das Wissen abzuleiten seien." "So gewiss wir die Idee des Wissens nicht aufgeben können, ebenso gewiss müssen wir auch dieses Ursein, in welchem der Gegensatz zwischen Begriff und Gegenstand aufgehoben ist, voraussetzen, aber ohne ein wirkliches Denken darüber vollziehen zu können." "Das Transcendente ist dasjenige, was wir niemals unmittelbar anschauen, sondern dessen wir uns nur als eines notwendig anzunehmenden bewusst werden können. … Also können wir auch nicht sagen, dass wir die Identität jener höchsten Differenz wissen, sondern wir setzen sie nur voraus zum Behuf des Wissens. Will man sagen, dass wir sie nur glauben und um des Wissens willen glauben müssen, so lassen wir uns das in dem Sinne des Wortes gefallen, in welchem es auch auf dem religiösen Gebiete vorkommt, wo es eine Gewissheit bezeichnet, die der letzte Grund aller Tätigkeit ist, denn die Annahme ist hier der Grund alles Wissens … Wir haben also hier den Grund des Wissens und Seins hinter dem Wissen und Sein gefunden, aber wir können ihn weder in Gedanken fassen noch das im Wissen dargestellte Sein aus ihm Ableiten." *Ibid.*, p. 80; quoted from *Dialektik*, p. 153, 145, 78 ff.

[2] DVG., p. 82.

[3] "Das unmittelbare Selbstbewusstsein ist nicht nur im Übergange; sondern sofern Denken auch Wollen ist und umgekehrt, muss es auch in jedem Moment sein. Und so finden wir auch das Gefühl als beständig jeden Moment, sei es nun vorherrschend denkend oder wollend, immer begleitend. Es scheint zu verschwinden, wenn wir ganz in einer Anschauung oder in einer Handlung aufgehen; aber es scheint nur. Es ist aber immer nur begleitend."
"Die Idee der Gottheit ist der transcendentale terminus a quo, und das Prinzip der Möglichkeit des Wissens an sich. … Sie liegt allem einzelnen Wissen, welches ohne sie nicht könnte vollzogen werden, auf gleiche Weise zum Grunde." "Der Parallelismus des Seins und Denkens führt schon auf ein absolut höchstes Sein… Das absolut höchste Sein und Denken in Seiner Identität ist nicht ein blosses Postulat, sondern es ist in jedem einzelnen Akt des Wissens das allein Reale und Gewisse." *Ibid.*, p. 83, 88. Quoted from *Dialektik*, p. 429.

that the recognition of the Absolute or the consciousness of God was a necessary presupposition for knowledge."[1]

Schleiermacher, unfortunately, according to Nygren, had "given his allegiance to a foreign philosophy of identity." Nygren found that Schleiermacher's failure at this point was due to "a confusion between an epistemology and an ontology." The transcendental method was the means by which one searched critically for the basic principles underlying all experience. Schleiermacher, according to Nygren, had confused the critical method with an uncritical philosophy of Identity. However, Schleiermacher could still be of some service, said Nygren, because he presented the correct problem for the contemporary philosopher of religion.[2] Schleiermacher discovered that the Absolute was the transcendental and necessary presupposition for knowledge and morality, and for knowledge and will. These constitutive elements of man's being were constructed upon "the idea of God." Therefore, for Schleiermacher, all experience, in its entirety, was dependent upon "the idea of God."[3]

II. NYGREN'S INTERPRETATION AND USE OF SCHLEIERMACHER'S CRITICAL METHODOLOGY

Schleiermacher, in his work, *Kurze Darstellung des theologischen Studiums*, presented what he believed to be the proper task of the Philosophy of Religion:[4]

1. To demonstrate in a "purely scientific way" the possible forms in

---

[1] DVG., p. 84.

[2] "Men om ock dialektikens transcendentala deduktion av religionen på grund härav måste betecknas såsom i grunden förfelad, så har dock detta Schleiermachers försök sin stora betydelse därigenom att han insett uppgiftens vikt och med så oöverträfflig klarhet och konsekvens uppställt problemet. Med lösningen må det förhålla sig huru som helst – att hava funnit och för första gången uppställt den moderna religionsfilosofiens grundproblem samt att hava pekat på den enda för dess lösning användbara metoden, den transcendentala metoden, är Schleiermachers ovanskliga förtjänst." *Ibid.*, p. 87.

[3] Schleiermacher expresses it this way: "Gott ist uns also als Bestandteil unseres Wesens gegeben. Das uns eingeborene Sein Gottes in uns konstituiert unser eigentliches Wesen, denn ohne Ideen und ohne Gewissen würden wir zum Tierischen herabsinken." DVG., p. 89. Quoted from *Dialektik*, p. 155.

[4] "auf welche Weise und in welchem Mass die eine (soil. fromme Gemeinschaft) von der andern verschieden sein kann, imgleichen, wie sich auf diese Differenzen das Eigentümliche der geschichtlich gegebenen Glaubensgenossenschaften bezieht." KD, Par. 23; cf. Par. 32.

which the different religious communities could express themselves,
that is to present the a priori;

2. To fix, in an empirical way, the historical uniqueness of the religious community, that is to present the a posteriori, that which was
given in the religious experience;

3. To place the a posteriori in relation to the a priori.

According to Schleiermacher, the critical method had the task of
relating the aposteriori to the apriori, the speculative and the ideal to
the empirical and the real.

Schleiermacher used the critical method in his *Apologetics* in which
he dealt with philosophical theology. Philosophical theology had the
task to present the essence of Christianity.[1] Philosophical theology had
to take as its starting point the Christian community, but it did so "in
the universal sense of the religious or believing community" ("in dem
allgemeinen Begriff der frommen oder Glaubensgemeinschaft").[2]
However, *Apologetics* dealt with the aposteriori element in the Christian
faith, that is, the conception of how the Christian faith expressed itself
in history.

The critical method was discussed in Schleiermacher's *Polemics*.
Polemics was the third discipline alongside of the Philosophy of Religion and Apologetics. Polemics presented the correspondence which
existed between the essence of Christianity and the historical forms of
Christianity.[3] The task of philosophy within Polemics was to demonstrate the congruence or divergence between the essence of the
Christian faith and its historical forms. Philosophy, therefore, had to
be "critical" philosophy. The critical method within Polemics was
therefore the same as it was within the Philosophy of Religion and
Apologetics, that is, it had as its task to relate the apriori to the
aposteriori.

Schleiermacher, therefore, employed the critical method within the
Philosophy of Religion, Apologetics, and Polemics, and believed that
it could be used wherever philosophy related itself to "Religions-

---

[1] "Da das eigentümliche Wesen des Christentums sich ebensowenig rein
wissenschaftlich konstruieren lässt, als es bloss empirisch aufgefasst werden kann:
so lässt es sich nur kritisch bestimmen durch Gegeneinanderhalten dessen, was
im Christentum geschichtlich gegeben ist, und der Gegensätze, vermöge deren
fromme Gemeinschaften können voneinander verschieden sein." *Ibid.*, Par. 32.

[2] *Ibid.*, Par. 33.

[3] "Wie sich irgend ein geschichtlich gegebener Zustand des Christentums zu
der Idee desselben verhält, das bestimmt sich nicht allein durch den Inhalt dieses
Zustandes, sondern auch durch die Art, wie er geworden ist." *Ibid.*, Par. 34.

wissenschaft." However, Schleiermacher did not define in a narrow way the tasks of philosophy and theology, but included Practical and Historical Theology within the total task of theology.[1] Schleiermacher asserted that the critical method provided the necessary philosophical presuppositions for the contemporary theological task.[2]

In the *Dialektikvorlesungen* of 1831, Schleiermacher contributed a new understanding of the apriori and the transcendental.[3] The transcendental was defined as that which preceded experience and was identical with the apriori. He identified, furthermore, "transcendentale Philosophie" with "Metaphysik."[4] He presupposed the relationship of "das transcendentale" to "das formale," that is, the relationship of Metaphysics to Logic. Philosophy, in the transcendental sense, related knowledge to being ("Feststellung des Wissens in Beziehung auf das Sein") and in a formal sense unified all knowledge ("Feststellung der Verknüpfung alles Wissens").[5]

---

[1] KD, Par. 31; "In dieser Trilogie, philosophische, historische und praktische Theologie, ist das ganze theologische Studium beschlossen." cf. also, Par. 28; "Die historische Theologie ist sonach der eigentliche Körper des theologischen Studiums, welcher durch die philosophische Theologie mit der eigentlichen Wissenschaft, und durch die praktische mit dem tätigen christlichen Leben zusammenhängt.", and Par. 27; "Wenn die historische Theologie jeden Zeitpunkt in seinem wahren Verhältnis zu der Idee des Christentums darstellt: so ist sie zugleich nicht nur die Begründung der praktischen, sondern auch die Bewährung der philosophischen Theologie." It is striking that in the term "jeder Zeitpunkt", the empirical, *das Aposteriorische*, is designated, and also "die Idee des Christentums", *das Apriorische* is used. The task of historical theology is not to present the *Idee des Christentums* but it is to employ the critical method, that is, to place the aposteriori element in relation to the apriori. Historical theology is "der eigentliche Körper des Theologischen Studiums", and is determined by the critical method to have a scientific and methodological function. Schleiermacher is, of course, in his *Kurze Darstellung des Theologischen Studiums* employing Kant in the area of theology in which Kant himself did not use the critical method.

[2] Cf. the following references where this is so: SW. III:4, 2, p. 23 ff.; KD, Erste Aufl., p. 11, Par. 1 and 2; Zweite Aufl., Par. 27, 35.

[3] "Man hat ... einen Unterschied gemacht zwischen transcendent und transcendental, von dem wir aber ganz abstrahieren. Das Denken welches wir hier suchen, geht über jede mögliche bestimmte Erfahrung und jedes mögliche bestimmte Denken hinaus, und darum nennen wir es transzendental." SW. III:4, 2, p. 385.

[4] "Logik, formale Philosophie, ohne Metaphysik, transcendentale Philosophie, ist keine Wissenschaft"; "Metaphysik ohne Logik kann keine Gestalt gewinnen als eine willkührliche und fantastische." SW. III:4, 2, p. 7.

[5] SW. III:4, 2, p. 33; cf. the following statements indicating Schleiermacher's relation to Kant: "Der Begriff des Dinges ist aber eben der ursprüngliche Zusammenhang zwischen Begriff und Sein, der Begriff des Geistes das Subject des Wissens ... Und die Idee der Gottheit ist doch nur der letzte Grund für das Wesen des Geistes und des Dinges und der Grund des Zusammenhanges beider."; "Kant polemeirte wol gegen die Metaphysik, ging aber doch davon aus, das eigentliche

Schleiermacher found that "final knowledge" ("das letzte Wissen"), that is, "die Idee von Gott als der Indifferenz des Dinges" was basically in accord with the Kantian critical philosophy.[1] But he became aware also of "the discernible modern fact" ("das unterscheidende moderne Factum")[2] of "the difference between constitutive and regulative principles" ("den Unterschied zwischen constitutiven und regulativen Principien"). Schleiermacher's interest and emphasis was different from Kant's, in that he made "die Idee der Gottheit" both the regulative (formal) and the constitutive (real) principle.[3] If "die Idee der Gottheit" is denied as the presupposition for all knowledge, then the idea of knowledge itself must also be denied.[4] If this is denied, then reason itself must be denied.[5] The fault that Schleiermacher found in Kant's critique of reason was that Kant had not found a necessary place for "die Idee der Gottheit" within reason, and had given it only an ancillary significance. Schleiermacher believed that the obvious conclusion of the Kantian critique was that "die Idee der Gottheit" must have, in addition to the *regulative* function in Ethics and Practical Philosophy, a *constitutive* function in knowledge and in Philosophy as a whole.[6] Schleiermacher, in other words, wished to bridge the gulf between Kant's theoretical and practical philosophies.

Wissen sei Uebereinstimmung des Denkens mit dem Sein, und zeigte nur, dass jene Art dies klar zu machen, nämlich das Wesen des Geistes als Subject und das Wesen des Dinges als Object in ein organisirtes Wissen auseinander zu legen, nichts tauge, denn das letzte Wissen sei nicht hinter sondern im realen Wissen." SW III:4, 2, p. 33 ff.

[1] SW. III:4, 2, p. 17. Schleiermacher refers specifically to the older metaphysics of Locke and Hume, cf. SW. III:4, 2, p. 16, 33 ff.

[2] "Ein positives Einlenken muss sich an das alte anschliessen mit beständigem Festhalten des unterscheidenden modernen Factum. Also das einwohnende Sein Gottes als das Princip alles Wissens, aber dieses Princip nicht anders haben wollen als in der Construction des realen Wissens." SW. III:4, 2, p. 17.

[3] "Die Idee der Gottheit könnte nicht regulativ sein, Princip des formalen, und zwar nicht bloss im Handeln sondern auch im Denken, wenn sie nicht constitutiv wäre." SW. III:4, 2, p. 171 ff.

[4] "Wenn und jemand die Idee des Wissens leugnet, können wir ihm auch nur zeigen, dass er die Vernunft mit leugnen müsse." SW. III:4, 2, p. 172.

[5] "Allein Kant hat den Ort der Idee der Gottheit und den Zusammenhang ihres Seins in der Vernunft nicht nachgewiesen, sondern er nimmt die Idee nur als er weiss nicht wie gegeben." SW. III:4, 2, p. 172.

[6] Cf. SW. III:4, 2, p. 48, "dem Correspondiren des Denkens und Seins"; cf. also SW. III:4, 2, p. 568 ff.; "Nun aber kennen wir alle als eine schon von je bei uns vorgekommene Thatsache das mit dem Denken über das Denken hinausgehen und es auf ein anderes beziehen, welches wir das Sein nennen, und welches sich uns von unseren Denkarten unzertrennlich von Anfang an ergiebt als das

"Die Idee des Wissens" was constructed by Schleiermacher in such a way that it corresponded to "ein Sein dem Wissen." There was, therefore, an opposition within Being itself.[1] Schleiermacher could speak of the "natural forms," which related to physics, and the "moral forms" which related to ethics. However, just as he presupposed a transcendental "ground" for the unity of *knowledge* in *being*, so he had to presuppose a transcendental ground for the union of *will* in *being*. These transcendental "grounds" could not be different, but had to be one and the same.[2] Because the transcendental "grounds" for theoretical knowledge and practical activity were one and the same, they appeared "in the relative identity of thought and will, that is, in feeling" ("in der relativen Identität des Denkens und Wollens, nämlich im Gefühl").[3] When "Gefühl" is religious, Schleiermacher wrote, "then religion stands over philosophy."[4] It was at this point that religion was defined by Schleiermacher as "the feeling of God ("Gefühl von Gott"),[5] and received the designation as the transcendental presupposition for all philosophy.[6]

Schleiermacher had identified the transcendental grounds of theoretical knowledge ("Denken") and practical activity ("Wollen") with "Gefühl," and had come to this conclusion in a "purely philosophical manner." The method he employed was the critical method, that is, the method which unified the apriori and the transcendental with the aposteriori and the empirical. The apriori never appeared as an empirical reality, but was "a higher knowledge in all real knowledge"

---

von aussen her zu unsern Affectionen mitwirkende und von unserm Heraustreten nach aussen leidende."

[1] On the one hand it "dasjenige (Sein), welches dem Denken vorangeht, in wiefern das Denken nur Betrachtung ist", on the other "dasjenige, welches auf das Denken folgt, in sofern das Denken ein Wollen ausdrückt." SW. III:4, 2, p. 148.

[2] SW. III:4, 2, p. 180. This transcendental ground is "die rein transcendentale Identität des idealen und realen." *Ibid.*

[3] Cf. SW. III:4, 2, p. 150, 151.

[4] SW. III:4, 2, p. 152. "Es ist aber nicht so" ... "wir sind hieher gekommen, ohne von dem Gefühl ausgegangen zu sein, auf rein philosophischem Wege." SW. III:4, 2, p. 152.

[5] SW. III:4, 2, p. 152.

[6] Schleiermacher calls this "die Anschauung Gottes", cf. "Die Anschauung Gottes wird nie wirklich vollzogen, sondern bleibt nur indirecter Schematismus. Dagegen ist sie unter dieser Form völlig rein von allem fremdartigen." *Ibid.*, and also "Das religiöse Gefühl ist zwar ein wirklich vollzogenes aber es ist nie rein, denn das Bewusstsein Gottes ist darin immer an einem anderen; nur an einem einzelnen ist man sich der Totalität, nur an einem Gegensatz (zwischen dem eigen Sein und dem ausser uns gesetzten) ist man sich der Einheit bewusst." *Ibid.*

("ein höheres Wissen in allem realen Wissen").[1] Schleiermacher found in "the God-idea" not only a *regulative* but a *constitutive* principle, that is, the transcendental identity of the ideal and the real.

How then does Nygren interpret Schleiermacher? Nygren had seen that Schleiermacher's *Dialektik* was similar to the Kantian transcendental critical method.[2] The transcendental deduction was a deduction which demonstrated what must be valid in order to have validity as a whole.[3] Nygren used the expression "the transcendental deduction" as synonymous with "the critical method." Nygren wanted to employ the transcendental deduction to demonstrate the formal and logical connection between the idea of validity and knowledge, that is, to demonstrate "that which must be present in all knowledge if knowledge is to be valid."[4] Schleiermacher had, however, in his philosophical system, defined all philosophy as "that which belongs to metaphysical or transcendental philosophy" (i.e. "Feststellung des Wissens in Beziehung auf das Sein"), and as "that which belongs to logic or formal philosophy" ("Feststellung der Verknüpfung alles Wissens"). The unity of these two functions of philosophy resulted in a unified scientific and critical system. Nygren's definition of the basic philosophical task, as the formal and logical demonstration of the validity of knowledge had no basis in Schleiermacher's own *Dialektik*.[5]

Nygren, furthermore, in reference to the problem in Schleiermacher of the relationship between the philosophical "Gottesidee" and the religious consciousness, misunderstood Schleiermacher's intention.[6] Schleiermacher did not treat religion in such a way that it had to be

---

[1] SW. III:4, 2, p. 152. This transcendental presupposition is "Grund der Zusammenstimmung unseres Wollens zum Sein, dass nämlich unser Thun wirklich ausser uns hinausgeht, und dass das äussere Sein für die Vernunft empfänglich auch das ideale Gepräge unseres Willens aufnimmt." SW. III:4, 2, p. 150.

[2] The apriori, "die jenseits aller Erfahrung liegende Voraussetzung alles Wissens und Handelns" or "die Gottesidee als die transzendentale Identität des Idealen und Realen", that is, "die Anschauung Gottes" was, according to Schleiermacher, "nie wirklich vollzogen". DVG, p. 70; cf. p. 75, also p. 72; cf. also *Religiöst Apriori*, p. 207.

[3] DVG., p. 73.

[4] *Ibid.*, p. 79.

[5] This is Nygren's "free construction" of Schleiermacher's thought as he called it. Much of Nygren's confusion rests upon his misunderstanding of Schleiermacher's use of the critical method. Schleiermacher orients his philosophy about both the logical and formal and the metaphysical and transcendental. Nygren insists upon the problem of the logical and formal proofs for validity.

[6] DVG., p. 69–91: Chapter, "Dialektikens transcendentala deduktion av religionen".

valid in order for there to be validity at all ("die Idee des Wissens"). However, Nygren interpreted him in this way.[1] Schleiermacher oriented his discussion about the idea of God, but he did so by means of a philosophical analysis, without presupposing any specific form of religion.[2] He could say "that the feeling for God is a religious feeling," but he differentiated very sharply between the purely philosophical idea of God, "die Anschauung Gottes," and "dem religiösen Gefühl."[3] Schleiermacher asserted that because the distinction between the two had not always been recognized, there had been a great deal of confusion as to the relationship of philosophy to religion.[4] Nygren did not see this distinction between the philosophical "Gottesidee" and the religious feeling, but rather identified them, and believed that therefore Schleiermacher had constructed a transcendental deduction of religion in his *Dialektik*. Religion, for Schleiermacher, was an empirical reality given in the consciousness of every man, which could not be related to a philosophical concept of God, which was "the idea of the highest unity." The "Gottesidee" was not an empirical reality, nor was it given in knowledge. Schleiermacher's "regressive method" could not be identified with Nygren's transcendental deduction.[5] A transcendental deduction of religion could not be found in Schleiermacher's *Dialektik*.

---

[1] Cf. DVG., p. 79: "Vad måste alltså den, som sin plikt likmätigt vill vetandet, förutsätta med avseende på tänkandet? Han måste i sista hand förutsätta det absoluta, det religiösa gudsmedvetandet."

[2] SW. III:4, 2, p. 152.

[3] *Ibid.*; In reference to "die Idee der höchsten Einheit", Schleiermacher writes, "Die Anschauung Gottes wird nie wirklich vollzogen, sondern bleibt nur indirecter Schematismus.", SW. III:4, 2, p. 152, also "Wir konnten das absolute als Begriff und Urtheil nicht finden; nur in negative Form konnten wir es aufstellen, und das ist unser Nichthaben.", SW. III:4, 2, p. 153. In reference to religion he writes, "Das religiöse Gefühl ist zwar ein wirklich vollzogenes, aber es ist nie rein, denn das Bewusstsein Gottes ist darin immer an einem anderen; nur an einem einzelnen ist man sich der Totalität, nur an einem Gegensatz (zwischen dem eignen Sein und dem ausser uns gesetzten) ist man sich der Einheit bewusst.", SW. III:4, 2, p. 153. "Während im religiösen Bewusstsein... das Bestreben das Bewusstsein Gottes zu isoliren gar nicht ist" "will das philosophische Bestreben es aber rein für sich haben, und es genügt ihm, sich desselben an und für sich als einer nothwendigen Voraussetzung bewusst zu sein, so dass es jedem nachweisen kann, so gewiss man wissen wolle, so gewiss bedürfe man dieser Voraussetzung des absoluten, in welcher allein das Wissen begründet und aus welcher allein die Regeln für das Wissen absuleiten seien.", SW. III:4, 2, p. 153. The philosophical idea of God, or "die Idee der höchsten Einheit" is the necessary presupposition for *Wissen* and *Wollen*.

[4] SW. III:4, 2, p. 152.

[5] As Nygren does in DVG, p. 79; cf. Schleiermacher, SW. III:4, 2, p. 609.

Nygren interpreted Schleiermacher in such a way that Schleiermacher identified the consciousness of God with the transcendental presupposition for all knowledge and will. The validity of the consciousness of God must be recognized if there is to be any knowledge or will.[1] Schleiermacher, Nygren believed, had come to this conclusion by a reliance upon the critical method (with the one exception that he had confused the theoretical and the ontological areas of philosophy).[2]

It would seem that Nygren misrepresented and misunderstood the philosophical structure of Schleiermacher's criticism. The critical method was a "Gegeneinanderhalten" and a "Vergleichung" or a "Schweben" between, on the one hand, the Idea, the universal form, the Principle, rational unity, and the apriori, and on the other, the experiential, the individual, the multiple, the diversified and the aposteriori.[3] "Die Idee der Gottheit" was the fundamental philosophical and transcendental concept which expressed the apriori, or that which was not given in experience. "Die Idee der Welt" as the fundamental philosophical and transcendental idea, expressed in a corresponding way the aposteriori, or that which was given in the world of sense experience. Criticism, as a philosophical method in *Dialektik*, contained the unity of the empirical and rational approaches to reality.[4] "Die Idee der Gottheit" and "die Idee der Welt" were related to one another, ("ein Verhältnis des Zusammenseins beider").[5] "Die Idee der Gottheit" as the expression of the apriori was "the principle of the possibility of knowledge in itself" ("das Prinzip der Möglichkeit des Wissens an sich") "Die Idee der Welt" was the expression of the aposteriori as "the principle of the reality of knowledge as it comes into existence" ("das Prinzip der Wirklichkeit des Wissens in seinen Werden").[6] This pair of ideas, possible knowledge and real knowledge, was constitutive for the philosophical structure of Schleiermacher's critical method.

Schleiermacher's philosophy of identity was, therefore, not as Nygren believed a confusion of the theoretical and the ontological,

---

[1] DVG., p. 66.
[2] *Ibid.*
[3] SW. III:4, 2, p. 166, p. 387 ff.
[4] Cf. SW. III:4, 2, p. 144; "Anstatt einer Durchdringung des speculativen und empirischen ist uns nur eine begleitende Beziehung des einen auf das andre möglich, oder eine wissenschaftliche Kritik."
[5] SW. III:4, 2, p. 165 ff; cf. KD, Par. 23, 32, 35.
[6] SW. III:4, 2, p. 164.

but was rather a conscious attempt to make not only "die Idee der Gottheit" a *regulative* principle for ethics and practical activity, but also a *constitutive* principle for knowledge and philosophy in general. Schleiermacher, as we have seen, had employed elements from a philosophy of identity to bridge the gulf which lies between Kant's theoretical and practical philosophy.

Nygren had, furthermore, constructed his transcendental deduction on the basis of Schleiermacher's thought in such a way that "the transcendental necessity of religion," that is, the idea of the validity of religion, led directly to the Christian faith.[1] This was the new form of the transcendental deduction of religion, asserted Nygren.[2] However, Nygren discovered that Schleiermacher had "psychologized" the Christian faith. Schleiermacher, however, in *Der christliche Glaube* had related religion to the Christian church, that is, as a special form of the total spiritual community, "Lehnsäze aus der Ethik." A feeling of immediate self-consciousness was identified with the religious feeling, which was distinct from all other experiences. Schleiermacher dealt with religion from an anthropological standpoint, not from a psychological standpoint. Religion was "ein wesentliches Element der menschlichen Natur." It was even the most essential element of human nature. Nygren had again misinterpreted Schleiermacher's critical position. Schleiermacher had clearly defined the critical method as the "Gegeneinanderhalten der apriorischen und der aposteriorischen Elemente der Erkenntnis." Dogmatics, for Schleiermacher, expressed the empirically given religious statements of a particular period in history, and attempted to show their relationship to one another.[3] However, only by means of the "Gegeneinanderhalten" of the apriori and aposteriori elements of the religious experience can the dogmatik task be a critical science, and orient itself to the religious expression

---

[1] DVG., p. 82, cf. p. 91 ff. "Religionens transcendentala nödvändighet enligt Der christliche Glaube".

[2] DVG., p. 115 ff; "I Dialektiken står giltighetsfrågan från början klart i förgrunden, och redan vid uppkastandet av Dialektikens problem kunde vi skönja den förknippning mellan giltighetsbegreppet och den religiösa erfarenheten, som det är religionsfilosofiens uppgift att söka rekonstruera. Men genom inblandning av identitetsfilosofiska tankar glider frågan snart in på metafysikens mark. I Der christliche Glaube möter oss en ny ansats till transcendental deduktion av religionen, denna gång i huvudsak utan metafysiska inblandingar; men nu är det i stället psykologismen som prevalerar."

[3] "Die zusammenhängende Darstellung der Lehre, wie sie zu einer gegebenen Zeit, sei es nun in der Kirche im allgemeinen wann nämlich keine Trennung obwaltet, sonst aber in einer einzelnen Kirchenpartei, geltend ist, bezeichnen wir durch den Ausdruck Dogmatik oder dogmatische Theologie. KD, Par. 97.

of a church.[1] Dogmatics was a critical and scientific discipline primarily because of its relationship to the principle science, "die Ethik," which Schleiermacher related to "die Elementarsphilosophie" or "die Dialektik."[2]

Nygren had not interpreted or employed the critical structure of Schleiermacher as Schleiermacher had himself presented it. The Kantian criticism, which Schleiermacher also employed, meant an investigation of the possibility of real knowledge. Criticism, furthermore, delimited the areas of dogmatics and skepticism. As a philosophical method it attempted to unify the apriori and the aposteriori, the rational and the empirical elements of knowledge. Nygren chose to employ the critical method to find "what must be valid if there is to be any validity." Nygren thereby used the critical method in a erroneous way.

---

[1] Gll. 2, Par. 4.
[2] Cf. SW. III:4, 2, p. 315, also p. 445, *Dialektik* as "Architektonik alles Wissens".

APPENDIX

ANDERS NYGREN'S RELIGIOUS APRIORI:
ANALYSIS AND CRITIQUE

I. *Introduction*

Nygren acknowledges that it was Kant who transformed philosophy from a "metaphysical ontology" to a "critical theory of experience," characterized by the transcendental method.[1] For this reason, says Nygren, philosophy must orient its methodological presuppositions about the problem of validity. Philosophy must differentiate between that which is valid and that which is not.[2] Kant, asserts Nygren, had employed the critical method most satisfactorily in his critique of knowledge, but less satisfactorily in his moral philosophy, and had failed entirely in his philosophy of religion.[3]

Nygren constructs his "transcendental deduction of the religious category" on the basis of Kant's deduction.[4] Nygren interprets Kant in such a way that he identifies *exactly* the transcendental deduction with the critical method in philosophy. Nygren interprets Kant in the following manner:

1. The task of the transcendental deduction is to show that objective experience may not be given if definite apriori ideas do not possess validity.[5]

2. The transcendental deduction is a deduction which demonstrates the necessity of accepting something as valid. It is therefore the presupposition for all of human consciousness.[6]

3. The transcendental deduction can never be interpreted in terms of a metaphysical or psychological system.

4. The transcendental deduction demonstrates what must be valid if there is to be any validity at all.[7]

---

[1] *Dogmatikens Vetenskapliga Grundläggning*, SKD, Stockholm, 1922.

[2] *Ibid.*

[3] *Ibid.*, p. 63.

[4] Cf. *Religiöst Apriori*, p. 207; DVG, p. 72, quoted from Kant, Kr.d.r.V., p. 109 ff., "Uebergang sur transcendental en Deduction der Kategorien." Nygren employs the following passages from the *Kritik der reinen Vernunft*: "Die transcendentale Deduction aller Begriffe a priori hat also ein Principium, worauf die ganze Nachforschung gerichtet werden muss; nämlich dieses: dass sie als Bedingungen a priori der Möglichkeit der Erfahrungen erkannt werden müssen. Begriffe, die den objectiven Grund der Möglichkeit der Erfahrung abgeben, sind eben darum nothwendig. Die Entwickelung der Erfahrung aber, worin sie angetroffen werden, ist nicht ihre Deduction (sondern Illustration) weil sie dabei doch nur zufällig sein würden. Ohne diese ursprüngliche Beziehung auf mögliche Erfahrung, in welcher alle Gegenstände der Erkenntnis vorkommen, würde die Beziehung derselben auf irgend ein Object gar nicht begriffen werden können."

[5] *Religiöst Apriori*, p. 207. Nygren refers to Hans Larsson's work, *Kants deduktion av kategorierna* (Lund: Gleerups, 1914).

[6] *Religiöst Apriori*, p. 207, 208; DVG, p. 80.

[7] *Ibid.*

It is this last emphasis which highlights Nygren's entire philosophical task. With Kant's apriori categories of the mind as the philosophical basis for his understanding of experience, he attempts to present religion as a "necessary and universal form of experience" which can never be superseded by the other forms of experience. Religion forms the basis for the claim of validity in reference to the forms of experience. Furthermore, the forms of experience are "realized" only in religion. Eternity is the apriori "ground form" or the fundamental category for the religious experience. But this same category of eternity is the foremost logical presupposition for all that validity means in the areas of knowledge, morality and aesthetics. Without the category of eternity, there can be no valid experience! What this means simply is that Nygren's conception of validity is all-embracing. Eternity is presupposed as basic to all experience, but somehow, the religious experience receives precedence over all of the other experiences by participating in the same category of eternity. The religious experience is not on the same plane with other forms of experience, but is more universal, more fundamental, and more primary for the whole of man's life. This is Nygren's transcendental deduction of religion. He begins with the concept of a valid experience, and from this leads to the presupposition that there must be some experience which makes all experience possible.

II. *An Analysis of the Category of Eternity*

Nygren has designated the task of the philosophy of religion to be "a search for the category which can form the apriori presupposition for the validity of religion and the religious experience." As we have seen, Nygren finds that the category of *eternity* is the transcendental category of religion. Eternity is the a priori "ground form" for the religious experience.[1] At the same time, the category of eternity is the presupposition for the validity of all of the other forms of experience. What does this mean for Nygren's transcendental deduction? Essentially Nygren has presented two different possibilities for the transcendental deduction:

1. Employing religious experience as it is expressed phenomenologically, he demonstrates what is valid about it, and from this discovers that the ultimate logical presupposition for religion is the idea of *eternity*. Eternity, therefore, is the presupposition for the religious experience as a valid form of experience.

2. Analyzing the religious experience and demonstrating that the idea of eternity is the "ground category" for this experience, he does not construct the validity and the religious a priori from this analysis, but from an analysis of experience as given in the forms of culture. Culture is demonstrated to contain the category of eternity which is at the same time the ultimate logical presupposition for its validity.[2]

Although Nygren had assigned to the transcendental deduction of religion the task of analyzing the religious experience, he digresses from the

---

[1] *Religiöst Apriori*, p. 239; cf. also A. Nygren, "Är evighetskategorien en religiös kategori?" *Kristendomen och vår tid*, (Upsala; 1922), p. 220 ff.

[2] *Religiöst Apriori*, p. 238, 239.

Kantian concept of a transcendental deduction by attempting "to prove that in religion there is a moment without which there cannot be anything valid or any experience at all."[1] Nygren constructs his transcendental deduction with reference to a particular area of experience,[2] that is, the area of experience which must be occupied by the religious experience. He then broadens this deduction to include the possibility of *all* experience. In the execution of this process, he loses his philosophical tool to analyze in a strict manner the religious experience as one of the forms of experience. A transcendental deduction is a deduction of the religious "ground category" and is the apriori presupposition for all religious experience. Does Nygren presuppose that the deduction of every form of experience can be constructed from an analysis of what is possible experience? Nygren has not distinguished sharply between the religious experience and the other experiences in his construction of his transcendental deduction. He has also arbitrarily employed the term experience to mean the theoretical experience.

Furthermore, the subsuming of religion under the concept of a valid experience, and then the subsequent elevation of religion above the other forms of culture and from all other forms of experience, provokes ambiguity in the meaning of religion as well as in the definition of its "ground category." For Nygren, the category of eternity is not only the ultimate formal category for the content of the religious experience (the "ground category" of religion), but is also the "foundation of validity" for religion.[3] The category of eternity has, therefore, two definitions: 1) It is a primary (fundamental) category, equal to the categories of causality and the moral imperative, and, at the same time, 2) It is the foundation for the validity of all experience.

Nygren does not make a distinction between a deduction which analyzes the forms of culture and a deduction which analyzes experience in general. They become, In Nygren's analysis, equated.[4] Nygren attempts to justify this ambiguity by saying that this interpretation is "the broad basis" for a transcendental deduction.[5]

In addition to this ambiguity, Nygren describes two principles of validity, one which he defines negatively, the other, positively.[6] Eternity is

---

[1] *Religiöst Apriori*, p. 215, 229, 233; cf. Kr.d.r.V., p. 233. Nygren indicates that the transcendental method must "also be employed within the religious area. This means that we must, in an analogous way, demonstrate that the religious ground-category is the foundation for all that experience means, and that without it, no experience is possible." After saying this, Nygren extends the meaning of the religious ground category to include it as the presupposition for every experience as well; cf. *Det religionsfilosofiska grundproblemet*, p. 96 ff.

[2] *Religiöst Apriori*, p. 241.

[3] Cf. *Religiöst Apriori*, pp. 224–242, the chapter entitled "Transcendental deduktion af religionens grundkategori," cf. *Kristendomen och vår tid*, (1922), p. 236.

[4] E. Tegen, "Är en transcendental deduktion av religionen möjlig," *Bibelforskaren*, (Uppsala: 1922–1923), pp. 300–319; 1–30, particularly p. 302.

[5] A. Nygren, "Transcendentala metodens användbarhet inom Religionsfilosofien," *Bibelforskaren*, (Upsala: 1923), p. 286 ff.

[6] J. Cullberg, "Den religionsfilosofiska apriorifrågan, Några randanmärkningar till det senaste svenska lösningförsöket," *Kristendomen och vår tid*, (1922), p. 18.

defined negatively as that which is "independent of time and space;" positively it is "participation in the life of God." The former is responsible for the determination of the validity of all experience, the latter the given content of the religious experience.[1]

However, can the mere negation of time and space be adequate as the "ground category" of religion?[2] Eternity presupposes that something is not characterized by time and space. Can this negative definition of eternity be what is the basis for all experience, as well as for the specific religious experience? Nygren has illustrated the nature of a religious statement by the Biblical expression "God is love." Does this religious statement say anything about the negation of time? Rather than the denial of time, this statement speaks of a certain quality, love, identified with a certain subject, God. It would appear that Nygren has deserted his definition of eternity as that which is independent of time and space, and introduced a positive definition, that which has a specific content. This is a further indication of the ambiguity found in Nygren's conception of eternity. Compare still another example:[3] Nygren speaks of the nourishment of birds as a "zoological" fact, but it can also be a religious statement, when one refers to the words of Jesus when he said, "Behold the fowls of the air: for they sow not, neither do they reap, nor gather into barns; yet your heavenly Father feedeth them. Are ye not much better than they?" (Matt. 6:26). The status of the birds in this latter instance is such, says Nygren, that they have been placed "sub specie aeternitatis." But what then of the negation of time and space? Rather, the statement regarding the birds possesses the character of eternity because, as Nygren says, "our heavenly Father feeds the birds." Nygren has, therefore, decided that the concept of eternity is to be more than the negation of time and space. However, Nygren has also said that, "from a religious viewpoint the eternal is that which participates in the life of God."[4] Eternity now receives the positive definition of participation in the life of God. The second definition of eternity, and, ultimately, the concept of validity, has not been deduced from Nygren's transcendental apriori system, but has come from Nygren's description of religion.[5] If the category of eternity is to remain as the basis for validity, then it must have only the negative definition of that which is independent of time and space. If eternity has a positive character, and is given a specific content, then it is clear that it has not received this from an analysis of experience.

Nygren's description of the category of eternity, which, he says, *has been* "*realized*" *in the factual historical religions*, is still another indication of the confusion which exists in his system. If eternity, as the "ground category" of the religious experience, is characterized in a negative way as independent

---

[1] *Religiöst Apriori*, p. 239. "Från religiös synpunkt är det eviga det som har del i Guds liv."

[2] Cullberg asks the question whether the category of eternity is religious, *Ibid.*, p. 17. N. H. Søe asks the same question, cf. *Religionsfilosofi*, (København, G. E. Gads, 1955) p. 51.

[3] Nygren, *Kristendomen och vår tid*, p. 227.

[4] Nygren, *Religiöst Apriori*, p. 239.

[5] E. Tegen, "Är en transcendental deduktion av religionen möjlig," p. 16 ff.

of time and space, then it is absurd to speak of religion as being "realized" in history.

Further ambiguity arises when the religious "ground category" is defined as "participation in God's life." A content has now been given, which cannot in any way correspond to the definition of a category in Nygren's thought. "Participation in God's life" can never serve as the "ground category" for religion. It is rather only a definition of a specific religious content, or that which is constitutive for religion.[1] The religious statement, therefore, must be subsumed under the theoretical category, and it thereby loses its priority as the foundation for all validity and all experience. Nygren's deduction was doomed to failure from the outset because his religious a priori was defined as *formal*. When applied to historical religions, however, its formal character was lost, and a qualitative content took its place. Nygren's conception of the transcendental deduction, finally, rests upon a faulty analysis of experience, and upon an inconsistent formulation of what is a category. The category of eternity is useless in the service of the transcendental deduction of religion.

It seems clear from the above analysis that religion must be located alongside the other forms of experience, and no priority can be claimed for the religious "ground category" as the "category's category." Religion is not the presupposition for all culture, but is only a part of culture. It takes its proper place alongside of, and in relationship to, the other forms of human experience in culture. Religion possesses no particular or individual norm for what is true and false, valid and invalid, but is only, once again, *one form of experience*.

III. *An Analysis of the Category of Reality in Relationship to the Category of Validity*

Nygren says that his critical method can never be confused with a metaphysical system or a psychological analysis. The importance of Kant for Nygren in this regard is that it was Kant, who as we have seen, transformed philosphy from a "metaphysical ontology" to a critical theory of knowledge. However, it is apparent that Nygren has lumped together metaphysical and critical approaches to philosophy and has confused the nature of Kantian critical philosophy.

Metaphysics, Nygren says, deals with the ultimate presuppositions for this world as well as with the nature of the Absolute. But Nygren refuses to acknowledge that metaphysics can also deal with "*Wissenschaft*," in relation to the empirical method and the knowledge of this world. Nygren's rejection of metaphysics in its entirety is a refusal to recognize this second function of metaphysics. Because of this refusal, for example, Nygren will not deal with the category of "reality." For him, the category of reality can only be handled in terms of a metaphysical approach to philo-

---

[1] Nygren has himself said that the religious statement is always characterized by the fact that it "receives its content from the eternal." *Kristendomen och vår tid*, p. 237.

sophical problems.[1] Philosophy, Nygren says, must have as its sole task the construction of a universal theory of experience.[2]

Nygren distinguishes very sharply between the category of reality and the category of validity.[3] If the category of reality is selected as the point of orientation for all of philosophy, then the question must be asked how "reality in its totality" is related to temporal and spatial realities? As soon as this question is answered, says Nygren, the answer which is given must include a metaphysical system.[4] To avoid such a conclusion, Nygren asserts that philosophy must concentrate itself about the problem of validity and never deal with reality.

Nygren has dealt with the category of reality in such a way that it must appear in a metaphysical system, where reality is defined as the "ultimate ground" for the world. This type of reality Nygren refuses to consider, because it has "metaphysical consequences." Thereby, for Nygren the only conclusion which one can reach is that all philosophy must deal solely with the problem of validity. Nygren has, however, failed to understand the concept of reality. According to the critical method, reality cannot be defined as a quality nor as a "definite quantity." Reality always presupposes something which lies outside of itself. However, because reality does not deal with the concepts of quality or quantity, this does not mean, as Nygren has interpreted, that the problem of reality must be taken away from philosophy, and replaced by the category of validity. When Nygren orients his philosophical program about the transcendental deduction of "what must be valid, if there is to be any validity," has he thereby eliminated the problem of reality? Validity must presuppose something in order for there to be any validity at all. Philosophy can never be reduced to the alternative methods of analyzing the categories of reality or validity![5] Nygren's con-

---

[1] Cf. his discussion with E. Tegen in *Bibelforskaren* 1923, p. 237 ff.

[2] Cf. A. Nygren, "Motivforschung als philosophisches und geschichtliches Problem," *Adolf Phalen in memoriam*, (Upsala: Universitets Bokhandeln, 1937), p. 229.

[3] "Mitt under denna både vidsträckta och djupgående överensstämmelse består det emellertid en fundamental åtskillnad mellan våra åskådningar såtillvida som verklighetsbegreppet kan betraktas såsom uppsalafilosofiens centralbegrepp, under det att för mig giltighetsbegreppet står i medelpunkten för filosofien." *Bibelforskaren*, p. 273 ff.

[4] "Enda utvägen att undgå allt vad metafysik heter är därför att frigöra den från befattningen med verklighstsfrågan och i stället koncentrera den kring giltighetsfrågan." *Bibelforskaren*, p. 274, 275. "Besvaras den uppställda frågan sålunda att den rumsligt-tidliga verkligheten icke är lika med verkligheten överhuvud, utan att det vid sidan av densamma gives en 'högre' verklighet, så är man tydligen, huru man än bestämmer denna högre verklighet, mitt inne i metafysiken. Men detsamma gäller också i det fall att man identifierar den rumsligt-tidliga verkligheten med verkligheten överhuvud och alltså fastslår, att det utom den rumsligt-tidliga verkligheten icke kan givas någon verklighet av annan art. Om detta påstående skall vara något annat än en jämnförelsesvis godtyckligt inskränkande definition av verklighetens begrepp, så är det ett metafysiskt påstående." *Bibelforskaran*, p. 275.

[5] As Nygren has done in *Religiöst Apriori*, p. 199: "Apriori varken är eller existerar eller har realitet, utan det gäller."

centration upon the problem of validity is based upon an uncritical assumption that critical philosophy is solely the attempt to avoid metaphysical problems.[1]

Nygren, in another reference, relates the category of reality to a "psychologism."[2] This association is bound up with Nygren's conception of reality as located within a metaphysical system, and his subsequent attempt to free philosophy from all psychologisms.[3] Philosophy is, for Nygren, an analysis of the presuppositions of experience, that is, it is "logische Veraussetzungsanalyse."[4] It is important to note now Nygren defines his logical analysis. It might be expected that the logical analysis would be interpreted in such a way that, by means of the law of contradiction, one could decide what was true or false in a given judgment. However, Nygren directs his discussion about the problem of *validity*. Something is valid when it belongs to knowledge. The critical theory of knowledge has to discover the logical presuppositions which are found within the principle of validity, and which conceive something to be either as "true" or "false". Nygren goes on to say that the theory of knowledge is not the whole of philosophy, but only a part,[5] and it is not completely freed from a psychologism. Nygren asserts that when a judgment is made in a theoretical sense, its content is con-

---

[1] Schleiermacher in *Dialektik* has identified transcendental philosophy and metaphysics; cf. Nygren's position in "Motivforschung als philosophisches und geschichtliches Problem," "Die Aufgabe der Philosophie ist es, allgemeine Erfahrungstheorie zu sein," p. 329.

[2] *Bibelforskaren*, p. 274; "Verklighetsbegreppet kan sättas i centrum för filosofien endast därigenom att man gör sig skyldig till en... förkastlig psykologism."

[3] "Motivforschung als philosophisches und geschichtliches Problem," p. 329: "Die Aufgabe der Philosophie ist es, allgemeine Erfahrungstheorie zu sein. Sie muss sich durch Analyse der gegebenen Erfahrungen zu den in ihnen enthaltenen Voraussetzung zurücksuchen, diesen Voraussetzungen, die erst den einzelnen Urteilen Zusammenhang und Sinn geben. Die Philosophie ist kurz gesagt logische Voraussetzungsanalyse."

[4] Nygren continues, "Die Gültigkeit eines Erkenntnisprinzips bedeutet nur, dass es logisch gesehen als notwendige Voraussetzung in jedem von uns als gültig aufgefassten und anerkannten einzelnen Urteil mitgegeben ist." *Ibid.*

[5] Furthermore, writes Nygren, "Die Erfahrung wird nämlich nicht mit nur theoretischem Konstatieren der gegebenen Sachverhältnisse erschöpft. Wir begegnen Sätzen und Urteilen, die dem Äusseren nach die Form der theoretischen Erfahrungsurteile tragen, die aber offenbar ihren Sinn verlieren, wenn sie unter die erkenntnistheoretischen Voraussetzungen oder Kategorien subsumiert werden. So verhält es sich z.B. mit den ethischen oder religiösen Urteilen. Wenn ich in einem ethischen Urteil eine Handlung als gut bezeichne, so unterscheidet sich dies Urteil in seiner sprachlichen Form nicht von einem gewöhnlichen theoretischen Urteil, aber meine Absicht damit ist eine ganz andere... Das ethische Urteil steht unter anderen Voraussetzungen und ist von anderen Kategorien bestimmt als das theoretische Urteil. Und ebenso ist es mit dem religiösen Urteil." "Motivforschung als philosophisches und geschichtliches Problem," p. 330. Although philosophy is a "logische Voraussetzungsanalyse" it remains within the area of our judgment, i.e., "In dem ethischen und dem religiösen Urteil, die der Form nach dem theoretischen Urteile gleich sind, ist unsere Absicht, unsere Intention, unser Zweck etwas ganz anderes als in dem theoretischen Urteile."

sidered to be valid. The task of logic is therefore limited by the demonstration that "truth," as the principle of knowledge, presupposes "validity." However, Nygren maintains that in the ethical and religious judgment, the form of the judgment is related to our "purpose," our "intention" and our "goal". By so doing, Nygren has designated the task of philosophy to be the investigation of those presuppositions upon which the theoretical, the ethical, and the religious judgments rest. At the same time, he has assigned to the theoretical judgment the category of "truth," and to the others, categories based upon purpose, intention, and one's goal. It is obvious that when Nygren speaks of purpose and intention that he too has *not* completely avoided a psychologism.

As well, Nygren has confused the different aspects of his "universal theory of experience." He calls one aspect of the theory, "the epistemological or the theory of the theoretical experience" ("die Erkenntnistheorie oder dis Theorie der theoretischen Erfahrung"), another "the ethical or the theory of the moral experience" ("Ethik oder die Theorie der sittlichen Erfahrung"), and the third, "the philosophy of religion or the theory of the religious experience" ("die Religionsphilosophie oder die Theorie der religiösen Erfahrung").[1] There is a general confusion between these different "branches" of philosophy, all of which he subsumes under the designation, "a universal theory of experience" ("allgemeiner Erfahrungstheorie."). Certain experiences are differentiated as qualitative experiences, others are simply empty names for experience.

IV. *An Analysis of the Concept of Religion*

Religion, according to Nygren, belongs to the "universal and necessary" forms of human culture. Religion is a part of those experiences of man which are universally valid, that is, (as in Kant) the theoretical, the moral and the aesthetic experience. Religion is not identical with any of these three, but it is closely related, nonetheless. However, religion does not give knowledge nor form a basis for morality nor initiate the aesthetic experience. A sharp distinction must be made at all times, says Nygren, between the religious and the theoretical areas of experience.[2] However, Nygren does define religion in such a way that it is positively related to knowledge, and he can say, that there is no religion which is not at the same time knowledge.[3] Religion is also defined as experience, in his "allgemeine Erfahrungstheorie."[4] The religious experience is unlike the theoretical and ethical experiences, however, for religion, as experience, is assigned an "over-individual validity."[5] Religion is, however, also a "form" of life.[6] It is universally

---

[1] *Ibid.*, also Nygren, *Religiöst Apriori*, p. 143.

[2] Nygren, *Religiöst Apriori*, p. 142 ff.

[3] *Ibid.*, p. 143.

[4] *Ibid.* "Die Erkenntnistheorie" is the first area of the general theory of experience, "die Theorie der sittlichen Erfahrung," the second, and "die Religionsphilosophie oder die Theorie der religiösen Erfahrung" the third.

[5] *Ibid.*

[6] *Ibid.*, p. 10.

present in consciousness.[1] It is a value, a form of culture, as well as a form
of the life of the spirit.[2]

It is possible now to summarize Nygren's definitions of religion. First,
it is knowledge, but it may not be subsumed under the theoretical category.
Second, it is "value," a "form of life," belonging to the life of consciousness, constituted by experience, but it is also elevated above the practical
experience. Religion is, on the one hand, related to that which is logically
demonstrable; on the other, it belongs to the area of the atheoretical and
the alogical. It is related to the concept of the apriori, and, on the other
hand, it is alogical.

However, religion for Nygren is defined primarily as *experience*. It is
possible therefore for Nygren to speak of religion as a form of culture, and
an experience found in the consciousness of every man, located in the same
structure of experience as the theoretical, the moral, and the aesthetic experiences. But as experience, religion must be more unique than simply a
form of culture. It must be constitutive for the theoretical, moral and
aesthetic experiences.[3]

There is also confusion in terms of the relationship between Nygren's
transcendental method and his concept of the nature of religion. The critical method and the transcendental deduction have been equated.[4] However,
in Nygren's writings there are other interpretations of the transcendental
method. Nygren says that the philosophy of religion investigates the phenomenon of religion to determine if there is a "moment" which can be
demonstrated to be a necessary and indispensable form of life. It investigates whether the religious value is a "ground value" or a derivative value,
and thereby, whether religion is an apriori form of life.[5] Therefore, according to this definition, the transcendental deduction has as its task to question
whether religion is "a necessary and universal form of life." When the
transcendental deduction is concluded, the validity of religion is legitimized.
However, this conception of validity had *not* been established from the
outset. In another reference, Nygren writes that there is a "ground fact,"
which is the "point of orientation" for all of the other apriori experiences.
This "ground fact" is the validity of experience in its different forms, that
is, the validity of the theoretical, the ethical, the aesthetic and the religious
experience.[6] The validity of religion or of the religious experience is not
established from the beginning of the deduction, but it is the presuppo-

---

[1] *Ibid.*, p. 12.

[2] *Ibid.*, p. 11.

[3] "Från denna synpunkt (d.v.s. erfarenhet fattad i kriticismens mening såsom
beteckning för en upplevelse med nödvandig och allmängiltig karaktär) kan den
kritiska filosofien karakteriseras såsom allmän erfarenhetsteori." *Religiöst Apriori*,
p. 143. cf. also "Motivforschung als philosophisches und geschichtliches Problem,"
p. 329.

[4] *Religiöst Apriori*, p. 10; cf. p. 206.

[5] *Ibid.*, p. 9.

[6] *Ibid.*, p. 133.

sition upon which the deduction stands. The validity of religion is the point
of orientation for the transcendental deduction and it has been taken for
granted. These different conceptions of religion and the religious experience are evident throughout.

Furthermore, upon what grounds can religion claim to have priority in
the matter of validity? When Nygren deals with this question, he introduces a third definition of religion in addition to the other two he has
already given. Religion, for Nygren, becomes an integrating part of the
spiritual and cultural life of man in its entirety. As such, it is autonomous
and independent.[1] The proof of the autonomy and independence of religion
leads Nygren to a discussion of the religious apriori.[2] When the philosophy
of religion deals with the religious a priori, it is dealing with that which is
specific in religion.[3] The investigation of the apriori is the basis for the proof
of the autonomy of religion. However, when the philosophy of religion
attempts to answer the question whether the religious apriori is given, the
relationship between the autonomy of religion and the religious apriori is
reversed. Is the proof for the autonomy of religion the basis for the investigation of the apriori or is it the establishment of a religious apriori?[4] Nygren,
on the one hand, says that the autonomy and validity of religion is something to be sought; on the other hand, its autonomy and validity is established from the very beginning. We encounter such a *circulus vitiosus*
throughout Nygren's discussion of the autonomy of religion.

This confusion is found also in the relation of religion to culture, and its
expression of science, morality, and art. Nygren can say that "religion is
universally present in consciousness," and also that "it is of great interest
to investigate that which is characteristically religious, that which separates
itself from everything which is similar in consciousness."[5] The philosophy
of religion, furthermore, deals with the specifically religious in religion.[6]
However, the universality and necessity of religion is based only upon the
meaning religion has within the culture system.[7] This oscillation between
the autonomy of religion and its relationship to culture appears throughout.
Religion is and is not a form of culture. As well, it is positively and negatively related to culture.

The transcendental deduction which Nygren employs to the different
forms of culture is not a formal and logical proof for their existence, but a

---

[1] "Religionen representerar gentemot övriga erfarenhetsområden en fullkomligt självständig och egenartad erfarenhetsform, som utvecklar sig efter en egen
autonom laglighet och alltså måste bedömas utifrån sitt eget centrum och ej i
första rummet efter dess förhållande till övriga erfarenhetsformer." *Religiöst
Apriori*, p. 12.

[2] *Religiöst Apriori*, p. 12.

[3] *Ibid.*

[4] Cf. *Religiöst Apriori*, p. 192 ff.

[5] *Religiöst Apriori*, p. 12.

[6] *Ibid.*

[7] *Ibid.*, p. 237.

demonstration of their cultural validity[1] and philosophical legitimacy.[2] The validity of knowledge, for example, is not demonstrated by a formal and logical proof for its necessity and validity, but by the fact that knowledge is recognizable as a cultural value. Religion, in relationship to culture, is transcendent to culture, and makes possible the validity of knowledge. The necessity of the religious "ground category" has been established. However, the transcendental deduction in the sense of a formal and logical demonstration of the validity of religion has demonstrated its relevance for the religious life, and only in a derivative way, for human life as a whole. When the philosophy of religion attempts to discover the category which is the basis for the religious experience, this task presupposes that the possibility or validity of the religious experience depends upon the possibility or validity of the religious "ground category." This, of course, results in a tautology, again, a *circulus vitiosus*. The validity of religion depends upon the validity of religion. Nygren must, thereby, attempt in another way to legitimatize the validity of religion, and he does so by using another definition of a valid religious experience, that is, it is the "ground category" for the validity of the three forms of culture, a validity which need not be formally and logically demonstrable. Their participation in cultural validity, which religion has established, is sufficient.[3]

Religion, finally, is defined both as cultural and as non-cultural throughout Nygren's transcendental program. Religion participates in the forms of life, but is also transcendent to them. It is one experience alongside others, but is also elevated above all experience and forms the ground of all experience.

In summary, Nygren's primary fault is the double definition he gives to the basic elements of his transcendental system. This criticism is relevant in relation to his definition of the category of eternity as the ground category of religion, his conception of the religious apriori, the idea of the transcendental deduction and the critical method as a philosophical method.

There is some confusion as well in Nygren's definition of the apirori. On the one hand, the apriori is defined as not simply another psychological fact beside other psychological facts, but it is *that moment* in experience upon which the validity of experience rests, that is, that moment which

---

[1] *Ibid.*, p. 235; also p. 234, "Man kunde vänta, att även religionsfilosofien kunde reducera sin bevisningsskyldighet därhän, att den fullgjort sin transcendentala uppgift genom att bevisa, att utan erkännande av den religiösa grundkategorien ingen religös erfarenhet vore möjlig. Men om religionsfilosofien gjorde anspråk på att få företaga en sådan reduktion skulle man med rätta förebrå den att dess bevisförfarånde innebure en circulus vitiosus."

[2] *Religiöst Apriori*, p. 235.

[3] "Vi måste påvisa, icke blott att ingen religiös erfarenhet, utan fastmer att överhuvud ingen erfarenhet är möjlig utan den religiösa grundkategorien, eller att det icke gives någon giltighet annat än på religiös grund. Om detta kan påvisas, så står icke längre den religiösa erfarenheten isolerad från de övriga erfarenhetsformerna." *Religiöst Apriori*, p. 236.

makes experience, logically (not psychologically) possible.[1] On the other hand, reality and existence are categories which are wholly inadequate to express the transcendental relationship. The transcendental category is validity. The apriori neither exists nor has reality, but is necessarily and universally valid.[2] According to these definitions, the apriori is defined in such a way that existence is attributed to it, then in the later reference, it has no existence.

Furthermore, Nygren speaks of the apriori as giving validity to knowledge, and again as the basis for the validity of the practical life.[3] The apriori thereby is partially a theoretical apriori, and partially an atheoretical apriori. The theoretical validity of experience is related to a logical apriori, but the religious validity, on the other hand, cannot be related in the same way, but must be related to the uniqueness of the religious experience.[4] Religion as a special form of experience makes a claim to validity upon the basis of its own particular kind of experience. The religious apriori is therefore not a logical apriori. However, Nygren has already defined the two distinct aprioris as, on the one hand, the logical apriori, which introduces a higher validity, and on the other, the psychological and generic apriori, which gives to the apriori the significance of temporal priority.[5] If the religious apriori is not a logical apriori, and is not an apriori in the sense of a psychological apriori, there is therefore some confusion as to what the religious apriori is.[6] Can the conclusion be, as Nygren asserts, that the religious apriori must be identified with the idea of *eternity* as the ground category of religion?

---

[1] *Religiöst Apriori*, p. 137 ff.

[2] *Ibid.*, p. 199.

[3] "Från transcendental synpunkt finns det ingen anledning att påstå, att blott en kunskap kan äga giltighet, men att giltighet icke kan tillskrivas t.ex. en viljeriktning, om icke denna i något avseende kan förvandlas i en kunskap." *Ibid.*

[4] "Även om det är ett gemensamt kännetecken för den teoretiska, etiska, estetiska och religiösa erfarenheten, att de alla göra anspråk på att gälla, så är det uppenbart, att den religiösa erfarenhetens sätt att gälla icke utan vidare kan vara att jämnställa med t.ex. vetenskapens sätt att gälla." *Ibid.*, p. 197.

[5] "å ena sidan den logiska linjen, där apriori innebär en högre giltighetsdignitet, å andra sidan den psykologiskgenetiska, där apriori får betydelsen av tidlig prioritet." *Ibid.*, p. 130.

[6] *Religiöst Apriori*, p. 137 ff., p. 241.

BIBLIOGRAPHY

Primary Sources

Nygren, Anders. *Agape and Eros.* 2 vols. London: Society for Promoting Christian Knowledge, 1932–1939.
— *Den kristna kärlekstanken genom tiderna.* Stockholm: Svenska Kyrkans Diakonistyrelses Bokförlag, 1938.
— *Det Religionsfilosofiska Grundproblemat.* Lund: Gleerupska Universitetsbokhandeln, 1921.
— *Die religiöse Erfahrung.* Lund: Gleerups, 1922.
— *Dogmatikens Vetenskapliga Grundläggning.* Stockholm: Svenska Kyrkans Diakonistyrelses Bokförlag, 1935.
— *Etiska Grundfrågor.* Stockholm: Sveriges Kristliga Studentrörelses, 1926.
— *Filosofi och Motivforskning.* Stockholm: Svenska Kyrkans Diakonistyrelses Bokförlag, 1940.
— *Filosofisk och Kristen Etik.* Lund: Håkan Ohlssons Boktrykeri, 1923.
— *Religiositet och Kristendom.* Uppsala: J. A. Lindblads, 1926.
— *Religiöst Apriori.* Lund: Gleerupska Universitets Bokhandeln, 1921.
— *Urkristendom och Reformation.* Stockholm: Svenska Kyrkans Diakonistyrelses Bokförlag, 1932.
— "Den metafysiska filosofiens betydelse för religionsvetenskapen – En metodisk studie," *Bibelforskaren*, 1918.
— "Motivforschung als philosophisches und geschichtliches Problem," *Adolf Phalen in memorium.* Upsala: Universitets Bokhandeln, 1937.
— "Religionen såsom 'Anschauung des Universums' hos Schleiermacher," *Studier tillägnade Magnus Pfannenstill.* Uppsala, 1923.
— "Till den nyaste religionsfilosofiska litteraturen," *Svensk Teologisk Kvartalskrift.* Lund: C. W. K. Gleerups Förlag 1926, pp. 52–74.
— "Till frågan om den transcendentala metodens användbarhet inom religionsfilosofien," *Bibelforskaren*, 1923, pp. 273–293.
— "Transcendental deduktion af religionens grundkategori," *Kristendomen och vår tid.* Uppsala, 1922.
— "Är evighetskategorien en religiös kategori?," *Kristendomen och vår tid.* Uppsala, 1922.
Schleiermacher, Friedrich D. E. *Sämmtliche Werke.* 31 vols.
Erste Abtheilung – Zur Theologie: 1–8, 11–13 Bd.;
Zweite Abtheilung – Predigten: 1–10 Bd.;
Dritte Abtheilung – Zur Philosophie: 1–9 Bd.;
Berlin: G. Reimer, 1835–64.
— *Werke, Auswahl in vier Banden.* Hrsg. v. O. Braun und J. Bauer. Leipzig: Meiner, 1910–1913.
— *Aus Schleiermachers Leben, in Briefen.* Hrsg. v. L. Jonas und W. Dilthey. 4 vols. Berlin: Reimer, 1858–1863.
— *Neue Briefe Schleiermachers aus der Jugendzeit, Niesky* 1784 *und* 1785. Hrsg. v., J. Bauer. *Zeitschrift für Kirchengeschichte.* 31 Bd., 4 Hft., 1910.
— *Briefwechsel mit J. Chr. Gass.* Hrsg. v. W. Gass. Berlin: Reimer, 1852.
— *Der christliche Glaube nach dem Grundsätzen der evangelischen Kirche im Zusammenhange dargestellt* (1821). Krit. Ausgabe v. C. Stange, Leipzig: Meiner, 1910. *Quellenschriften zur Geschichte des Protestantismus.* 9 Hft.
— *Dialektik.* Krit. Ausgabe v. J. Halpern. Berlin: Reimer, 1903.
— *Grundlinien einer Kritik der bisherigen Sittenlehre.* Krit. Ausgabe v. N. H. Mulert. Leipzig: Meiner, 1908.

— *Kurze Darstellung des theologischen Studiums*. Krit. Ausgabe v. Heinr. Scholz. Leipzig: Meiner, 1910. *Quellenschriften zur Geschichte des Protestantismus*. 10 Hft.
— *Monologen – Eine Neujahrsgabe* (1800). Krit. Ausgabe v. F. M. Schiele. Leipzig: Meiner, 1914.
— *Über die Religion – Reden an die Gebildeten unter ihren Verächtern* (1799). Hrsg. v. R. Otto. Göttingen: Vanderhoeck und Ruprecht, 1920.
— *Weihnachtsfeier*. Krit. Ausgabe v. H. Mulert. Leipzig: Dürr, 1908.

SECONDARY SOURCES

Allgemeine Literatur Zeitung. Von Jahre 1789, I–III.
Athenaeum. – Eine Zeitschrift von August Wilhelm Schlegel und Friedrich Schlegel. I–III. Berlin: Frederick Wieweg, 1798–1800.
Aulen, Gustaf. *Den allmänneliga kristna tron*. Stockholm: Svenska Kyrkans Diakonistyrelses Bokförlag, 1923.
— "En modern strideskrift mot Schleiermacher," *Svensk Teologisk Kvartalskrift*. 1 årg. 4 hft., 1925.
Baillie, John. *The Interpretation of Religion*. New York: Scribners, 1928.
Barth, Karl. *Die protestantische Theologie im* 19. *Jahrhundert*. Zürich: Evangelischer Verlag AG Zollikon, 1947.
Bauer, Joh. *Schleiermacher als patriotischer Prediger*. Giessen: Töpelmann, 1908.
Beck, Lewis W. *Immanuel Kant – Critique of Practical Reason*. New York: Liberal Arts Press, 1956.
Bender, W. *Schleiermachers Theologie*. Nördlingen: Beck, 1876.
Beth, K. *Die Grundanschauungen Schleiermachers in seinem ersten Entwurf der philosophischen Sittenlehre*. Göttingen: Vanderhöck und Ruprecht, 1898.
Billing, Einar. *De Etiska Tankarna i Urktistendomen*. Stockholm: Sveriges Kristliga Studentrörelses, 1936.
Bleek, H. *Die Grundlagen der Christologie Schleiermachers*. Berlin: Reimer, 1898.
Bornhausen, K. "Das religiöse Apriori bei Ernst Troeltsch und Rudolf Otto," *Zeitschrift für Philosophie und philosophische Kritik*, Band 139. 1910.
Bring, Ragnar. *Kristendoms Tolkningar*. Stockholm: Svenska Kyrkans Diakonistyrelses Bokförlag, 1950.
— *Teologi och Religion*. Lund: C. W. K. Gleerups, 1937.
— *Till Frågan om den Systematiska Teologiens Uppgift*. Lunds Universitets Årsskrift N. F. Avd. 1 Bd. 29., Nr. 1. Lund: Håkan Ohlssons Boktryckeri, 1933.
Brunner, Emil. *Das Symbolische in der religiösen Erkenntnis*. Tübingen: J. C. B. Mohr (Paul Siebeck), 1914.
— *Die Mystik und das Wort*. Tübingen: J. C. B. Mohr (Paul Siebeck), 1924.
Carstensen, G. *Individualitetstanken hos Schleiermacher*. Lund: Gleerupska Universitets Bokhandeln, 1924.
Cohen, Hermann. *Der Begriff der Religion im System der Philosophie*. Berlin: Bruno Cassirer, 1915.
— *Kants Theorie der Erfahrung*. Berlin: Dümmlers Verlagsbuchhandlung, 1871.
— *Religion und Sittlichkeit*. Berlin: Bruno Cassirer, 1907.
Cullberg, D. "Det religionsfilosofiska apriori frågan," *Kristendomen och vår tid*. Uppsala, 1922.
Dilthey, Wilhelm. *Denkmale der innere Entwicklung Schleiermachers*. Appendix to *Leben Schleiermachers*. Edited by Mulert. Berlin and Leipzig: DeGruyter, 1922.
— *Leben Schleiermachers* (Vol. I). Berlin: Reimer, 1870.
— "Schleiermacher," *Allgemeine Deutsche Biographie*. 31 Bd. Berlin: Reimer, 1890.

Dunkmann, D. "Der Religionsbegriff Schleiermachers in seiner Abhängigkeit von Kant," *Zeitschrift für Philosophie und philosophische Kritik.* 151 Bd. 1913.

Dunkmann, K. *Das religiöse Apriori und die Geschichte.* Berlin: Reimer, 1910.

— "Die theologische Prinzipienlehre Schleiermachers," *Beiträge zur Förderung christlicher Theologie.* 20 Jrg. 2 Hft., 1918.

— *Religionsphilosophie.* Berlin: Reimer, 1917.

Eberhard, J. A. *Neue Apologie des Sokrates oder Untersuchung der Lehre von der Seligkeit der Heiden.* I–II. Halle: 1772–1778.

— *Neue vermischte Schriften.* Halle: 1788.

— *Sittenlehre der Vernunft.* Halle: 1786.

Eck, S. *Ueber die Herkunft des Individualitätsgedankens bei Schleiermacher.* Berlin: Reimer, 1908.

Eklund, Harald. *Die Religiöse Qualität und die Sittlichkeit.* Åbo: Acta Academiae Aboensis, 1942.

Engstrand, C. J. H. *Expose och kritik av pligtbegreppet enligt Schleiermacher.* Upsala: Upsala Universitets Årsskrift, 1962.

Fichte, J. G. *Werke.* Auswahl in VI Bänden. Berlin: 1910.

Fries, Martin. *Metafysiken i Modern Svensk Teologi – En systematisk undersökning.* Stockholm: Bokförlaget Natur och Kultur, 1948.

Friess, Horace. *Schleiermacher's Soliloquies – An English Translation of the Monologen.* Chicago: The Open Court Publishing Co., 1926.

Gundolf, Fried. "Schleiermachers Romantik," *Deutsche Vierteljahrsschrift für Literaturwissenschaft und Geistesgeschichte.* Bd. II. Heft. 3, 1924–25.

Günther, W. *Die Grundlagen der Religionsphilosophie Ernst Troeltsch.* Tübingen: J. C. B. Mohr (Paul Siebeck), 1914.

Gyllenkrok, Alex. "Liberalteologi och Lundateologie," *Kristen Humanism.* Årsbok. Lund: C. W. K. Gleerup, 1953, pp. 9–23.

Görland, A. *Mein Weg zur Religion.* Göttingen: Vanderhoeck und Ruprecht, 1910.

Halpern, H. J. *Schleiermachers Dialektik.* Berlin: Reimer, 1903.

Harnack, Adolf. *Das Wesen des Christentums.* Leipzig: J. C. Hinrich, 1900.

Hedenius, Ingemar. *Att Välja Livsåskådning.* Stockholm: Albert Bonniers Förlag, 1951.

— *Tro och Vetande.* Stockholm: Albert Bonniers Förlag, 1949.

Hering, H. "Samuel Ernst Timotheus Stubenrauch und sein Neffe Friedrich Schleiermacher," *Beiträge zur Förderung christlicher Theologie.* 34 Bd. 1919.

Herrmann, W. *Ethik.* Tübingen: J. C. B. Mohr (Paul Siebeck), 1901.

— *Religion och historia.* Lund: Gleerups, 1912.

Hillerdal, Gunnar. *Teologisk och filosofisk etik.* Stockholm: Svenska Bokförlaget, 1958.

Huber, Eugen. *Die Entwicklung des Religionsbegriffes bei Schleiermacher.* Leipzig: 1901.

Hägerström, Axcl. *Religionsfilosofi.* Stockholm: Natur och Kultur, 1949.

Jacobi, F. H. *Ueber die Lehre des Spinoza in Briefen an den Herrn Moses Mendelssohn.* München; 1785.

Kade, R. *Rudolf Euckens neclogische Methode in ihre Bedeutung für die Religionsphilosophie.* Göttingen: Vanderhöck und Ruprecht, 1912.

Kalweit, P. "Das religiöse Apriori," *Theologische Studien und Kritiken,* 1908.

— "Religion und Allgemeingültigkeit," *Zeitschrift für Theologie und Kirche.* 1907.

Kant, Immanuel. *Die Religion innerhalb der Grenzen der blossen Vernunft.* Leipzig: Reclams Universal Bibliothek, Text der Ausgabe 1793, (1794).

— *Grundlegung zur Metaphysik der Sitten.* Leipzig: Reclam, Text der Ausgabe 1785.

— *Kritik der praktischen Vernunft.* Leipzig: Reclam, Text der Ausgabe 1788, (1792, 1797).

— *Kritik der reinen Vernunft.* Leipzig: Reclam, Text der Ausgabe 1781, (1787).
— *Kritik der Urteilskraft.* Leipzig: Reclam, Text der Ausgabe 1790, (1793, 1799).
— *Prolegomena zu einer jeden künftigen Metaphysik, die als Wissenschaft wird auftreten können.* Leipzig: Reclam, Text der Ausgabe 1787.
Köhler, R. *Der Begriff a priori in der modernen Religionsphilosophie.* Tübingen: J. C. B. Mohr (Paul Siebeck), 1920.
Larsson, Hans. *Den Intellektuella Åskådningens Filosofi.* Stockholm: Albert Bonniers Förlag, 1920.
— *Kants deduktion av kategorierna.* Lund: Gleerups, 1914.
Lindroth, Hjalmar. "Anders Nygrens Kriticism i förhållande till Kants och Schleiermachers," *Nordisk Teologie, Ideer och Män* – till Ragnar Bring. Lund: C. W. K. Gleerups, 1955, pp. 169–186.
— "Anders Nygren und die Kritizismus," *Studia Theologica* Vol. X, Fasc. II, Lund: Gleerups, 1957.
— *Schleiermachers Religionsbegrepp* Vols. I, II. Uppsala Universitets Årsskrift, 1926–1930. Uppsala: A.–B. Lundequistska Bokhandeln, 1926–1930.
Litt, Theodor, *Ethik der Neuzeit.* München und Berlin: R. Oldenbourg, 1927.
Loew, W. *Das Grundproblem der Ethik Schleiermachers in seiner Beziehung zu Kants Ethik.* Berlin: 1914.
Lütgert, W. "Die Religion des deutschen Idealismus und ihr Ende I–II," *Beiträge zur Förderung christlicher Theologie.* 2. Reihe 6 u. 8 Bd., 1923.
Løgstrup, K. E. *Den Erkendelsesteoretiske Konflikt Mellem Den Transcendentalfilosofiske Idealisme og Teologien.* København: Samlarens Förlag, 1942.
Mackintosh, Hugh Ross. *Types of Modern Theology.* London: Nisbet, 1937.
Mehlis, G. *Einführung in ein System der Religionsphilosophie,* Tübingen: J. C. M. Mohr (Paul Siebeck), 1917.
Meyer, E. R. *Schleiermacher und C. G. Brinkmanns Gang durch die Brüdergemeine.* Berlin: Reimer, 1905.
Natorp, P. *Religion innerhalb der Grenzen der Humanität.* Tübingen: J. C. B. Mohr (Paul Siebeck), 1908.
Nystedt, Hans. *Plikt och Kärlek* – Studier i Anders Nygrens etik. Stockholm: Svenska Kyrkans Diakonistyrelses Bokförlag, 1951.
Otto, Rudolf. *Das Heilige.* Breslau: Trewendt und Granier, 1922.
— *Kantisch – Fries'sche Religionsphilosophie, und ihre Anwendung auf die Theologie.* Tübingen: J. C. B. Mohr (Paul Siebeck), 1921.
Paton, H. J. *Kant's Metaphysic of Experience.* Vol. I, II. A Commentary on the first half of the *Kritik der Reinen Vernunft.* London: George Allen and Unwin, 1936.
Pfleiderer, Otto. *The Development of Theology in Germany and its Progress in Great Britain since* 1825. Trans. by J. Frederick Smith. London: George Allen and Unwin, 1890.
Philosophisches Archiv I–II. Hrsg. v. J. A. Eberhard, 1792–1795.
Philosophisches Magazin I–IV. Hrsg. v. J. A. Eberhard, 1788–1792.
Philosophisches Magazin I–IV. Hrsg. v. J. A. Eberhard, 1788–1792.
Rickert, H. *Der Gegenstand der Erkenntnis.* Tübingen: J. C. B. Mohr (Paul Siebeck), 1913.
Rodhe, Edvard. "Nutida Tendenser inom den Svenska Systematiska Teologien," *Svensk Teologisk Kvartalskrift.* Lund: C. W. K. Gleerups Förlag, 1932, pp. 207–226.
Rosenqvist, G. G., and Nygren, Anders. "Religionens sanningsfråga och religionsvetenskapen. Ett Meningsutbyte," *Svensk Teologisk Kvartalskrift.* Lund: C. W. K. Gleerups Förlag, 1928, pp. 192–206.
Sahlin, C. Y. *Schleiermachers, Kants, och Boströms etiska Grundtankar.* Upsala Universitets Årsskrift, 1877.

Fr. Schlegels Briefe an seinen Bruder August Wilhelm. Edited by O. Walzel. Berlin: Reimer, 1890.

Spranger, E. *Ernst Troeltsch als Religionsphilosoph.* Tübingen: J. C. B. Mohr (Paul Siebeck), 1906.

Stange, Carl. *Christentum und moderne Weltanschauung: I. Das Problem der Religion.* Leipzig: A. Deichert'sche Verlagsbuchhandlung, 1913.

— *Die Ethik Kants.* Leipzig: A. Deichert, 1920.

— *Einleitung in die Ethik; I. System und Kritik der Ethischen Systeme.* Leipzig: Deichert'sche Verlagsbuchhandlung, 1900.

Strauss, David Fr. *Charakteristiken und Kritiken.* Berlin: 1839.

Süskind, H. *Der Einfluss Schellings auf die Entwicklung von Schleiermacher's system.* Tübingen: J. C. B. Mohr (Paul Siebeck). 1909.

— "Die religiöse Apriori bei Schleiermacher," *Religion und Geistkultur.* 1914.

Søe, N. H. *Religionsfilosofi.* G. E. C. Gads Förlag, 1955.

Tegen, Einar. "Är en transcendental deduktion av religionen möjlig?." *Bibelforskaren.* 1923, pp. 1–30.

Tillich, Paul. "Über die Idee einer Theologie der Kultur," *Philosophische Vorträge.* (Kant-Gesellschaft), Berlin: Reuther and Reichard, 1920, pp. 29–58.

Traub, F. *Theologis und Philosophie.* Göttingen: Vanderhöck und Ruprecht, 1910.

Troeltsch, Ernst. *Die Absolutheit des Christentums und die Religionsgeschichte.* Tübingen: J. C. B. Mohr (Paul Siebeck), 1912.

— *Gesammelte Schriften II, Zur religiösen Lage, Religionsphilosophie und Ethik.* Tübingen: J. C. B. Mohr (Paul Siebeck), 1913.

— *Psychologie und Erkenntnistheorie in der Religionswissenschaft.* Tübingen: J. C. B. Mohr, 1905.

Troeltsch, E., Natorp, P., et. al. *Schleiermacher der Philosoph des Glaubens.* Berlin: Schöneberg, 1910.

Ueberweg, Friedrich. *Grundriss der Geschichte der Philosophie.* Neu, bearb. u. hrsg. v. K. Oesterreich, 11 Aufl. Berlin: Reimer, 1916.

Wehrung, G. *Der geschichtsphilosophische Standpunkt Schleiermachers zur Zeit seiner Freundschaft mit den Romantikern.* Strassbourg: 1907.

— *Die Dialektik Schleiermachers.* Strassbourg: 1920.

— *Die philosophisch – theologische Methode Schleiermachers – Eine Einführung in die Kurze Darstellung und in die Glaubenslehre.* Strassbourg: 1911.

Wendland, J. *Die Stellung der Religion im Geistesleben.* Tübingen: J. C. B. Mohr (Paul Siebeck), 1920.

— "Neuere Literatur über Schleiermacher," *Theologische Rundschau,* 1914.

Windelband, Wilhelm. *Die Geschichte der neueren Philosophie.* Freiburg; 1911.

— *Einleitung in die Philosophie.* Tübingen: J. C. B. Mohr (Paul Siebeck), 1920.

— *Lehrbuch der Geschichte der Philosophie.* Tübingen: J. C. B. Mohr (Paul Siebeck), 1910.

Wingren, Gustaf. *Predikan – En Principiell Studie.* Lund: C. W. K. Gleerups Förlag, 1949.

— *Teologiens Metodfråga.* Lund: C. W. K. Gleerups Förlag, 1954.

Wobbermin, G. *Die religionspsychologische Methode.* Tübingen: J. C. B. Mohr (Paulr Siebeck), 1913.

Zeller, Eduard. *Geschichte der deutschen Philosophie seit Leibnitz.* München: Oldenbourg, 1873.

INDEX